ROUTLEDGE LIBRARY EDITIONS: BRITISH IN INDIA

Volume 26

WOMEN OF INDIA

WOMEN OF INDIA
An Annotated Bibliography

HARSHIDA PANDIT

Routledge
Taylor & Francis Group

LONDON AND NEW YORK

First published in 1985 by Garland Publishing Inc.

This edition first published in 2017
by Routledge
2 Park Square, Milton Park, Abingdon, Oxon OX14 4RN

and by Routledge
711 Third Avenue, New York, NY 10017

Routledge is an imprint of the Taylor & Francis Group, an informa business

British Library Cataloguing in Publication Data
A catalogue record for this book is available from the British Library

ISBN: 978-1-138-22929-7 (Set)
ISBN: 978-1-315-20179-5 (Set) (ebk)
ISBN: 978-1-138-29227-7 (Volume 26) (hbk)
ISBN: 978-1-138-29229-1 (Volume 26) (pbk)
ISBN: 978-1-315-23306-2 (Volume 26) (ebk)

Publisher's Note
The publisher has gone to great lengths to ensure the quality of this reprint but points out that some imperfections in the original copies may be apparent.

Disclaimer
The publisher has made every effort to trace copyright holders and would welcome correspondence from those they have been unable to trace.

WOMEN OF INDIA
An Annotated Bibliography

Harshida Pandit

GARLAND PUBLISHING INC. • NEW YORK & LONDON
1985

Library of Congress Cataloging in Publication Data

Pandit, Harshida, 1927–
  Women of India.

  (Garland reference library of social science ;
vol. 152)
  Includes index.
  1. Women—India—Bibliography. 2. Women—India—
Social conditions—Bibliography. I. Title. II. Series:
Garland reference library of social science ; v. 152.
Z7964.I5P36   1985   016.3054   82-49172
[HQ1742]
ISBN 0-8240-9175-2

ACKNOWLEDGMENTS

This bibliography would not have been conceived without Dr. Esther Steinman's inspiration and insistence. I had to visit different libraries in Bombay to look at various publications for annotation. I must confess that not only the librarian friends at Shrimati Nathibai Damodar Thackersey University Library, but also librarians at the American Library, British Council Library, Institute of Social Sciences, Tata Institute of Social Sciences, Bhavan's library, Maniben Nanavati College Library were most generous and helpful. I am thankful for all the help they rendered.

My special thanks to Miss Hilda Sales-Pontes, Miss Leena Pandya, Miss Jayshree Patel, Mrs. Rani Ghosh, Miss Tara Sheth, and Miss Minal Gandhi for helping me in listing, annotating, classification and also for guiding me in getting specific library assistance. I want to express my heartfelt thanks to them.

My thanks are due to Mr. K. Venkatraman for going through the draft manuscript and rendering editorial assistance and to Miss Carmel Dias for typing the manuscript so accurately. Lastly, I must express my grateful thanks to my husband Mr. Ramu Pandit, who always encouraged and guided me in my moments of disappointments and diffidence in completing this stupendous task.

My former student and close friend Ms. Ila Doshit who is now settled in the United States also showered me with new ideas, suggestions, and literature with great enthusiasm. I shall ever remain thankful to her for her generous assistance.

The completion of this project took much longer than I had envisaged. I am grateful to Ms. Marie Ellen Larcada of Garland Publishing, Inc., for understanding my difficulties and encouraging me to complete the assignment.

I will appreciate it very much if the users send me their reactions, suggestions, and criticisms.

Harshida Pandit
Department of Psychology
S.N.D.T. Women's University
Bombay 400 020
India

CONTENTS

INTRODUCTION

The status and position of Indian women have undergone many changes since the high status they enjoyed in the Vedic era yielded to forced suicide during the dark ages, female infanticide, purdah, child marriages, the prohibition of widows' remarriages, the denial of property rights, or the right to inheritance and the denial of freedom to participate in political movements both during the past and pre-Independence days.

The advent of the 19th century ushered in a new era in the liberation of women. This was possible due to the relentless struggle fought by women on the socio-political and legal fronts. The social reform movements turned public opinion against the earlier practices of Sati, child marriages, infanticide of female children, and enforced widowhood. Progressive legislation as well as the social reform movements led by Iswarchandra Vidyasagar and Raja Rammohan Roy and later by the All-India Women's Conference and Mahatma Gandhi helped ease the restraining yoke. The progressive steps taken by the Indian government since Independence by way of granting certain rights and principles and doing away with some evil practices have brought about definite changes. The passing of the Hindu Code Bill in 1956, though welcome, cannot be deemed sufficient in itself to lead to the acceptance of women as equals in every walk of life. Much remains to be done to accomplish this objective.

Women in India's Population

Since 1901, when census taking began in India, the female-male population ratio has consistently declined: in 1901, it was 972 women per 1,000 males; in 1911, it was 964; 955 in 1921; 950 in 1931; 945 in 1941; 946 in 1951; 941 in 1961; 930 in 1971; and 935 in 1981. These declining figures could be explained in various ways: perhaps more boys are born than girls; the survival rate for female infants may be lower than for males; or the decline may be due to the recent trend towards aborting females. Whatever the reason, the fact remains that the population ratio is unfavorable to females, as are the life expectancy figures: 47.1 years for Indian males and 45.6 years for females.

Similarly, the figures for literacy are also disheartening. Indian women are lagging behind, for lack of opportunities. In 1901 the literacy rate among women was 0.8%; by 1981, it had increased to only 24.8%. Enrollment of women in institutions of higher learning is not as high as it should be.

Legal Rights

The legal rights of women in India under the Civil Laws are extensive. The Hindu Code Bill (1956), the Special Marriage Act (1954), the Hindu Marriage Act (1955), and the Hindu Succession and Adoption and Maintenance Acts (1956) do fulfill the need of doing away with the injustices suffered by the women of India. But translating these rights into reality is another matter, and women do not benefit as much as they should. For example, polygamy still exists, despite the law forbidding it; moreover, in recent years it has acquired the form of Friendship Contracts, very similar to a man's keeping a concubine or a mistress. Even when valid grounds for divorce exist, uneducated and economically dependent wives often cannot take recourse to law as legal proceedings against their husbands may lead them to face social ostracism since public opinion still favors men.

Therefore, one frequently comes across reports of dowry deaths or suicides in the newspaper. Murdering of brides, or bride-burning by husbands and in-laws, has acquired shocking dimensions in cases where the brides' parents are not able to satisfy the material demands of husbands and their families. Although the Dowry Prohibition Act of 1961 prohibits dowry in any form, the incidence of dowry is not decreasing. Many loopholes need to be eliminated. The National Committee on the Status of Women, which was appointed by the government of India in 1971, is pressuring the government to strengthen the law so that more women will not die unnatural deaths. Every day

12 women commit suicide and 12 are raped. Unfortunately, most rapists and murderers are never brought to trial.

Thus, the journey toward equality has never been easy for women of India. The male child is preferred and the female child is often neglected, rejected, and in many cases allowed to die. Family members in many cases mete out differential treatment to the female child; when it comes to sending children to school, male children are the first to be educated. The daughter is still considered a burden to the parents, needing to be protected until she marries at an early age. As a wife, her position is lower than that of her husband. If she lives with her husband's family, she is mostly ill-treated by her in-laws, either as an unpaid servant-cum-cook or as a slave with no self-respect. The formidable mother-in-law is still the boss to whom the daughter-in-law owes complete obedience and devotion and who invariably treats her with harshness and vengeance. A divorced woman commands no respect and a widow is considered an unimportant person. A woman's position is still determined by her father's or husband's status. She is perceived as an object for man's physical pleasure and a nonentity.

Since India was until recently governed by a woman Prime Minister, people elsewhere assume that the women of India have achieved an almost equal status with men. Nothing can be further from the truth. The country's first Parliament (House of Representatives) included 23 women; the second Parliament, 27; the third Parliament, in 1967, included 34 women; and in the fourth (1971), fifth (1977), and sixth (1980) the representation of women declined to 31, 22, and 19 respectively. Because of this insufficient representation in political life, women's share in decision-making is also meagre and programs for the welfare of women and children in the districts suffer a great deal.

The status of working women in India is also not what it should be. Of 35 million working women of India, fewer than a million are educated. Women constitute about 2.5% of the total working population, but 90% of working women are carriers of wood for fuel and drawers of water. The educated women workers are employed mainly as schoolteachers, clerks, nurses, midwives, and telephone operators. Most women university degree holders work in colleges and universities, although a few of them work in law, medicine, or architecture. As a result of recent developments in the mass media, some women have entered advertising, journalism, and the commercial arts. Women's menial jobs are mostly found in household industries, e.g., weaving, oil pressing, rice-pounding, and leather processing.

Because tradition and custom still govern the destinies of Indian women, reaching the top is not yet possible. Hidden or subtle discrimination still exists. Despite their abilities, Indian women suffer lack of opportunities, encouragement, or appreciation. Moreover, the double standard also holds them back.

Nevertheless, in spite of these limitations, Indian women are becoming increasingly aware of the status they can achieve and the role they can play in society. This holds out some hope for the future status and position of Indian women.

Women of India

I

GENERAL AND HISTORICAL SURVEY

The entries in this section mainly concern Hindu women
from ancient times to the present. The ages covered are:
Vedic, Epic, Moghul, British, and post-independence India.
During the Vedic age the Indian woman enjoyed complete
equality of status, but her position regressed considerably
during the Epic and Moghul ages. The British period, however,
brought some new thoughts and fresh ideals for Indian women,
and changes introduced in that era raised their status. This
section provides statistical information about women from
census data, yearbooks, and general studies. Such entries
as "The Female Element in Indian Culture" by Hannah Fane,
Cultural History of Gujarat by M.R. Majumdar, and *Hindu
Social Organisation* by P.H. Prabhu do not deal directly with
women as such, but they throw much light and provide authentic
material on Indian culture and the place of women in it.

1. Altekar, (Dr.) A.S. *The Positions of Women in Hindu
   Civilization from Prehistoric Time to Present Day.*
   Delhi: Motilal Banarasidas, 1962, xii + 380 pp.

   The book attempts to survey the position of women in
   Hindu civilization from prehistoric times to the present.
   It also contains information about childhood, education,
   marriage, divorce, the position of widows in society,
   women in public life, women and religion, proprietary
   rights, dress and ornaments, general attitudes toward
   women, and problems faced by them. An index, bibliography, and eleven plates are provided.

2. Ambedkar, B.R. *The Rise and Fall of Hindu Women.* Jullundur: Bheem Patrika Publications, 1970, 28 pp. (Reprinted from *Journal of Maha Bodhi Society*, Vol. 59,
   May/June 1951.)

   The author of this article was a prominent leader and
   a constitutional lawyer who was born an untouchable,
   later embraced Buddhism, and inspired many untouchables
   to convert to Buddhism. This article was primarily

written to refute a charge that Buddhism has caused the
downfall of Hindu women. Manu, not Buddhism, was responsible for the decline in the status of women. Ambedkar proves this by quoting Pali literature.

3. Bader, Clarisee. *Women in Ancient India: Moral and
      Literary Studies.* 2nd ed. Varanasi: The Chowkhamba
      Sanskrit Series, 1964, 338 pp.

    Translated from the French by Mary E.R. Martin, the
    book discusses the role played by Indian women in the
    Hindu pantheon and culture from the time of Aryan symbo-
    lism to the age of Krishna. The various roles of women,
    e.g., as daughters, wives, mothers, and widows from
    Vedic times to the present, are described.

4. Bazaz, Premnath. *Daughter of the Vitasta: A History of
      Kashmiri Women from Early Times to the Present Day.*
      New Delhi: Pampost Publication, 1959, vii + 279 pp.

    This is a poetic description of Kashmiri women in
    different periods of history, including their past
    achievements and present struggle for emancipation.
    Most of the material is gathered from various books such
    as *Raj Tarangini* (12th century) and other documents. The
    book also contains biographical sketches of Kashmiri
    queens and highly accomplished women, a select bibliog-
    raphy, and index.

5. Chakraborti, Usha. *Condition of Bengali Women around
      2nd Half of the 19th Century.* Calcutta: Author, 1963,
      iii + 232 pp. (K.L. Mukhopadhyay, sole distributor.)

    The life of Bengali women during the 19th century is
    the subject of this book. Life prior to marriage and the
    social, political, and religious status of married women
    are described. The social evils prevalent in the 19th
    century are described, and 16 brief life sketches of
    eminent Bengali women are offered. Appendices list books
    by Bengali women, names of Bengali women in journalism,
    periodicals, women editors, Bengali women university
    graduates and post-graduates, and references for each
    chapter. An index is provided.

6. Das, R.M. *Women in Manu and His Seven Commentators.*
      Varanasi: Kanchana Publ., 1962, xv + 288 pp.

    Das presents a picture of the social history of Indian
    women to the 16th century. The subject is treated com-
    prehensively with regard to both status and rights.

7. Das, Sudhirranjan. "The Position of Women in Kautilya's
   Arthasastra." In *Indian History Congress*, 3, Calcutta,
   1939; *Proceedings* 3, Calcutta: Bhupendralal Banerjee,
   1940, pp. 537-563.

   Kautilya was a minister and a statesman who wrote the
   first book on Indian economics, *Arthasastra*. In this
   epoch-making book, he laid down certain rules regarding
   marriage, widowhood, prostitution, sexual crimes, property rights, etc. He framed strict rules restricting the
   liberty of women. Das's paper, written in an analytical
   style, examines the position of women in Indian society
   as envisaged by Kautilya.

8. DeSouza, Alfred (ed.). *Women in Contemporary India*.
   New Delhi: Manohar, 1975, xxvi + 274 pp.

   This book contains 11 articles on various contemporary
   topics, e.g., health, education, marriage, and aging.
   Written by specialists, the articles offer a perspective view. This is a reprint from the special International Women's Year issue of *Social Change*. A relevant
   bibliography is provided.

9. Dharma, P.C. "Women during the Ramayana Period." *Journal of Indian History*, Vol. 17, No. 1 (1938), pp. 1-
   28.

   During the epic period, polygamy existed, but women
   were allowed to choose their life partners. The life
   styles, customs, education, achievements, status, and
   rights of women are discussed in this research paper.

10. Dharma, P.C. "The Status of Women During the Epic
    Period." *Journal of Indian History*, Vol. 27, No. 1
    (1949), pp. 69-90.

    The status of women declined quite a bit during the
    Epic age from their status in the Vedic age. Freedom
    was curtailed and intellectual activities among women
    were at a standstill.

11. Fane, Hannah. "The Female Element in Indian Culture."
    Asian Folklore Studies, Vol. 34, No. 1 (1975), pp. 51-
    112.

    This long research paper surveys the image of women,
    Indus valley goddesses, the matriarchal as well as
    patriarchal form of family, legal status, feminine
    religious traditions and cults, etc., and brings out

the fact that the ancient Indian culture was female-
centered but that the effects of foreign invasions re-
versed this condition.

12. Gandhi, M.K. *Women and Social Justice*. 2nd ed. Ahmed-
     abad: Navjivan Publishing House, 1945, vii + 212 pp.

     This is a collection of articles by Mahatma Gandhi
     written on various occasions and published in *Harijan*
     and *Young India*. Many of these articles were written
     in response to the letters Gandhi received from his
     readers, or are reactions to current events. But each
     article has something to do with the problems of women
     and the injustices suffered by them in Indian society.
     The foreword is by Amrit Kaur, a freedom fighter and
     ardent feminist who created an awareness among women
     of the need to create their own independent identity.
     A good index is included.

13. Gaur, Albertine. *Women in India*. London: British
     Library Board, 1980, 29 pp.

     This volume examines the relevant historical informa-
     tion about the position of Indian women of all religions:
     Muslim, Parsi, Jain, Jew, Christian, and Hindu. The
     book presents a wall painting (in folkart style) by
     Indian women; 14 black-and-white plates of women's daily
     activities as well as the ordeal of Sita and Draupadi;
     and 8 multi-color plates depicting a Parsi woman, Hindu
     marriage, and Muslim family courtesans; along with the
     translation of some North Indian folk songs. A short
     reading list is an added attraction of this beautiful
     production.

14. Ghosha, Jogeshchandra. *Hindu Woman of India*. Delhi:
     Bimla Publishing House, 1982, 140 pp. (First printed
     in 1928 by Sen Brothers, Calcutta.)

     This book, first published in 1928, is relevant even
     after more than 50 years. Although women are organizing
     to protest against eve-teasing and rape, the evils of
     dowry and women's feelings of degradation are still
     problems, and women still suffer at the hands of men.
     To quote the author, "If every man is what he has made
     of himself, every woman is what man has made her."
     Chapters include such topics as the victim of power,
     the revolt of woman, the ideal of Hindustan, the fortunes
     of the Hindu girl, marriage, the Hindu widow, social re-
     lations, and education. No index or bibliography is
     provided.

15. Gross, Susan Hill, and Marjorie Wall Bingham. *Women in India--Vedic to Modern Times*. Hudson, Wisc.: Gary E. Mecuen, 1980, 110 pp.

     Written under Women in World Area Studies, an ESEA, Title IV-C Federal Project granted by the Minnesota Department of Education, this is a well-illustrated and readable book on Indian women. Women in early Indian history, the complexities of Hindu marriage, the diversities of women's roles, 19th- and 20th-century reforms, and the status of women are the topics covered. A selected bibliography on women in India, a glossary, and a chronology of Indian women's history and culture are also included.

16. Hate, Chandrakala A. *Hindu Woman and Her Future*. Bombay: New Book Comp., 1948, 293 pp.

     A sociological study reporting the socioeconomic situation of Indian women. The data from Bombay and Pune and some North Indian cities are interpreted. A short history of the women's movement and a review of legislation and important resolutions passed by the All-India Women's Conference and the Indian National Social Conferences are included in the appendices.

17. Indira, V.V. *The Status of Women in Ancient India*. 2nd ed. Varanasi: Banarasidas, 1955, 278 pp.

     The social, religious, political, and legal status of women in Ancient India is presented in this book. Also discussed are polygamy, monogamy, divorce, and the status of widows. Education and legal rights are explained, along with the status of women in Buddhism and Jainism. Quotations from the scriptures, a useful bibliography, and an index are provided.

18. Jayal, (Dr.) Shakambari. *The Status of Women in the Epics*. Delhi: Motilal Banarasidas, 1966, xvi + 323 pp.

     The book examines the status of women in epics from the historical and legal viewpoints. The author has tried to locate primary and secondary sources and has quoted extensively from the epics *Mahabharata* and *Ramayana*. The epilogue and 5 appendices explain various forms of marriage in detail. A good bibliography is found at the end.

19. Krishnamurthy, Vaidehi A. "Position of Women." Pp. 51-73. In her *Social and Economic Conditions in Eastern Deccan from A.D. 1000 to A.D. 1250*. Madras: No

publisher; printed at Kabeer Printing Works, 1970.

In addition to examining those women who stayed at home, the writer discusses the economic conditions of temple dancers, courtesans, and prostitutes and the educational and occupational opportunities enjoyed by women during the 250 years under study.

20.   Mahindra, Indira. *The Rebellious Homemakers*. Bombay: S.N.D.T. Women's University, 1980, 213 pp.

Through references from ancient scriptures tinged with sarcasm, the author moves to the inherent barbarism of man toward woman. Her conclusion is that male criminals escape punishment after causing grievous physical and irreparable psychological harm to women. Man has not harnessed the brute inside him. The author asks: "Is there any place on earth where women walk fearlessly?" She further observes: "There is no sympathy for the raped woman, only curiosity. It is well known that society stones an adulteress, not the adulterer. The egalitarian society is our ideal, but when will it be achieved?" Quoting extensively from the Vedas and Indian mythology, the author has tried to raise certain crucial issues. The book contains a bibliography.

21.   Majmudar, M.R. *Cultural History of Gujarat: From Early Times to Pre-British Period*. Bombay: Popular Prakashan, 1965, 364 pp.

The book includes topics primarily pertaining to women of Gujarat. Besides the cultural history of Gujarat, it covers marriage, family, religion and art, widowhood, female infanticide, child marriage, Sati, and Gujarati literature. The volume is quite useful from the point of view of references quoted from primary sources of information and illustrations.

22.   Misra, Rekha. *Women in Moghul India (1526-1748 A.D.)*. New Delhi: Munshiram Mancharlal Publ., 1980, 177 pp.

During the Moghul period, women lived in seclusion and avoided public appearances. Their social life was, therefore, quite limited. Depicted here are the life styles of noble as well as ordinary women during that period. The relevant information is drawn from Persian sources and travellers' accounts.

23. Mitra, Veda. *Happy Married Life in Ancient India*. New
     Delhi: Arya Book Depot, 1965, 176 pp.

     The philosophy of marriage as depicted in the ancient
     Hindu scriptures is explained here. Citations from the
     texts, i.e., *Sruti* and *Smruti*, as well as various as-
     pects of marriage have been graphically described.

24. Mukherjee, Prabhati. *Hindu Women*. New Delhi: Orient
     Longman Ltd., 1978, 118 pp.

     This book studies the past history of Indian women.
     It also examines Hindu ideals of womanhood--chastity
     and fidelity--by citing textual authorities. The woman
     question in India is examined from the historical angle.

25. Murdoch, J. *The Women of India and What Can Be Done for
     Them*. Madras: Christian Vernacular Education Society,
     1888, vi + 150 pp.

     The book deals with the position of Hindu women from
     the Vedic period to the present. It is enriched by ab-
     stracts and quotations from ancient Hindu literature.
     Social customs concerning child marriage, widowhood, and
     Sati (wife's burning herself on the funeral pyre of her
     husband) are discussed, and legislative measures to
     overcome them are highlighted. Regional-language sources,
     books, and periodicals for women are also listed.

26. Nanda, B.R. (ed.). *Indian Women: From Purdah to Modern-
     ity*. New Delhi: Vikas Publishing House, 1976, 187 pp.

     A collection of essays about Indian women in the 20th
     century covers a wide range of themes--upper-class women's
     participation in the freedom movement to speculative
     psychology. Rama Mehta, Veena Das, and Ashish Nandy's
     articles discuss economic independence, the relationship
     between work, status, and power, and the structure of
     defense, etc. At the same time the writers drag readers
     into the realm of jargon, which raises more questions
     rather than providing answers. The forms of oppressing
     women may have changed but oppression still remains--
     this is the central thought.

27. Pandita, Ramabai Sarasvati. *The High-Caste Hindu Women*.
     New York: F.H. Ravell, 1901, 42 pp. (Reprinted, West-
     port, Conn.: Hyperion Press, 1976.)

     Primarily written for American women with the plea:
     "Will you not, all of you, read this book, think of these,

my countrywomen, and rise, moved by a common impulse,
to free them from life-long slavery and internal misery?"
This book describes the difficult conditions in which
Hindu women live. Photographs of the author (a Christian
missionary) and of the welfare work she carried out are
included.

28. Pinkham, Mildreth Worth. *Women in the Sacred Scripture
    of Hinduism*. New York: Columbia University Press,
    1941, 239 pp.

    The author analyzes the influence of the Hindu scrip-
    tures on the life style and status of Indian women. She
    has quoted and discussed important passages from the
    scriptures for the purpose of analyzing and validating
    arguments.

29. Prabhu, P.H. *Hindu Social Organisation: A Study in
    Socio-Psychological and Ideological Foundations*.
    Bombay: Popular Prakashan, 1971, xiv + 389 pp.

    Education, marriage, family, and the attitude of the
    Hindu community toward women through various ages are
    the topics discussed in this book. A very authentic and
    objective rendering of Hindu social institutions, this
    is the only book of its kind.

30. Puri, Omanandaswami. "Women in the Brihadaranyaka Upani-
    sad." *Modern Review*, Vol. 86, No. 3 (1949), pp. 238-
    239.

    A very brief review of the famous women scholars Gargi
    and Maitreyi's accomplishments is given with the help of
    Vedic texts.

31. Rajgopal, T.S. *Indian Women in the New Age or Women in
    Young India*. Mysore: Jaya Stores, 1936, 246 pp.

    The book presents a clear picture of the position of
    women in India and suggests some measures for improve-
    ment, e.g., raising the age for marriage, eliminating
    the hurdles in the way of women's progress, and uplifting
    women's status.

32. Sengupta, Padmini. *The Story of Women in India*. New
    Delhi: Indian Book Co., 1974, 273 pp.

    A broad historical panorama with major sections on
    the ancient, medieval, and British periods as well as
    the post-Independence years, this book describes the

women's movement toward equality. A chapter on Indira
Gandhi and her achievements appears at the end.

33. Shastri, Shakuntala Rao. *Women in Vedic Age*. 4th ed.
     Bombay: Bharatiya Vidya Bhavan, 1969, 187 pp.

     This title discusses the social, religious, and
     political position of Indian women from *Rig Veda* to the
     Griha Sutra.

34. Shridevi, S.A. *A Century of Indian Womanhood*. Mysore:
     Rao & Raghavan, 1965, 161 pp.

     A historical study from 1857 to 1957 tracing the
     achievements of Indian women in all spheres of life,
     from education to business, this volume explains how
     the Indian renaissance guided Indian women from a lowly
     condition to one of high responsibility.

35. S.N.D.T. Women's University. *Women in India: A Handbook*.
     Bombay: Research Unit on Women's Studies, Shreemati
     Nathibai Damodar Thackersey Women's University, 1975,
     84 pp.

     The handbook reviews many facets of women's lives,
     e.g., education, economic participation, political par-
     ticipation, legal status, and women's organization.
     Presentation of data is in tabular form. Detailed and
     good demographic information is included.

36. Thomas, Paul. *Indian Women through the Ages*. Bombay:
     Asia Publishing House, 1964, x + 392 pp.

     This book surveys the position of Indian women from
     prehistoric times to the present. It traces the origin
     and development of the institution of marriage and
     family, morals, and social theories as they relate to
     the women of India. It throws some light on marriage
     laws and customs of Buddhists, Jains, Christians,
     Parsis, and other minority sects.

37. Upadhyaya, Bhagvat Saran. *Women in Rigveda*. 2nd ed.
     New Delhi: S. Chand & Co., 1974, 243 pp.

     The status of women in Rigvedic times and the problems
     of morals and manners faced by them are described.

II

THE POSITION, ROLE, AND STATUS OF WOMEN

This section deals with the role, position, and status
of Indian women. Some items are general surveys, some spe-
cifically refer to the higher status enjoyed by women in recent times. Many symposia/seminars and research projects
were organized in India during the International Women's
Year in 1976, and some foreign authors who evinced interest
in the status of Indian women have also found a place in
this section. Opinions expressed in these publications are
at times self-contradictory, but that is a reflection of the
condition of Indian women. On the one hand, one finds women
who are well educated, aware of their rights and status, and
possessed of a good standard of living, and on the other,
women who are illiterate, unaware, and struggling for survival. There are two important publications: (1) *Women in
Developing Countries* and (2) *Women in India*, which can provide guidelines in arriving at the objective assessment of
Indian women.

38. Amritkaur, Rajkumari. *To Women*. Ahmedabad: Navjivan
     Publishing House, 1948, 31 pp.

     How can underprivileged women be helped through
     planning various activities like spinning and weaving
     and how, through medical aid and literary programs, can
     less fortunate women be helped? These are the issues
     discussed in this book.

39. Avasty, Indira. *Rural Women of India*. New Delhi: D.K.
     Publishers, 1982, 482 pp.

     Although the rural women studied in this book belong
     to the village of Jagti in Jammu and Kashmir, they are
     representative in character of those women living in
     faraway villages elsewhere in India. Women belonging
     to Brahmin, Thokkars, Lohars, Carpenters, Gujjars, and
     Scheduled castes are studied. Their attitudes toward
     various aspects of life, i.e., divorce, childbirth,
     education and employment, and marriage and dowry are

neatly documented in tables. The book is extremely
readable because of the narrative style and because of
the compassionate attitude toward women. The author
has succeeded in inducing the village women to express
their views frankly.

40. Baig, Tara Ali (chief ed.). *Women of India.* National
    Council of Women in India, Delhi: Publications Division,
    Govt. of India, 1958, viii + 276 pp.

    This is a broad survey of Indian womanhood covering
    various aspects such as women in ancient India, the
    middle period (12th to 15th century), the struggle for
    freedom, law as it affects women, participation in
    politics, influence of religion, education, creative
    art, handicrafts, women writers, women in sports, women
    in government, and women in voluntary social service.
    The foreword is by the late Prime Minister Pandit
    Jawaharlal Nehru. Women authors in particular fields
    are identified. The book contains rare photographs of
    women social reformers, women participants in the freedom
    movement, women in the performing arts, and also those
    women who fulfill traditional roles and rituals.

41. Bhasin, Kamla (ed.). *The Position of Women in India.*
    Proceedings of a Seminar held in Srinagar, Sept. 1972.
    Bombay: Leslie Sawhny Programme of Training for De-
    velopment and Friedrich-Naumann-Stiftung, 1972, 131 pp.

    This collection of papers, ably edited by Kamla Bhasin,
    frankly discusses various aspects of female status and
    multiple roles, trials and tribulations, economic and
    sexual exploitation, etc. Some bold suggestions to im-
    prove women's condition are also offered.

42. Billington, M.E. *Women in India.* London: Chapman and
    Hall, 1895, 342 pp. (Reprinted, New Delhi: Amarka
    Book Agency, 1973.)

    This book is a compilation of an earlier series that
    first appeared in *Daily Graphic*, for which the author
    toured India. This work considers the status of Indian
    women at the turn of the century. It includes informa-
    tion about customs and religious practices, occupations,
    dress, needlework, education, marriage, health care,
    crime and criminals, death, and funerals. Illustrated
    with numerous drawings of Anglo-Indian Society; the
    notes on travelling and dress are not included in the
    Indian reprint edition.

43. Chitnis, Suma. "International Women's Year: Its Sig-
     nificance for Women in India." *Social Action*, Vol. 25,
     July-Sept. 1975, pp. 203-220.

     The author discusses the significance of three objec-
     tives of International Women's Year, namely, equality,
     development, and peace in the Indian context. This
     paper focuses attention mainly on those problems faced
     by women as a result of the general attitudes of society.
     Female population, participation in agricultural ac-
     tivity, trends in urban occupation, education, and un-
     employment, political participation, modernization and
     change, redefining sex roles, assertion of equal rights,
     etc., are discussed in a scholarly manner with the help
     of available data in the form of statistical and tabular
     presentation. This objectively written research paper
     is an eye-opener about the status of Indian women.

44. Cormack, Margaret. *Hindu Woman*. New York: Bureau of
     Publications, Teachers' College, Columbia University,
     1953, ix + 205 pp.

     Reviewing the various life stages of Hindu women from
     birth and infancy to childhood, puberty to betrothal,
     marriage to motherhood, this is a theoretical as well
     as an empirical study. The author interviewed 10 Indian
     women studying at Columbia University, New York, for her
     doctoral dissertation. The limitations of the conclu-
     sions drawn from such a study are obvious because the
     author met only progressive and educated women. Rural
     women were not even encountered. A select bibliography
     appears at the end of the volume.

45. Cousins, M.E. *Indian Womanhood Today*. Allahabad:
     Kitabistan, 1947, 207 pp.

     This book gives an account of the changes occurring
     in the cultural and social life of Indian women through
     short biographies. It describes how women joined hands
     and participated in the struggle for freedom as well as
     in the fields of art and education.

46. Cousins, M.E. *Awakening of Asian Womanhood*. Madras:
     Ganesh & Co., 1922, viii + 160 pp.

     As a joint Secretary of the Women's Indian Association,
     the writer noticed that Indian women were in the process
     of making history. A discussion of the women's movement,
     characteristics of Asian womanhood, and biographical

sketches of Ramabai Ranade, Sarojini Naidu, and Abala
Bose are also included.

47. Desai, Neera. *Woman in Modern India*. Revised ed. Bom-
    bay: Vora Publication House, 1977, 314 pp.

    Many facets of the changing status of Indian women
    in the 19th and 20th centuries are described. The posi-
    tion of Indian women as a result of the reform movements
    and the British impact on culture are described in de-
    tail. This is a revised edition (earlier ed., 1957)
    and includes updated statistical tables, bibliography,
    and index. This work was originally written as an M.A.
    thesis at the University of Bombay.

48. Deshpande, Gauri. *Position of Women in India*. Deolali:
    Sawhny Programme of Training for Democracy, Leslie
    Sawhny Centre, n.d., 16 pp.

    This small pamphlet deals with the position of women
    in India from ancient to present times. Their economic
    and legal status is described aptly: "We, the Women of
    India, are most fortunate in our laws and most unfortu-
    nate in our traditions, history and religions."

49. Dhillon, Gurmet. "The Changing Role of Rural Women."
    Social Change, 11 (2), June 1981, pp. 21-28.

    The study reveals that change encompasses various
    socio-economic spheres of women's work. It also points
    out that improved economic status has not resulted in
    improvement in the working conditions of a housewife.

49a. Dhindsa, Ragwinder Kaur. "Changing Status of Women in
    Rural India." Ph.D. Dissertation, Department of
    Sociology, University of Illinois, 1968, 250 pp.
    (University Microfilms 69-10-682.)

50. Hate, Chandrakala A. *Changing Status of Women*. Bombay:
    Allied Publishers, 1969, xiii + 284 pp.

    Chandrakala Hate's study of the changing status of
    women is based on a sample of 1,534 educated, wage-
    earning women from the middle class and another sample
    of 239 non-wage-earning women from 143 families. Both
    the samples are from four urban centers in Maharashtra
    State: Bombay, Poona, Nagpur, and Sholapur. This study
    highlights some of the changes taking place under the
    influence of education and employment on the attitudes,
    values, problems, and status of the educated earning

women from the middle class. Since this book is not
designed to be an analytical study, firm conclusions are
not drawn.

51. India. Ministry of Education and Social Welfare. Com-
     mittee on the Status of Women in India. *Towards
     Equality: Report of the Committee on the Status of
     Women in India.* New Delhi: Ministry of Education and
     Social Welfare, Dept. of Social Welfare, 1974, xiv +
     480 pp.

     The report covers a wide spectrum of all important
     aspects of the life of Indian women, e.g., demography,
     images of women in religious traditions, law, roles,
     opportunities for economic participation, educational
     development, political status, etc. The report was
     submitted to the Indian Parliament. It is rich with
     tables, graphs, and findings of specially conducted
     studies.

52. Jacobson, Doranne, and Wadley, Susan S. *Women in India:
     Two Perspectives.* New Delhi: Manohar, (Also published
     by Columbia 1977: Montana, South Asia Books), 144 pp.

     Two anthropological essays are included in this book.
     The first is "The Women of North and Central India: God-
     desses and Wives" by Doranne Jacobson, and the second,
     by Susan S. Wadley, is "Woman and the Hindu Tradition."
     The Jacobson essay describes the various roles of women
     in modern India, especially in Madhya Pradesh, and
     presents the diversities among women in such variables
     as geography, occupation, economics, religion, and caste.
     It also gives a comparative picture of women in Uttar
     Pradesh and Madhya Pradesh and covers the issues of
     separation of the sexes, hierarchy, and restraint as
     well as rural-urban contrast. The details may be in-
     teresting to Westerners. The second essay attempts to
     define femaleness in a common structural line from
     sources as diverse as classical Hindu laws, mythology,
     and the folklore tradition. It tries to provide role
     models for the changing position of women in Indian
     society. The author states that while classical litera-
     ture emphasizes a woman's duties to her husband, there
     are almost no role models for husbandly behavior. Taken
     together, these two essays provide a perspective on the
     duality of femaleness in Indian society. Jacobson's
     introduction to the two essays is informative and con-
     tains a bibliography of recent publications.

53. Jain, Devki (ed.). *Indian Women*. New Delhi: Publica-
     tion Division, Ministry of Information and Broad-
     casting, Government of India, 1975, xxii + 312 pp.

     The editor has tried to include various facets of
     Indian womanhood, e.g., women and the national movement,
     marriage, upbringing of a girl, woman in the labor market,
     legal provisions, Muslim women, tribal women, prosti-
     tutes, women in politics, women and the performing arts,
     etc. The contributors are all known specialists in
     their respective fields. A scholarly introduction is
     offered by the editor. Relevant statistical information
     is made available, and many empirical studies provide
     rich information.

54. Khan, Mumtaz Ali. *Status of Rural Women in India*. New
     Delhi: Uppal Publishing House, 1982, xiv + 219 pp.

     Books on Indian rural women are extremely limited in
     number. The Joint Women's Programme of the William
     Carry Study and Research Centre and the Christian Insti-
     tute for the Study of Religion and Society sponsored this
     project. Chapters discuss participation in educational,
     economic, and social organizations as well as social
     legislation. All aspects of rural women's life are
     covered. The authors conclude that rural women's lot
     has not changed much; formal education still has not
     reached all the rural areas, and women's organizations
     have not significantly penetrated these areas, and
     where they have penetrated, they have not made adequate
     arrangements for non-formal education. Tables, a bib-
     liography, and an index are included.

55. Khanna, Girija, and Mariamma A. Verghese. *Indian Women
     Today*. New Delhi: Vikas Publishing House, 1978,
     vi + 212 pp.

     This book discusses various roles of women, e.g.,
     wife and mother, and covers working women's views on
     sex, marriage, family planning, adoption, fashions,
     social issues, religion, etc. A bibliography and index
     are provided.

56. Mehta, Hansa. *Indian Woman*. Delhi and Baroda: Butala
     and Company, 1981, xi + 206 pp.

     This is a collection of Mehta's articles, speeches,
     radio talks, and addresses delivered at various times
     and places. The main areas covered are women's educa-
     tion, the status of women, impact of Gandhiji, and legal

rights. The book is dedicated to Sarojini Naidu, a
freedom fighter and a poet of eminence. The work provides some insight into the changing status of Indian
women and their problems.

57. Mehta, Sushila. *Revolution and the Status of Women in
     India*. New Delhi: Metropolitan Book Co., 1982, v +
     278 pp.

     This book is a sociological study of women's status
     in India. The topics covered are the position of women,
     image of women in India, purdah, polygamy, prostitution,
     devdasi and sati, new social roles of Indian women,
     women in unusual professions, rape, bride-burning, social
     structure, etc. A bibliography for further reading is
     appended. The book includes a word index.

58. Menon, Laxmi N. *The Position of Women*. London: Oxford
     University Press, 1944, 31 pp.

     The writer compares the position of women and men in
     Hindu law. She also discusses property rights of
     Hindu widows and their educational level.

59. Mies, Maria. *Indian Women and Patriarchy: Conflicts and
     Dilemmas of Students & Working Women*. New Delhi:
     Concept Publication, 1980, 311 pp.

     The conflicts and dilemmas faced by Indian female
     students as well as working women in an authoritarian
     patriarchal family system are discussed in a frank
     manner. An important contribution to women's studies, it
     offers a new perspective on Indian family. Translation
     from German by Saral K. Sarkar. Has references as well
     as tables illustrating the advancement of women.

60. Mukerjee, Ila. *Social Status of North Indian Women
     (1526-1707 A.D.)*. Agra: Shiva Lal Agarwala & Company,
     1972, x + 172 pp.

     The North Indian woman's social status is described
     from cradle to grave, through Hindi and Bengali litera-
     ture as well as foreign travellers' accounts. Information
     about food, dress, customs (Sati-Jauhar), education of
     Hindi and Muslim women, the conditions of widows and
     prostitutes, and women's contributions to music and the
     other arts is also provided. A bibliography on sources
     is included.

61. Nehru, Shyamkumari (ed.). *Our Cause: A Symposium by
     Indian Women*. Allahabad: Kitabstan, n.d., xvi + 419 pp.

This is a collection of seminar papers dealing with
various aspects--social, legal, educational, health,
and economic--that affect the position of women in family
and society in India.

62. Pandit, Harshida R. *The Status of Women in India: Nation-
    al Survey (1930-1972). A Qualitative Content Analysis
    of Newspapers and Magazines in Gujarati Language.*
    Sponsored by the Indian Council for Social Science
    Research, New Delhi, 1974, 150 pp. (mimeographed).

    In all, 1,436 entries are analyzed and interpreted in
    chapters on the position of women; organizations; legal,
    economic, and political participation; social problems
    faced by women; women in the arts; and Gandhiji and
    women. Many tables, excerpts, and quotations are in-
    cluded. Data presented here are gathered from Gujarati
    newspapers and magazines. A comprehensive report cover-
    ing all regions was presented to the Indian Parliament
    during the International Women's Year in 1976.

63. Phadnis, Urmila, and Malani, Indira. *Women of the World:
    Illusion and Reality.* New Delhi: Vikas Publishing
    House, 1978, 259 pp.

    This is a collection of papers on the status of women
    in 11 American, European, Asian, and African countries.
    Indian women are compared with the women of other coun-
    tries where the status of women is much better. Indian
    males can accept women either as slaves or as goddesses,
    but not as equals--this fact is brought out by the
    authors very emphatically.

64. Ross, Aileen D. *The Hindu Family in Its Urban Setting.*
    Toronto: University of Toronto Press, 1967, xiv + 325
    pp.

    The traditional urban joint family in Bangalore is
    the focus of this study, and the ways in which changes
    are brought by industrialization and urbanization with
    regard to authority, family sentiments, work, education,
    friendship, and marriage are shown. This is not a book
    on Indian women themselves, but one that can throw much
    light on relevant aspects of women's life.

65. Rothfeld, Otto. *Women of India.* London: Simpkin Mar-
    shall, Hamilton Kent & Co., 1920, 22 pp.

    The author was a political agent posted in Rajkot
    during the British regime. The book deals with his ob-
    servations of the marriages and married life of aristo-
    cratic Indian women of the period; their life styles

and the self-sacrificing attitudes of women are explained
in detail. There are 48 illustrations in color by M.V.
Dhurandhar of women belonging to different communities.

66. Sashi, S.S. *Tribal Women of India*. Delhi: Sundeep Pra-
     kashan, 1979, 153 pp.

     The tribal women of India, especially in the context
     of the socioeconomic changes brought about in their life
     style after Independence, are the subject of this book.
     The author has made an attempt to explore the effects of
     modernization on their lives.

67. Sharma, N.A. *Women and Society*. Baroda: Padmaja Pub-
     lication, 1947, 120 pp.

     This book traces the general conditions of life of
     women from ancient times to the present, examining
     various factors. It also considers the higher status
     enjoyed by women in India in ancient times, and dis-
     cusses the selfless and humane role of women in Indian
     families and the social problems faced by them.

68. Shrinivas, M.N. *Changing Position of Indian Women*.
     Delhi: Oxford University Press, 1978, 30 pp.

     The author approaches the problem by keeping in view
     the processes of urbanization and Sankritization, the
     effects of social reform as well as the freedom movement,
     and by reference to the recent interest in studying
     women in general and Hindu women in particular.

69. Singh, Andrea Menefee. "The Study of Women in India:
     Some Problems in Methodology." *Social Action*, Vol.
     25, Oct.-Dec. 1975, pp. 340-364.

     This paper provides a comprehensive and critical view
     of the methodological problems inherent in studies of
     women in India. During International Women's Year,
     these problems came to the forefront as it was noticed
     that a focus on women was new. Factors of special rele-
     vance in the study of women are discussed with a rare
     insight.

70. *Status of Women in India: A Synopsis of the Report of
     the National Committee on the Status of Women, 1971-74*.
     New Delhi: Indian Council of Social Science Research,
     1975, 188 pp.

     Intended to reach a wider audience, this volume presents
     a synopsis of the original report, "Towards Equality,"
     presented to Parliament. The seven chapters deal with
     demographic perspectives; sociocultural setting; women
     and the law; roles, rights, and opportunities for

economic participation; educational development; political status; and policies and programs for women's welfare and development. 40 tables and 12 graphs and a list of the committee members are given.

71. Venkatarayappa, K.N. *Feminine Roles*. Bombay: Popular Prakashan, 1966, vi + 139 pp.

   This book attempts to present the basic facts on feminine roles by examining morphology, the psyche, and social roles. The author rejects the traditional Indian notion that women are inferior to men. Appropriate examples are provided.

72. Vivekanada, Swami. *Our Women*. Almora: Advaita, Ashram, 1961, x + 59 pp.

   Swami Vivekananda in this book attributes the downfall of India to the continued neglect of women and replies to the questions put by disciples on women, marriage, education, etc.

73. Wadia, A.R. *The Ethics of Feminism: A Study of the Revolt of Women*. New Delhi: Asian Publication Services, 1977, 256 pp.

   Discusses mostly 19th- and 20th-century feminist ideas of the Western world. Only the concluding chapter deals with issues pertaining to Indian womanhood and the status of Hindu, Muslim, and Parsi women. The problems of feminism in the East and West are quite different; a comparison is offered in this publication.

74. Ward, Barbara E. (ed.). *Women in the New Asia: The Changing Social Roles of Men and Women in South and South-East Asia*. Paris: UNESCO, 1963, 523 pp.

   This volume contains mainly socio-anthropological papers concerning India and other Southeast Asian countries, presented at a meeting of social scientists in Calcutta in 1958 as a part of UNESCO's project for the mutual appreciation of Eastern and Western cultural values. Photographs are included.

75. *Women in Developing Countries: Case Studies of Six Countries*. Stockholm: Swedish Development Authority, 1974, 98 pp.

   This small book provides valuable resource material and comparative background data on the position of

women in six developing countries, including India.
The report on the contribution of the United Nations
and other international organizations working in the
field of women's development, along with the bibliography, will prove useful.

76. *Women in India: A Statistical Profile by Government of
    India*. New Delhi: Dept. of Social Welfare, 1978,
    xvii + 477 pp.

   Data are presented on various aspects concerning women,
   e.g., demographics, vital statistics, health, education,
   employment, political participation, social welfare and
   defense, social work, education and training. Extensive
   data are illustrated through numerous tables. This is
   an informative and invaluable source on Indian women.

77. Zeitler, Misquita, C., and J. Tellis-Nayak (eds.). *Women
    in India and in the Church*. Pune: Ishvani Kendra,
    1978, 278 pp.

   This book is a collection of interesting articles by
   such eminent people as N.N. Shrinivas, Margaret Khalakdina,
   Kamala Mankekar, and Kamlesh Nischol. All papers give a
   rounded picture of the status of women in India and the
   different ways in which they are participating actively
   in the socioeconomic, cultural, and religious spheres
   of life. A useful bibliography is an added advantage.

III

ECONOMIC PARTICIPATION

India's working women do not have an enviable lot. They
are subject to sexual discrimination, low and unequal wages,
sexual exploitation, insecurity, etc. Certain areas are the
exclusive preserve of men. There is sex-typing of occupations;
women work as teachers, professors, clerks in factories and
offices, nurses, etc. They also find a place in the field
of medicine and in research laboratories. Uneducated women
are involved in construction and agricultural activities.
Many of them serve as domestic servants since very little
help is available from male members of the family. Role conflict is a common malady from which most working women suffer.
Automation also adversely affects female employment. The
entries in this section throw more light on this subject.
Some foreign scholars have also been attracted to this area
of study, and references to their work have been included
even though these books were not published in India.

78. Number omitted.

79. Adyanthaya, N.K. "Women's Employment in India." *Inter-
    national Labour Review*, Vol. 70, No. 1, July 1954, pp.
    44-46.

    This article discusses the extent of and trends in
    women's employment in India. Information regarding
    working conditions, wage structure, and legislative
    measures taken by the central as well as state governments
    is provided.

80. Agarwal, B. "In Employment." *Seminar*, No. 165, May
    1973, pp. 21-24.

    This article gives an account of rural working women
    and their role in society. Data on urban employed women
    are also provided. The injustices to blue-collar women
    workers are stressed, and the need for equality in edu-
    cational facilities for girls is reiterated.

81. Andiappan, P. *Women and Work: A Comparative Study of
     Sex Discrimination in Employment in India and U.S.A.*
     Bombay: Somaiya Publications, 1980, ix + 155 pp.

     Sex-typing of jobs and sex discrimination in jobs are
     not new occurrences in India and the U.S.A. Equal pay
     is not granted for the same jobs. The difference be-
     tween the two countries is only one of degree; in India
     more women work in agriculture and other unorganized
     sectors. There is no unemployment insurance, and the
     condition of Indian women workers is degraded and
     pathetic. References at the end of every chapter,
     tables, and a good bibliography on this subject are
     provided.

82. *Banking with Poor Women.* Ahmedabad: Mahila Sewa Sahakari
     Bank Ltd., 1980, 12 pp.

     The Self-Employed Women's Association, a sort of trade
     union, was set up in 1972 with the object of assisting
     the unorganized sector of poor women who are small,
     home-based producers, e.g., patch workers, seamstresses,
     carpenters, vegetable and fruit vendors, hand-cart
     pullers, etc. The Mahila Sewa Sahakari Bank extends
     credit to members. In addition to tables and other
     information, photographs of these women are given.

83. Bhatia, K.K. (director). *Women in Industry.* Ministry
     of Labour, Labour Bureau, Government of India, Simla:
     1975, iv + 241 pp.

     The sharing of economic activities by women is the
     main subject of this book. Women workers in agriculture,
     factories, mines, and plantations in organized as well
     as unorganized sectors, their demands and prospects,
     facilities for training and vocational guidance, and
     some laws covering women workers and their participation
     in trade union activities are discussed. I.L.O.'s
     recommendations are reproduced. Comparative tables
     from all states and all jobs are made available in one
     publication.

84. Bhatt, Ela R. *Economic Role of Cottonpod Unshellers and
     Handloom Weavers.* Ahmedabad: Gandhi Majoor Sevalaya,
     n.d., 28 pp.

     The first study deals with the socioeconomic condition
     of 500 cottonpod shellers. The work involved is manual
     labor and seasonal. The women employees are so poorly
     paid that most of them have to borrow money in order to

make ends meet. At times fingers of workers may bleed
in the process of work, but no provision has been made
for rendering first aid. The second study, concerning
women weavers in Khambat in Gujarat State, also brings
out similar facts. Tables indicate the women's miseries.

85. Bhatt, Ela R. *Profiles of Self-Employed Women.* Ahmeda-
    bad: Self-Employed Women's Association, Gandhi Majoor
    Sevalaya, 1976, 87 pp.

    A short history of the Association and its role in
    alleviating the sufferings of women and making them
    self-supporting. One thousand women who were occupied
    in sewing were studied. Their education, socioeconomic
    background, the kind of clothes they stitched, and their
    expectations from the Association are examined in this
    survey. Information about hand-cart pullers, vegetable
    vendors, junk-smiters (collectors and sellers of recyclable
    material), and milk producers is also given. This is a
    very useful study, revealing the trials and tribulations
    of women workers who are struggling to be independent
    and improve their situation.

86. "Bidi Workers of Nipani." *Economic & Political Weekly.*
    July 22, 1978, pp. 1177-1178.

    Nipani is in Karnatak, but it is a Marathi-speaking
    area. The whole town smells of tobacco. About 17,000
    women are engaged in tobacco pounding, sifting, and bidi-
    rolling activities. They earn 5Rs. (50 cents) a day,
    work 8 hours, walk 5 to 6 miles from their villages,
    and bring their lunches; sometimes they are manhandled
    and deprived of their personal belongings and sexually
    exploited by the checkers and bosses.

87. Chakraborty, Krishna. *Conflicting Worlds of Working
    Mothers.* Calcutta: Progressive Publishers, 1978,
    305 pp.

    The author is an ardent feminist; she feels that
    division of labor based on sex is unjustified and un-
    reasonable. Middle-class women seeking gainful employ-
    ment are trying to combine both roles--homemaking and
    breadwinning--and the reactionary forces are not sym-
    pathetic. Supported by case studies and statistical
    data, this survey has a strong academic bias.

88. D'Souza, Victor S. "Family Status and Female Work Par-
    ticipation: An Empirical Analysis." *Social Action*,
    Vol. 25, July-Sept. 1975, pp. 267-276.

Women need to supplement the low income of their husbands; and with the socioeconomic changes in society, women's representation in occupations of importance is increasing. These two hypotheses are tested in this survey with the help of research data and census information.

89. Dalaya, Chandra K. *A Socio-Economic Study of Unorganised Women-Workers in Slum Areas of Bombay City*. Bombay: Research unit on women's studies of S.N.D.T. Women's University, 1978, 72 pp. (mimeographed).

This survey conducted by the National Service Scheme Volunteers of Ramnarain Ruia, Bombay, is the first of its kind covering unorganized women workers. In all, 391 women residing in 3 slums were interviewed in 1978 about their family background and socioeconomic status. Type of work, working conditions, and general way of life were also studied. This is an informative survey but does not really examine the plight of slum women.

90. *Defending Our Rightful Place*. Ahmedabad: Self-Employed Women's Association, 1981, 8 pp.

Women vegetable vendors, fish-sellers, old garment sellers, etc. often do business with small capital that is sometimes borrowed. Money-lenders often exploit these women, and police harass these hawkers. This pamphlet maintains that these women can organize and defend themselves with the help of SEWA.

91. Desai, Jayshree. *Some Aspects of Socio-Economic Conditions of Women Workers in Certain Textile Mills of Ahmedabad*. *Vidya*, Jan. 1967, pp. 77-82.

Ahmedabad is the Manchester of India. Women work in many textile mills, although the number is declining. Social customs, lack of guidance, and religious taboos were found to be responsible for the state of affairs in this study of 500 women laborers. Women complained that they were hired only for temporary jobs. Rationalization means retrenchment for women. Frequent childbearing and fatigue from their dual roles act as social barriers for women.

92. Desai, Jayshree. *Report on a Study of Socio-Economic Conditions of Women Workers in Certain Textile Mills of Ahmedabad*. Ahmedabad: Gujarat University, 1966, 66 pp.

The city of Ahmedabad has nearly 100 textile mills.
The women working in these mills are given mostly class
IV workers' jobs. Some of these women have just migrated
to Ahmedabad in order to work here, so this survey was
planned to study their attitudes to work and their problems. 500 women were interviewed for this purpose to
ascertain their socioeconomic background, their health
problems, use of health services, husbands' cooperation
in family planning, etc.; the findings are interpreted
with the help of 53 tables. The interview schedule and
some references are at the end.

93. Dixon, Ruth B. "The Roles of Rural Women: Female Seclu-
     sion, Economic Production, and Reproductive Choice."
     Pp. 290-321 in Ronald G. Ridkar (ed.). *Population and
     Development: The Search for Selective Interventions*.
     Baltimore: Johns Hopkins University Press, 1976.

     Seclusion inhibits female participation in economic
     and social activities. Early marriage prevents girls
     from resorting to birth control practices. The author
     proposes a program of small-scale, labor-intensive
     industry cooperatives employing only women as a way to
     make up for the lack of opportunities.

94. Dixon, Ruth. *Rural Women at Work: Strategies for Develop-
     ment in South Asia*. Baltimore: Johns Hopkins Univer-
     sity Press, 1978. (Not seen by compiler.)

     The author draws heavily on her experiences in Bangla-
     desh, India, Nepal, and Pakistan. She proposes a plan
     for small rural cooperatives and consciousness-raising
     through functional literacy and access to family planning
     information.

95. Gadgil, D.R. *Women in the Work Force in India*. Bombay:
     Asia Publishing House, 1965, 33 pp.

     Available facts are brought together, and tentative
     conclusions on the nature and extent of participation
     in economic activity are arrived at.

96. Gangadhar, V. "Handcart-Pullers of Ahmedabad." *Illus-
     trated Weekly of India*, Dec. 24, 1972, pp. 21-23.

     The miserable life of women hand-cart pullers is de-
     picted in this article. Looking after too many people
     in the family, carrying heavy loads long distances, fre-
     quent pregnancies, and ill-health are some of the problems
     these women face. The article is illustrated with color
     photographs.

97. Garza, I.M., and N. Rao. "Attitudes Towards Employment
     and Employment Status of Mothers in Hyderabad." *Jour-
     nal of Marriage and the Family*, 34(6), Aug. 1972, pp.
     153-155.

     Dissatisfaction with husbands' level of income, desire
     for material comforts, educational aspirations of off-
     spring, desire for increased social contact, and the
     perceived image of the working mother are significantly
     related to mothers' employment status. Authors studied
     40 pairs of sisters, one a typical housewife and another
     gainfully employed but comparable on chosen variables.

98. Ghosh, S.K. *Women in Policing*. New Delhi: Light and
     Life Publishers, 1982, 155 pp.

     The author is an ex-police officer and with the help
     of documentation traces the history of women's entry
     into the police force and the duties prescribed for
     them. Policewomen in India constitute 0.20% of the
     total police force; hence the representation is rather
     inadequate. 95% of the duties and functions do not
     require physical strength, and female qualities are
     valuable. Also there are certain duties which only
     women can perform, such as treatment of rape victims,
     juvenile delinquents, runaway women and adolescent
     girls, and the guarding of women prisoners in police
     lockups, security search of women passengers, etc.

99. Giri, V.V. "Economic and Social Conditions of Women
     Workers." Pp. 374-408 in *Labour Problems in Indian
     Industry*. 2nd ed. Bombay: Asia Publishing House,
     1959.

     Discussed here are employment patterns, the nature
     of skilled and unskilled jobs, recruitment and training,
     wage structure, trade union participation, and problems
     of health and welfare. Most of the women perform un-
     skilled jobs, and their problems therefore need to be
     tackled differently.

100. Goldstein, Rhoda L. *Indian Women in Transition: A
      Bangalore Case Study*. Metuchen, N.J.: Scarecrow
      Press, 1972, viii + 172 pp.

      This study, undertaken by an American researcher, of
      the women students of Bangalore University, in South
      India, throws light on the socioeconomic awakening
      among women today as compared to their awareness in

the past. The study deals with women's views of education, employment, and marriage.

101. Goyal, S. "Effective Utilisation of Womanpower Resources in India." *All India Congress Committee
Economic Review*, Vol. 20, No. 3, Aug. 15, 1968, pp.
15-20.

Womanpower resources--the growth of the female population, women's education and their role in the economic
development of the country--are studied here. The areas
where most women can be employed have been identified.
This article deals with the problems faced by women and
the regional disparities in such problems.

102. Gulati, Leela. "Profile of a Female Agricultural
Labourer." *Economic and Political Weekly*, 13, 12,
March 25, 1978, pp. A 27-A 35.

Profile of a 35-year-old female agricultural laborer
of a scheduled caste, named Kalyani, who lives in a settlement in Trivendrum. The chances of her coming
out of this cycle of deprivation, frustration, and indebtedness are explained.

103. Gulati, Leela. "Unemployment among Female Agricultural
Labourers." *Economic and Political Weekly*, 11, 13,
March 27, 1976, pp. 31-39.

The Rural Labour Enquiry Report (1964-65) is analyzed.
The unemployment rate among female agricultural workers
is double that of male agricultural workers. Tables
substantiating rural-urban unemployment according to
state are reproduced.

104. Gulati, Leela. "Occupational Distribution and Working
Women: An Interstate Comparison." *Economic & Political
Weekly*, 10, 43, Oct. 25, 1975, pp. 1692-1704.

Drawing from the census data about work performed by
women, the writer discusses problematic categories as
far as working women and their work situations are
concerned. Self-explanatory tables are included.

105. Gulati, Leela. "Female Work Participation: A Study of
Interstate Differences." *Economic and Political
Weekly*, 10, Jan. 11, 1975, pp. 35-42.

Gulati's paper examines the relationship between female employment and different economic and demographic

factors, e.g., per capita income, literacy levels, sex
ratio, male employment rates, scheduled caste, and
tribal proportion. According to Gulati, these factors
are not significant.

106. Gulati, Leela. *Profiles in Female Poverty: A Study of
     Five Poor Working Women in India*. Delhi: Hindustan
     Publishing Corporation, 1981, xii + 180 pp.

     The author documents five case studies of working
     women on the outskirts of Trivandrum, South India:
     Kalyani, an agricultural laborer; Jayama, a brick
     worker; Sara, a fish vendor; Devki, a construction
     worker; and Kesari, a coir worker. These five women
     all live in abject poverty. They work for low wages;
     they are discriminated against; they have no upward
     mobility as they are unskilled workers. They toil and
     suffer. Their husbands and sons are either sick or
     vagabonds. Therefore, they have to take care of their
     families. Their daughters share the domestic chores
     at the cost of their education. The author questions
     this legacy of discrimination in a very outspoken way.

107. Iyer, Rupa. "Women Handcart Pullers." *Illustrated
     Weekly of India*, Oct. 12, 1972, 28 pp.

     There are nearly 1,000 women hand-cart pullers operating
     in the mill-center of Ahmedabad, where Gandhiji issued
     various calls for justice to women. Citing some typical
     cases of women engaged in their work, the writer speaks
     against their miserable lives. Even after a day's hard
     work, they cannot afford a meal. Now they have begun
     to organize by joining the self-employed women's union
     in order to save themselves from exploitation.

108. Jain, Devki. *Women's Quest for Power: Five Indian Case
     Studies*. Delhi: Vikas Publishing House, 1980, 268 pp.

     The book discusses five case studies of women workers
     who have organized themselves in large numbers. One
     such association is the Self-Employed Women's Associa-
     tion, as part of which vegetable vendors, junk collec-
     tors, milkmaids, used garment dealers, hand-cart
     pullers, and fire-wood pickers have also established
     a bank. Other similar organizations are the home in-
     dustry for making Lijjat Papad (an Indian delicacy),
     the Amul Milk Producers' Union, and the Madhubani
     Painters' Association. Information is reproduced about
     all these associations engaged in helping achieve economic

independence and uplifting the status of women workers. This is a valuable addition to women's studies.

109. Jain, Devki. *From Dissociation to Rehabilitation.* New Delhi: Indian Council of Social Science Research, Allied Publishers, 1976, 39 pp.

Part of a series titled "Women in a Development Economy" published by I.C.S.S.R. and edited by Vina Mazumdar, the aim of this monograph is to provide information on women workers in the unorganized sector of the economy. This is a report of the Self-Employed Women's Association (SEWA), which was established in Ahmedabad, giving its history and discussing how 5,000 women workers are earning a living as vegetable vendors, garment workers, and cart-pullers. SEWA has a bank which helps self-employed women. The book is quite informative but lacks a critical approach.

110. Jeffers, Hilde. *Organising Women Petty Traders and Producers: A Case Study of Working Women's Forum.* Madras; Berkeley, University of California, 1981, 83 pp. (mimeographed).

This study was conducted in partial fulfillment of the requirements for the Master of City Planning degree. Women engaged in selling remnants, vegetables, wire bags, and flowers were interviewed about their education, marital status, earnings, skills, instruments required for their business, types of transaction, credit facilities created through the Working Women's Forum, and benefits drawn from these.

111. Kakar, D.N. *Dais: The Traditional Birth Attendants in Village India.* Delhi: New Asian Publishers, 1980, 151 pp.

Dais (untrained midwives) are traditional practitioners catering to the needs of rural populations. The author studies 42 dais of Harayana and their role in promoting an indigenous system of health. Rural populations hold these dais in high esteem; some of them are very experienced. The book also discusses pregnancy, childbirth, family planning, abortion, infanticide, etc.; it is informative enough but the material is poorly organized.

112. Kalanidhi, M.S. "Problem of Job Satisfaction among Women Workers in Industry." Pp. 273-300 in T.E.

Shanmugam (ed.). *Researches in Personality and Social
Problems*. Madras: University of Madras, 1973.

Through a questionnaire and also by personal interview, 195 women working in 5 factories around Madras
city were questioned about job satisfaction. Jobs
provided security and income to these women. They
preferred good human relations and liked to work in a
clean environment. Strained social relations at home
affected their emotional adjustment.

113. Kalarani. *Role Conflict in Working Women*. New Delhi:
     Chetna Publications, 1976, 242 pp.

This report of interviews with educated and employed
mothers in Patna examines the conflicts between domestic
and employment roles. Literature on employed women,
role theory, the socioeconomic background of these
women, motivations and attitudes and activities, and
the problems of employed widowed, separated, and
divorced women are discussed. 10 brief life histories
are included.

114. Kamerkar, Mani, et al. *Economic Opportunities for
     Women in India*. Bombay: Forum of Free Enterprise,
     1975, 19 pp.

Compiled in this leaflet are three relevant speeches
delivered by eminent persons about (1) equality in employment; (2) economic status and career opportunities for
in India today; and (3) property law and women.

115. Kanhere, Sujata, and Mira Savera. *A Case Study on the
     Organising of Landless Tribal Women in Maharashtra,
     India*. Bangkok, Thailand: Asian and Pacific Centre
     for Women and Development, June 1980, 13 pp.

Almost 51% of working women in India are agricultural
workers, unorganized, unlettered, and oppressed. This
is a field study of 150 villages in Dhulia District
in Maharashtra where, in 1972, agricultural rural women
from the tribal communities went around to all the
liquor dens and broke the liquor pots. This particular
act against drinking by their husbands was a revolt
against wife beating. How they decided to do this and
the nature of leadership and structure of the protest
movement are analyzed in this brief report.

116. Kapoor, R. *Role Conflict among Employed Housewives*. New Delhi: Shri Ram Centre for Industrial Relations, n.d., 29 pp.

    The author examines the role conflicts of women employed as nurses, social workers, and researchers in Delhi. Considered as independent variables are traditional or modern values, economic or noneconomic motivation to work, job satisfaction, job tenure, age, family income, family dependency load, duration of marriage, availability of household help, and coping facilities.

117. Kapur, Promilla. *Marriage and the Working Woman in India*. Delhi: Vikas Publishing House, 1970, xv + 528 pp.

    The volume is divided into four parts: methodology, quantitative analysis of the data on working women who held jobs prior to marital maladjustment, case studies, and conclusions. The author interviewed 300 working women in Delhi in this connection. Findings indicate that the husbands of working women felt that the housekeeping chores were entirely women's province and they never helped. They seemed to consider their wives' income as a matter of their own legitimate right. Furthermore, they did not miss a single opportunity to insult or taunt their wives. Case studies throw light on the conditions of wage-earning women, which have obviously not improved much.

118. Kapur, Promilla. *The Changing Status of the Working Woman in India*. Delhi: Vikas Publishing House Pvt. Ltd., 1974, ix + 178 pp.

    In this book Promilla Kapur summarizes the findings of her earlier research studies, *Marriage and the Working Woman in India* (1970) and *Love, Marriage, and Sex* (1973). Also included are two chapters based on speeches she delivered at Baroda University in 1973. The author prepared some material for the National Commission on the Status of Women which is presented here. Not only does the book not add much to existing knowledge, but it also suffers from feminist bias and stray generalizations. An excellent bibliography is provided.

119. Karlekar, Malavika. *Poverty and Women's Work: A Study of Sweeper Women in Delhi*. New Delhi: Vikas Publishing House, 1982, 158 pp.

The views of 80 sweeper women have been ascertained
by the author through participant observation, ques-
tionnaires, and interviews to determine whether or not
the impact of rapid urbanization and their economic
independence have made any difference in their status.
The author concludes that urbanization and mechanization
have an adverse impact on women's employment. Most
women laborers are still classified as unskilled, and
young girls are dropping out of school to push brooms
because of economic pressures. Most women are not
allowed to keep their earnings; health facilities are
inadequate; and there is really no change in their
status. The author has suggested ways and means of
improvement; a questionnaire is appended, as are a list
of books and an index.

120. Krishnaraj, Maithreyi. *Approaches to Self-Reliance for
      Women: Some Urban Models*. Bombay: S.N.D.T. Women's
      University Research Unit on Women's Studies, 1980,
      50 pp.

      This brief monograph examines some economic schemes
      for women. The author thinks that the schemes need
      close scrutiny, as they sometimes act as traps for women.

121. Krishnaraj, Maithreyi. "Working Women: Science Degree
      Holders in Bombay, 1976-78." Bombay: S.N.D.T. Women's
      University, Research Unit on Women's Studies (Summary
      Report), mimeographed.

      This survey was undertaken to find out how science
      degree holders are employed, what obstacles they en-
      counter from the family and organization, and what
      science education has meant to them. For this purpose,
      400 women were studied through a self-administered
      questionnaire and in-depth interviews. Their socio-
      economic, educational, and career achievements, working
      conditions, and job satisfaction were also studied.
      The women agreed that they are not getting recognition
      at work, have very little job satisfaction, suffer from
      lack of support from family members, and receive prac-
      tically no encouragement for advancement. The findings
      indicate negative feelings. The study lacks statistical
      sophistication.

122. Kumarappa, J.M. "The Woman as Wage Earner." *Indian
      Journal of Social Work*, Vol. 1, No. 2 (1940), pp.
      162-178.

A majority of women work to supplement a low family
income. But performing two roles creates pathological
problems, with the result that both the family and
society become losers. Many tables show women's economic participation in society.

123. Labour Bureau. "Socio-Economic Conditions of Women
      Workers in Mines." Chandigarh: Labour Bureau, Minis-
      try of Labour, Government of India, 1978, 107 pp.
      (mimeographed).

An empirical study of illiterate and unskilled women
working in mines, describing their employment patterns,
earnings, working conditions, welfare amenities, recrea-
tion facilities, economic and living conditions. A
questionnaire was used to study nearly 400 female miners,
most of whom are coal miners or manganese, iron ore,
stone, limestone, china clay, fire clay, and gypsum
miners. Their living as well as working conditions
are subhuman. In addition to 8 hours of work, they
spend 6-7 hours in housekeeping, fetching water,
walking long distances for shopping, groceries, washing clothes, etc. Family members do not help with any
of these tasks. The women have no leisure time and
are in poor health because of frequent pregnancy.
Theirs is a miserable lot. Many tables substantiate
these findings.

124. Labour Bureau. "Study on Employment of Women in Selec-
      ted Industries (1977)." Chandigarh: Labour Bureau,
      Ministry of Labour, Government of India, 1977, 32 pp.
      (mimeographed).

Industrialization has brought many women into the
work force in the cotton, jute, mica, and mining industries. The studies conducted during the International
Women's Year showed a decline in the number of women
employed in some of these industries. The government
therefore decided to study the problem in depth. This
is a questionnaire study that tries to probe into the
distribution of women workers in selected occupations,
segregation by sex in these jobs, turnover, absenteeism,
and benefits. The findings indicate that these jobs
do not pay well, the facilities are not adequate, and
even the creches maintained by industries are not
properly managed. Some of these jobs present health
hazards to women and the added responsibility of household work makes their lives really miserable. Many
tables are given comparing men and women workers.

125. Lalitha Devi, U. *Status and Employment of Women in
        India*. Delhi: B.R. Publishing Corporation, 1982,
        186 pp.

      Women holding white-collar jobs are studied to see
      whether higher education and top jobs promote an egali-
      tarian relationship with men and raise women's status.
      Does employment increase a woman's status in society?
      This study was conducted in Trivendrum District of
      Kerala State. Out of 6,036 women employees, 300 women
      were studied and compared with 1,000 randomly selected
      unemployed women. The results indicate positive
      trends: working women's participation in decision
      making is accepted, they have more freedom in spending
      the family income, they receive help with household
      responsibilities, and they are exempt from many ritual-
      istic or religious activities. But male subordinates
      resist them in the workplace. Many tables explain
      these findings. The questionnaire used for this study
      is reproduced. A bibliography and index are included.

126. Mahajan, Amarjit. *Indian Police Women*. New Delhi:
        Deep Publications, 1982, 197 pp.

      The author is an academic sociologist. She analyzes
      the occupational choices, the role of women, and the
      role of policewomen. Mahajan thinks that the police-
      woman's role is not a noble one, as adoption of third-
      degree methods sometimes becomes necessary for obtaining
      confessions. She suggests that training is inadequate
      and the work includes mostly protective and oppressive
      duties. The book suffers from too much theoretical
      discussion, but this is the only such work in the
      field.

127. Mazumdar, Vina (ed.). *Role of Rural Women in Develop-
        ment: Report of an International Study*. Seminar
        held at the Institute of Development Studies, Univer-
        sity of Sussex, U.K. 5th Jan. to 10th Feb. 1977.
        Bombay: Allied Publishers, 1977, 125 pp.

      Task force reports prepared by participants are re-
      produced in this volume. Family, marriage, and law
      reports, access to rural services and case studies, and
      appendices providing guidelines for planners, research-
      ers, and field personnel are included. The book also
      carries a directory of projects with contact addresses
      that might interest sociologists and other field workers.
      This is a useful publication.

128.   Mies, Maria. *Indian Women and Patriarchy: Conflicts
       and Dilemmas of Students and Working Women*. Delhi:
       Concept Publishing, 1973, 266 pp.

   The well-known German sociologist deals with the
   problems and conflicts of Indian women brought up in an
   authoritarian and patriarchal family system, where a
   feudal system still prevails. Dr. Mies, through 15
   biographical case studies, has tried to reveal the in-
   compatible roles and conflicting situations that arise
   in present-day Indian society. The study is confined
   to a small, educated urban middle class which consti-
   tutes hardly 5% of India's population. The role conflicts experienced by these women are crushing.
   Shrinking job markets and women workers who cater to
   family needs rather than fulfilling their own needs
   are the root cause of this alarming situation.

129.   Mitra, Asok. "Employment of Women." *Frontier*, Vol. 9,
       No. 46 (1977), pp. 6-9.

   This article gives an assessment of the status of
   Indian women and an outline of a program to bring about
   the most basic and essential changes.

130.   Mitra, Asok. *Status of Women: Literacy and Employment*.
       Bombay: Allied Publishers, 1979, 74 pp.

   Trends in literacy and employment are discussed. The
   author points out with the aid of tables that illiteracy
   is more pronounced among Indian women, since it is
   linked with economic strata, lack of cultural freedom,
   and sexual inequality. This study substantiates many
   such disturbing conclusions with facts and figures.

131.   Mitra, Asok. *Implications of Declining Sex Ratio in
       India's Population*. Bombay: Allied Publishers, 1979,
       85 pp.

   This pamphlet examines the nature and causes of the
   declining sex ratio from 1901 through 1971. Numerous
   districtwide tables, both urban and rural, make the
   picture clear. Until women receive a technical education combined with managerial skills, their economic
   opportunities will be limited.

132.   Mitra, Asok; Adhir K. Srimany; and Lalit P. Pathak.
       *The Status of Women: Household and Non-Household
       Economic Activity*. Bombay: Allied Publishers, 1979,
       78 pp.

This brief essay considers trends in the relative
participation of men and women in household and non-
household economic activities in rural and urban areas
in India as reflected in the 1961 census. There are
tables in this joint project of ICSSR and Jawaharlal
Nehru University. The author feels that until women
get technical education and equip themselves with
managerial skills, their economic participation will
not increase.

133.   Mitra, Asok, et al. *The Status of Women: Shift in Occu-
       pation, 1961-71.* New Delhi: Abhinav Publication,
       1980, 78 pp.

This study examines the occupational participation
of women and men as recorded in the Indian census of
1961-1971. The focus is primarily on nonagricultural
occupations. The study also highlights certain socio-
economic and institutional policies necessary for increasing women's employment opportunities and for
raising their standard of living.

134.   Murickan, J. "Women in Kerala: Changing Socio-Economic
       Status and Self-Image." *Social Action*, Vol. 25
       (July-Sept. 1975), pp. 249-55.

Kerala is one of the most progressive states in India.
The women of Kerala have many firsts to their credit.
This state with a favorable sex ratio also has the
highest literacy rate among women. Even so, the lot
of women workers in Kerala is not better than that of
the female working population elsewhere in India.
Politically, the women in Kerala are alert and they
have participated in the freedom struggle. The social
evil of dowry still exists. Most of the women serve
as nurses; others work as domestic servants. This compilation of several small research studies is a useful
publication.

135.   Nath, Kamla. "Urban Women Workers: A Preliminary Study."
       Economic and Political Weekly, 17, 37 (11 Sept. 1965),
       pp. 1405-1412.

This preliminary study surveys the diversified occupations of women. Participation by state and education
level, based on the 1961 census, is compared with that
of the period 1901 to 1961 in 15 major cities.

136.   Nath, Kamla. "Female Work Participation and Economic

Development: A Regional Analysis." *Economic and Political Weekly*, 5 (21 May 1970), pp. 846-849.

The author laments the rate of decline in economic participation among women and suggests the desirability of undertaking further research to locate the causes, so that remedial steps can be taken to improve women's position.

137. Nath, Kamla. "Women in Service Occupations." *Economic and Political Weekly*, 2, 1 (Jan. 1967), pp. 25-30.

This article points out that even educated women are not interested in public service or foreign service occupations. With the help of the census figures of 1951 and 1961, the author gives future projections and stresses the need for change in educational curricula.

138. Nath, Kamla. "Women in the New Village." *Economic and Political Weekly*, 17, 20 (15 May 1965), pp. 813-816.

Jitpur village in Ludhiana District is undergoing some technological changes. The author discusses the effects of these changes on economic conditions of Jat cultivator women, their work patterns, day-to-day life, medical practices, and attitudes toward education of women.

139. Nerurkar, Amaraja. "Segmentation of Labour Market in India" (with special reference to women). *Indian Journal of Labour Economics*, Vol. 23, 1 and 2 (April-July 1980), pp. 52-65.

Nerukar considers the employment rate of women in the organized as well as the unorganized sector. Illiteracy among women is a grave limiting factor to suitable employment, either semi-skilled or skilled. Family responsibilities and lack of adequate child care facilities are restricting forces. She further suggests that women's organizations should try to bring about some changes in labor legislation to eliminate discrimination against women and differential wages. This is a highly theoretical article.

139a. *A New Deal for the Self-Employed*. Ahmedabad: Self-Employed Women's Association, 1981, 5 pp.

Presenting profiles of self-employed women engaged in making various handicrafts, this pamphlet suggests im-

proved techniques of preparing and marketing these
articles. Some suggestions are made as to how the
municipal corporation could make certain facilities
available to the craftswomen.

140. Omvedt, Gail. *We Will Smash This Prison*. Bombay:
        Orient Longman Ltd., 1980, 189 pp.

        During the International Women's Year, the author, a
        sociologist teaching at the University of California,
        San Diego, came to India and toured through the rural
        areas in Maharashtra. She met socialist and leftist
        Indian women workers who were beginning to organize
        and fight for their rights. Women laborers weary of
        double work, pining for freedom from oppression and
        exploitation from foremen as well as the men in their
        family, fall into the hands of Marxist activists. Case
        studies and firsthand information and observations are
        included.

141. Omvedt, Gail. "College Girls." *Frontier*, Vol. 8, No.
        26/27 (8/15 Nov. 1975), pp. 11-15.

        Omvedt tries to explain why militant middle-class
        women have not provided leadership for rural women
        workers in India. Middle-class women's lives revolve
        around cooking, rituals, and vows.

142. Omvedt, Gail. "Women and Rural Revolt in India." *South
        Asia Papers*, Vol. 1, 4/5 (1977), pp. 1-59.

        Examined here are factors underlying women's work
        participation and changes occurring in methods of agri-
        culture. Militant middle-class women trying to organize
        poor women workers and develop a sort of movement are
        depicted here.

143. *Organising Self-Employed Women: The SEWA Experiment*.
        Ahmedabad: Self-Employed Women's Association, 1981,
        15 pp.

        This pamphlet explains how self-employed women were
        brought under the banner of this organization and how
        their economic exploitation was stopped. Training,
        legal aid, and bank loans are provided by this organiza-
        tion, and protection is sought against any kind of
        harassment. Flow charts explain the field and functions.

144. Oza, Ghanshyambhai. "Role of Women in Rural Industries."
        Khadi Gramodyog, Vol. 22, No. 1 (1975), pp. 9-14.

The article examines the trends of women's participation in various rural and cottage industries, e.g., spinning, weaving, pottery, etc. Participation rates are shown in many tables. This is a very informative article by a sincere Gandhian worker.

145. Patel, Tara. *Report on a Socio-Economic Survey of Women in Professions in the City of Ahmedabad*. Ahmedabad: Gujarat University, 1958, 66 pp.

355 professional women (teachers, professors, telephone operators, social workers, researchers, and office workers) were interviewed and asked to complete a questionnaire. Their age, education, marriage, and work attitudes are studied. It was found by the author of this report that the working women are middle-class; they prefer teaching jobs; and in offices they would like to work at the clerical level. Not very eager to reach the top, they think that their duty lies in doing household work joyfully; husband, home, and children come before any profession. The questionnaire is reproduced at the end.

146. Ramanama, Angora. *Graduate Employed Women in an Urban Setting*. Poona: Dastane Ramchandra, 1979, 159 pp.

A sample of 505 women from Poona is examined. Changes taking place in joint families, patterns of friendship and marriage, and the roles and status of educated and employed women are discussed. Some changes have taken place in households as a result of office work and insistence on equality. The sad truth is that the status of working women has not risen a bit, and lending a helping hand to the working wife in domestic chores has not become a reality. Men's assumption of superiority creates annoyance and conflicts in women.

147. Ranade, S.N., and P. Ramchandran. *Women and Employment: Devnar*. Bombay: Tata Institute of Social Science, 1969, 88 pp.

Higher education among women has the positive effect of causing them to enter the work force, but this trend is not welcomed by some segments of society. This report statistically analyzes the role conflicts that married women face. The findings indicate the preference of married working women for part-time jobs so that they can utilize their education and training for creative expression of their abilities and at the same time

contribute to the family income, thereby raising the
standard of living. The need for training facilities
for such jobs is recommended. The sample (920 women)
studied was from Delhi and Bombay.

148. Ranadive, Vimal. *Women Workers of India*. Calcutta:
        National Book Agency, 1976, 100 pp.

        Dwindling job opportunities, wage discrimination,
        lack of maternity benefits, the need for effective
        legislation to protect women's interests, and the
        formation of trade unions are discussed with a Marxist
        slant. The conditions of women workers in capitalist
        and socialist countries are compared.

149. Rothermund, Indira. "Women in a Coal-Mining District."
        Economic and Political Weekly, Vol. 10, No. 31
        (2 Aug. 1975), pp. 1160-1165.

        Rothermund attempts to assess rural-urban differences
        in the political participation of women in Dhanbad dis-
        trict. She finds urban women to be mostly interested
        in their homemaking and to possess more vices than the
        rural women.

150. Sachidananda. "Social Structure, Status and Mobility
        Patterns: The Case of Tribal Women." *Man in India*,
        Vol. 58, No. 1 (1978), pp. 1-32.

        Tribal women are not a homogeneous group, and their
        traditional roles are not identical. In this article,
        the author examines the structure of tribal societies;
        their ethos, occupational distribution, and mobility;
        and the economic roles tribal women play all over India.
        Discussed also are the trends of change. Good refer-
        ences and useful tables conclude the article.

151. Sandhu, H.K. "Technological Development Versus Economic
        Contribution of Women in Rural Punjab." *Social
        Change*, Vol. 6, Nos. 3-4 (Sept.-Dec. 1976), pp. 18-
        21.

        Women's participation in family farming as well as
        household activities is proving to be unremunerative.
        Technological advances are responsible for much female
        unemployment. As the production of grain per acre is
        increased, the standard of living is improving. Men
        are not training women to use tractors and modern
        methods of irrigation, so the economic status of women
        is going down. The study was conducted with the help

of rural samples of Punjab State and provides detailed
data of household activities.

152. Sengupta, Padmini. *Women Workers of India*. Bombay:
    Asia Publishing House, 1960, 296 pp.

    This survey encompasses a wide range of occupations
    to give a complete picture of employment patterns.
    Numerous tables illustrate and analyze the situation,
    using data based on the 1951 census report. General
    conditions--e.g., housing, health, trade unions, and
    the activities of middle-class working women--are
    studied. Women working as fourth-class workers in muni-
    cipal jobs, as domestic servants, as social workers,
    and in administrative services are discussed. Future
    employment trends are also indicated. A bibliography
    is attached.

153. Sethi, Rajmohini. *Modernisation of Working Women in
    Developing Societies*. New Delhi: National Publishing
    House, 1976, vi + 168 pp.

    This revised version of a Ph.D. thesis submitted to
    Punjab University offers a comparative study of women
    in two less-developed societies following two different
    religions, i.e., Hindu and Muslim. Some chapters deal
    with the attitudes of women in Ankara, Turkey, and
    Chandigarh, Punjab, toward their education and their
    changing status. The sample was comprised of 120 work-
    ing women from Ankara and 125 from Chandigarh. The
    data were collected through interviews; the index of
    modernity by Smith and Inkles was adapted for the pur-
    pose. Freedom of selection of a marriage partner and
    favorable attitudes toward coeducation are considered
    indicators of modernity.

154. *SEWA Goes Rural*. Ahmedabad: Self-Employed Women's
    Association, 1981, 5 pp.

    This is a leaflet describing the SEWA's programs for
    helping rural women attain economic independence through
    activities such as spinning, weaving, dairy, poultry,
    and sewing. As most of India's population stays in
    villages, the condition of rural women must be improved
    for the national good.

155. Shah, K.T. (ed.). *Woman's Role in Planned Economy*.
    National Planning Committee, 6. Bombay: Vora & Co.,
    1947, 265 pp.

The National Planning Committee set up a subcommittee
to study every field in which women were working in
1938. This report reviews such fields, suggests new
areas of employment, and shows that women could participate effectively in the national development.

156. Singh, Andrea Menefee. "Women and the Family: Coping
      with Poverty in the Bastis of Delhi." *Social Action*,
      Vol. 27, No. 3 (July-Sept. 1979), pp. 241-265.

The problem of urban poverty and how it affects the
women in the family are studied in this research paper.
Data are collected from the women staying in four un-
authorized squatter settlements (Bastis) in New Delhi
during 1975-1976. Their physical environment, migration, kinship and family structure, decision making,
employment, health and nutrition, etc. are analyzed
through tables, references, and quotations from other
such studies. This is a purely sociological study
that provides understanding of many urban problems.

157. Singh, Andrea Menefee. "Rural Urban Migration of Women
      Among the Urban Poor in India: Causes and Consequences."
      Social Action, Vol. 28, No. 4 (Oct.-Dec. 1978), pp.
      326-356.

In this important article, the writer brings out some
of the patterns and trends of rural-urban migration of
women as revealed by the data collected at the national
level, i.e., census and the National Sample Survey.
By focusing on the urban poor of major cities of India,
Singh analyzes the consequences of migration at length.
The list of references at the end of the article is
quite comprehensive.

158. Singh, K.P. "Career and Family--Women's Two Roles (A
      Study in Role Conflict)." *Indian Journal of Social
      Work*, Vol. 33, No. 3 (1972), pp. 277-281.

Working women have to perform dual domestic and
occupational roles, and often experience role conflict.
This study reports on interviews with 171 women and
finds that women who choose to work do not perceive employment as interfering with child care, but women who
are forced into employment experience role conflict.

159. Singh, K.P. "Economic Development and Female Labour
      Force Participation: The Case of Punjab." *Social
      Action*, Vol. 30, No. 2 (April-June 1980), pp. 128-
      137.

This paper attempts to determine the reasons for
women's participation in the economic activities in
Punjab. In Punjab more women prefer to work and their
per-capita income is the highest in India among women.
The article is enriched with many tables indicating
rural and urban differences in certain types of women's
occupations.

160. Singh, K.P. "A Comparative Study of the Attitudes of
Working and Non-Working Women Towards Women's Educa-
tion and Employment." *Inter Discipline*, Vol. 2, No. 3
(Summer 1974), pp. 88-89.

Using data collected from 311 married working and non-
working women, Singh analyzes their views on suitable
education for women, whether women should work or not,
appropriate jobs, economic dependence, and independence.

161. Singh, K.P., and S.N. Ranade. *Women Construction
Workers*. Indian Council of Social Science Research.
New Delhi: Allied Publishers, 1976, 79 pp.

This brief monograph examines two surveys of construction workers in Delhi and Bihar. The authors
present the tabulated data without any attempt to in-
terpret their sociological significance. Written in a
pedestrian style, the booklet lacks a theoretical
dimension. However, it is relatively informative
about wages, recruitment methods, family, marriage,
income levels, and welfare facilities.

162. *Social Scientist* (Special Number on Women), Vol. 4/5,
1975, 160 pp.

Various aspects of women's life are discussed by
specialists and famous writers. Women's movements,
liberation and productive activities, patriarchy and
matriarchy, women office workers, problems of working
women in urban areas, literacy, etc. are the areas
covered.

163. Srivastava, Vinita. *Employment of Educated Married
Women in India: Its Causes and Consequences*. New
Delhi: National Publishing House, 1978, 192 pp.

A research study of employment patterns in Chandigarh
for which unemployed women were also interviewed.
Socioeconomic correlates of the two groups, prestige
from husbands' positions, effects of occupation on fertility, and social interaction between the two groups

were studied as were attitudes of working women toward
homemaking and children. A considerable difference
between the two groups was noted by the author. This
book was originally written as a doctoral dissertation.
Tables, a bibliography, and an index are included.

164. Sunder, Pushpa. "Khadgodhra: A Case Study of a Women's
      Milk Co-Operative." *Social Action*, Vol. 31, No. 1
      (Jan.-March 1981), pp. 79-98.

This well-researched paper describes a primary milk
co-operative in the Khedas district of Gujarat, which
was the first and one of the few milk co-operatives
managed entirely by women. The paper examines the impact of the co-operative on the lives of women and also
critically evaluates women as managers. This case study
is important to an understanding of the role of women
in economic development. The case study is well illustrated by tables providing comparative statistics.

165. *Survey of the Economic and Social Conditions of the
      Women Firewood Pickers from Mount Girnar.* Junagadh,
      Gujarat State (India), Self-Employed Women's Associa-
      tion, c/o Ahmedabad: Textile Labour Association,
      1978, 12 pp. (mimeographed).

Girnar is one of a range of mountains in Gujarat
3,000 feet above sea level. Poor women here live on
the produce of the forest. The women who pick up firewood are known as "Bharawali" (firewood pickers). This
survey collects the basic information from 300 women,
who pay a toll to go and collect firewood from the
government-owned forests. Most of these women work
hard, walk 3 to 4 miles before sunrise carrying an axe,
earn a meager amount after the hard day's labor, and
are harassed by the government personnel. Schemes for
their welfare are suggested.

166. Wadhera, Kiron. *The New Bread Winners (A Study on
      Situation of Young Working Women).* New Delhi: Vishwa
      Yuvak Kendra, 1976, 377 pp.

Most women work because of economic need, and at low-
paying jobs. They do not enjoy any status and often
are exploited. Because of the semifeudal socioeconomic
structure of Indian society, working women suffer.
These are the conclusions the author has arrived at
after interviewing 1,000 working women in Delhi. This
survey reveals that these women have low self-esteem

except for perhaps a few women who are highly qualified
and occupy key positions. The author wants working
women to cultivate a positive self-awareness. 45 tables,
5 graphs, a questionnaire, glossary, and some reference
books are listed at the end.

167. *Women as Partners in Progress*. Report of a Conference
      Organised by Governor of Gujarat in Collaboration
      with the Self-Employed Women's Association (25 Feb-
      ruary, 1979). Gandhinagar: Directorate of Informa-
      tion, Government of Gujarat, 1979, 36 pp.

      This report contains a keynote address by Sharda
      Mukherjee, the Governor of Gujarat, who presided over
      the conference. Other papers include the subjects of
      women and public policies by Ela Bhatt, Chairman of the
      Self-Employed Women's Association; women in rural India;
      employment problems of rural women in Gujarat; and the
      role of voluntary agencies. The booklet presents a
      comparative picture of the different districts of
      Gujarat State, focusing attention on various problems.
      Reports of three groups with suggestions to improve
      conditions are useful. The fact that the Governor took
      an interest in problems of such small scale is note-
      worthy.

168. *Women in Industry*. Delhi: Labour Bureau, Ministry of
      Labour, Government of India, 1975, iv + 241 pp.

      This extremely useful report on women in industry
      is divided into two sections, the first dealing with
      factual analysis of the proportion of women employed
      in the various sectors and the second with the services
      available to women job seekers, the demand for women
      workers, and the factors (e.g., vocational training
      and conditions of work including wages) affecting the
      employment of women in general.

169. Wood, M.R. "Employment and Family Change: A Study of
      Middle-Class Women in Urban Gujarat." *Social Action*,
      Vol. 25, No. 3 (July-Sept. 1975), pp. 221-234.

      On the basis of the data collected from 32 women in
      Ahmedabad through in-depth interviews, the author con-
      cludes that most middle-class women are satisfied with
      familial roles. Education, birth order, desire to
      work, intrafamilial relationships, life styles, and
      ritualistic behaviors are studied at great length.
      The tables provide interesting reading.

170.   "Working Class Women and Working Class Families in
        Bombay--Report of a Survey." *Economic and Political
        Weekly* (22 July 1978), pp. 1169-1173.

        Poorly paid women and their family background are
        dealt with in this article. The subjects have come to
        Bombay and do not own property. They have no educa-
        tion; their average age at marriage was 15; they lived
        in joint families with occasional conflicts. As a re-
        sult of protein-deficient food, their children's growth
        was stunted. Most either worked in the factories or
        were domestic laborers. Altogether, this is not a very
        happy picture of women workers.

IV

EDUCATIONAL STATUS

The educational status of Indian women is a tricky subject. No doubt Indian women have come a long way, but there
is still much to be accomplished. The literacy rate among
women is shocking. A few social reformers and missionaries
at the dawn of the present century focused attention on the
lack of educational facilities, and they established institutions to remedy the situation. However, the different
treatment and inferior status meted out to daughters at home
acted as deterents to education. Two institutions--the John
Bethune Educational Society in the east and S.N.D.T. Women's
University in the western region--have done yeoman's service
in the education of women.

The entries in this section are diversified in subject--
purdah and education, socioeconomic background of women students, their problems, separate schools and colleges for
women, curriculum, utility of education, etc. Several institutions dedicated to women's education deserve to be compli-
mented for their outstanding contribution over a period of
many decades.

171. Agarwal, J.C. *Indian Women: Education and Status, Including Major Recommendations of the Report of the
National Committee on the Status of Women in India
1971-1974.* New Delhi: Arya Book Depot, 1976, 106 pp.

The report contains miscellaneous materials, e.g.,
recommendations of various committees on different
aspects of female education, a historical review of
female education in India, demographic tables, and constitutional rights.

172. Ahmed, Shadbano. "Education and Purdah Nuances: A Note
on Muslim Women in Aligarh." *Social Action*, Vol. 27,
No. 1 (1977), pp. 45-52.

This paper reports the findings of a study of the
relationship between education and variations in the
observance of purdah among middle-class Muslim women in

Aligarh City. Of those with a secondary school education, over one-fourth continued to observe strict,
partial, or intermittent purdah. While Muslim women
value secular education for the sake of higher social
status, after marriage they fall back on traditional
conventions. An appendix, tables, and references
giving primary sources are included.

173. All India Women's Conference, Cultural Section. *Educa-
    tion of Women in Modern India*. Aundh: Aundh Publish-
    ing Trust, 1946, 87 pp.

    Papers on aims and objects of women's education,
    physical education, home-science education, art educa-
    tion, college curriculum, and professional education
    are edited and presented in a form that may be useful
    for curricula planners.

174. Bagal, Jogeshchandra. *Women's Education in Eastern
    India: The First Phase*. Calcutta: World Press Private
    Ltd., 1956, xi + 128 pp.

    Jadunath Sarkar writes in the foreword to this book:
    "The greatest benefit that India has derived from the
    influence of English society and European thought is
    a social revolution which has transformed our religion,
    literature, social rules and domestic life." As far
    as women's education is concerned, the British govern-
    ment and foreign missions played a pioneering role.
    In this book, the contribution of various women's asso-
    ciations--missionary and non-missionary--is reviewed
    with awe. A bibliographical index and photographs of
    missionaries and students are attached.

175. Basu, A.N. "Women's Education in India in 19th and
    20th Centuries." *Calcutta Review*, 3rd Series, Vol.
    60, No. 1 (1936), pp. 67-80.

    The history of women's education is divided into four
    sections: (i) 1820 to 1850 when British government
    lacked a definite policy and interest although private
    but ineffectual efforts continued; (ii) 1850-1882 when
    the State policy and initiative began; (iii) 1882-1900
    when, as a result of the movement of religious and
    sociopolitical reforms, some awakening began; and
    (iv) 1900 to the modern period in which these move-
    ments continue to promote female education, which has
    brought about good results.

176. Basu, B.D. "Female Education Was Not Encouraged by the East India Company." Pp. 174-185 in his *History of Education in India Under the Rule of the East India Company*. Calcutta: Modern Review Office, 1922.

   Basu deals with the provisions concerning female education in the educational "Dispatch of Wood," 1854, in which women's education was mentioned by the Indian government, but without any strong suggestion or plan to promote it.

177. Basu, Jogiraj. "The Education of Women in Vedic India." *Visvabharati Quarterly*, Vol. 37, No. 2 (1971/72), pp. 121-133.

   Women were obtaining the opportunities for intellectual, moral, spiritual, aesthetic, and physical education in Vedic India, as Basu demonstrates by quoting extensively from Vedic literature. Women were considered equal partners, and adequate opportunities for educational advancement were provided. Education was considered essential for the overall development of the personality.

178. Bhownaggree, Mancherjee M. "The Present Condition and Future Prospects of Female Education in India." *Journal of the Society of Arts*, Vol. 33, No. 1687 (1885), pp. 452-462 with a discussion, pp. 462-467.

   This article reviews trends in female education in India over the centuries and refers to governmental involvement in this task. Expansion in education is discussed and the influence of medical missions on educational aims is also noted. Educational facilities were meager in the last century and the article deals with this fact at length.

179. Blumberg, R.L., and Leela Dwarki. *India's Educated Women: Options and Constraints*. Delhi: Hindustan Publishing Corp., 1980, ix + 172 pp.

   This book presents the findings of a longitudinal study of educated women in Banglore between 1967 and 1977. In the 1967 study the size of the sample was 97; in the follow-up study of 1977, the sample was 33. What one would expect from such a study is an analysis of the changes that occurred during the decade. But this book is disappointing in this regard, and is likely to create some confusion in the mind of the reader. The educated women, their career choices and

conceptions of different roles, and their attitude
toward tradition and modernity could have been interpreted sociologically.

180. Brockway, Nora K. *A Larger Way for Women. Aspects of
      Christian Education for Girls in South India, 1712-
      1948.* Madras: Oxford University Press, 1949, viii +
      189 pp.

      This book traces the development of education for
      Indian girls in South India under the patronage of
      non-Roman missions and churches from the year 1712
      until 1948. Female education made a very modest be-
      ginning in the early days, as it was considered purely
      a work of faith in India. However, since the national
      awakening, there has been considerable improvement in
      the position of women. A comprehensive account is pre-
      sented in these pages, with photographs of several
      missions and missionaries. An index and references
      are included.

181. Brown, Edith M. "Medical Training for Women in India."
      Double Cross and Medical Missionary Record, Vol. 11,
      No. 5 (May 1896), pp. 97-100.

      This article (apparently reprinted from *The Missionary
      Review*) summarizes the outcome of a conference of women
      medical missionaries held in Ludhiana in 1893, when it
      was proposed that a nondenominational Christian medical
      school for Eurasian and native Christian girls be es-
      tablished. It was felt that such a school was needed
      because medical missionaries were among the most useful
      agents in the evangelization of a country. A sexually
      segregated school was thought to be necessary on the
      assumption that association with male students presents
      a moral danger at a susceptible age. Propositions for
      the establishment of the school are summarized.

182. Brown, Edith M. "Making Doctors of India's Daughters."
      Medical Woman's Journal, Vol. 36, No. 12 (Dec. 1929),
      pp. 328-329.

      Dr. Brown relates how she came to the conclusion,
      through her work as a medical missionary in India, that
      a school should be started to train Indian women to be
      doctors and nurses. A medical school for Indian girls
      was opened in 1894 in Ludhiana, Punjab. The author
      describes at length the coming into being of this school
      and a subsequent hospital.

183. Chaudhuri, Roma. "Women's Education in Ancient India."
      Pp. 88-111 in Swami Madhavananda and Ramesh Chandra
      Majumdar (eds.). *Great Women of India*. Mayavat, Al-
      mora: Advaita Ashram, 1953.

      Using ancient scriptures (e.g., Vedas, epics, Jaina
      and Buddhist literature), educational opportunities
      and patterns are reviewed. The ancient system was
      residential, i.e., students stayed with their teachers
      in *ashramas*. The emphasis was not on reading and
      writing but on moral training, religious principles,
      and self-realization. The education was secular and
      women were given equal opportunities to learn and de-
      velop. This is an informative essay.

184. Chiplunkar, G.M., and S.B. Hudlikar (eds.). *The Scien-
      tific Basis of Women's Education*. Poona: S.B. Hud-
      likar, 1930, 4 + xxvii + 333 pp.

      The editors suggest that the educational system and
      methods introduced by the British were not suitable
      for Indian girls. Education should inculcate in stu-
      dents a sense of duty, motivating them to participate
      in the national movement.

185. *Compilation of Opinions on the Subject of the Education
      of Girls and Women Called for by Government Order,
      Educational Department*. No. 1268, 15 May 1916.
      Calcutta: Government Printing Press, 1916, 473 pp.

      The definition of female education, the primary and
      secondary curricula for girls, the utility of educa-
      tion, and allied topics are discussed by quoting
      opinions of prominent Indian citizens. Rules laid down
      by the British government are listed, and reactions to
      those rules are given verbatim. Documented nicely,
      this book is useful for researchers.

185a. Cormack, Margaret Lawson. "Traditional Patterns in the
      Internalization of the Ideals of Womanhood by Hindu
      Girls with Special Reference to Urban Educated Women."
      Ph.D. Dissertation, Department of Sociology, Columbia
      University, 1951, 261 + 88 pp. (University Microfilms
      2802.)

186. Cowan, Minna G. *The Education of the Women of India*.
      Edinburgh: Oliphant, Anderson and Ferrier, 1912, 256 pp.

      The book traces the progress made in the field of
      female education and the part played by government,

missions, and private efforts by the Indian public.
Included are a discussion of university education and
many photographs.

187. Dasgupta, Jyotiprova. *Girls' Education in India in the
      Secondary and Collegiate Stages*. Calcutta: University
      of Calcutta, 1938, ix + 269 pp.

      The progress of female education in various states
      is reviewed. Reorganization at various levels of edu-
      cation is suggested. The author proposes schemes for
      vocational and physical education. The statistical
      data on the state of girls' education in various states
      are very useful.

188. Datta, Kalikinker. *Education and Social Amelioration
      of Women in Pre-Mutiny India*. Patna: Patna Law Press,
      1936, iv + 126 pp.

      The history of female education, widow remarriage,
      and the social welfare and anti-sati movement from the
      1750s to 1857 is traced with the help of primary sources.
      Very useful documentation regarding sati, with the
      necessary statistics, is reproduced in 31 pages with
      many appendices.

189. Desai, Chitra. *Girls' School Education and Social
      Change*. Bombay: A.R. Seth and Company, 1976, 293 pp.

      The social environment of 19th- and 20th-century
      Gujarat and the changing pattern of primary and secon-
      dary education for girls are discussed. Through a re-
      view of the literature, collection of data from secon-
      dary sources, and interviews with parents and educators,
      the author has done a thorough job of compilation.

190. Deshmukh, Laj. *Women and the Continuing Education
      Programme of S.N.D.T. Women's University*. Bombay:
      Research Unit on Women's Studies, S.N.D.T. Women's
      University, 1979, x + 104 pp. (mimeographed).

      This is a feedback study conducted by the research
      unit on women's studies to determine the utility of
      the courses offered by the department and the feasibility
      of continuing education at the university in collabora-
      tion with a voluntary women's organization in a suburb
      of Bombay. Based on the response received from 300
      participants and nonparticipants, the author has ana-
      lyzed what sort of courses could be offered in the
      future, timing, duration, place, the effective speakers

and their age, education, responsibilities at home, husbands' education and occupation, etc. Participants responded in a favorable manner, and nonparticipants also expressed their views about their interest, timing, etc. This is a sociological study.

191. Doraiswami, S. *Educational Advancement and Socio-Economic Participation of Women in India*. Teheran: International Institute for Adult Literacy Methods, 1975, 38 pp.

    The educational advancement of women in India cannot be viewed as significant since there has been little change in role expectations, although the concepts of equal status and equal opportunity are beginning to translate these constitutional rights into reality. This research paper prepared for a conference cites a higher rate of illiteracy among women and drop-outs, which amounts to wastage of education. Women are thus deprived of their legitimate role in the process of national development.

192. Gokhale, G.K. "Female Education in India." Pp. 177-186 in his *Speeches and Writings of Gopal Krishna Gokhale*. Ed. D.G. Karve and D.V. Ambekar. Bombay: Asia Publishing House, 1967.

    This article is based on a paper read at the Education Congress held in connection with the women's section of the Victorian Era Exhibition, 1897. Gokhale compares the educational opportunities in ancient India with 19th-century efforts to promote female education.

193. Goldstein, Rhoda L. *Indian Women in Transition: A Banglore Case Study*. Metuchen, N.J.: Scarecrow Press, 1972, viii + 172 pp.

    Goldstein, a Fulbright scholar at Banglore University in 1966-67, took a sample of 20% of the women graduates of a class in 1965. In all, she ascertained the views of 99 Hindu, Muslim, and Christian women students through a questionnaire. Goldstein was shocked to find that women students desired higher education chiefly as a means to kill time, although some hoped it would better their chances in the marriage market. Dr. Goldstein's study demonstrates that the educated woman in India still thinks and acts in the traditional way. Tables, case studies, a bibliography, and an index are useful.

194.   Gorwaney, Naintara. *Self-Image and Social Change: A
       Study of Female Students*. New Delhi: Sterling Pub-
       lishers, 1977, 276 pp.

       Female students of Rajasthan University, Jaipur, are
       studying for the sake of studying. What is worth con-
       sidering is whether education has changed their ideas
       and attitudes toward themselves as well as their tradi-
       tions and customs. Their family background and its
       relationship to their self-esteem, modern ways of
       thinking, and attitudes toward certain roles are ex-
       amined in this technical and theoretical study.

195.   Hartog, Lady (Mabel Helene Kisch Hartog). "The Educa-
       tion of Girls in India." *Journal of the Royal Society
       of Arts*, Vol. 84, No. 4348 (March 1936), pp. 499-514
       with discussion, pp. 514-517.

       The article summarizes the progress of formal educa-
       tion for girls in India at various levels in 1936.
       Lady Hartog considers the recent influx of girls into
       schools, the financial implications, and the future
       requirements of teachers. This paper was originally
       presented before the Royal Society of Arts. It pro-
       vides useful information, and demonstrates a sympathetic
       attitude toward education for women.

196.   India Information Service. *Women in India*. Delhi:
       India Information Service, n.d., 58 pp.

       Women's education in other countries is compared
       with that of Indian women. Information about girls'
       schools and universities from 1950 to 1960 is given.
       Also discussed are the position of Indian women and their
       role during the freedom movement.

197.   Jesudasonn, Victor; Prodipto Roy; and T.A. Koshy (eds.).
       Non-Formal Education for Rural Women. New Delhi:
       Allied Publishers, 1981, vi + 419 pp.

       UNICEF and the Council for Social Development spon-
       sored an experimental project to develop an integrated
       program to educate rural women by nonformal education.
       This book is a report on such objectives as decreased
       infant mortality and morbidity, improved physical
       health and nutritional status of young children and
       pregnant women as well as lactating mothers. The study
       reports the methods, target group, and different pro-
       grams in regard to functional literacy and cost effec-
       tiveness, etc., but it does not mention whether the

objectives were fulfilled. The report is confusing because of the jargon and quantitative and qualitative
analysis of the program. An index is provided.

198. Jhabvala, Renana, and Pratima Sinha. "Between School
and Marriage: A Delhi Sample." Pp. 283-287 in
Indian Women. Ed. D. Jain. New Delhi: Publication
Division, Govt. of India, 1975.

A questionnaire and case study-cum-interview method
were used for collecting data about women students at
Delhi University. The findings indicate that most female students attend college to keep themselves busy
until marriage. But there are some exceptions, who
have a definite purpose, e.g., self-development.

199. Krishnaraj, Maithreyi. "The Status of Women in Science
in India." *Journal of Higher Education*, vol. 5, No. 3
(Spring 1980), pp. 381-393.

Women in science education and the scientific professions are few. The occupational pattern of women
scientists of India is studied here vis-à-vis Swedish
and Soviet scientists to provide a comparative picture.
Few women receive a scientific education because it is
expensive, time-consuming, and few women really benefit
from science education. The societal attitudes create
hindrances. Tables and other data from national and
international sources are presented.

200. Law, Narendranath. "Female Education." Pp. 200-205 in
his *Promotion of Learning in India during Muhammadan
Rule by Muhammadans*. London: Longmans, Green, 1916.

The opportunities available for upper-class Muslim
women during the Moghul period are surveyed briefly.
Because very few public and private schools existed in
those days, upper-class families hired governesses.

201. Mathur, Y.B. *Women's Education in India, 1813-1966*.
Bombay: Asia, 1973, 208 pp.

This survey of women's education includes a basic
bibliography and key documents reproduced in the appendices. It is a very useful publication from the point
of view of historical perspective. Information about
S.N.D.T. Women's University is also given.

202. Mazumdar, Vina, and Kumud Sharma. "Women's Studies:
New Perspectives and the Challenges." *Economic and
Political Weekly* (20 Jan. 1979), pp. 113-120.

New perspectives for changing times are suggested in
this article. Contemporary programs on women's studies
are evaluated.

203. Misra, Laxmi. "Democratic India and Women's Education."
      Education Quarterly, Vol. 13, No. 50 (1961), pp. 119-
      122.

      Government programs to promote female education in
      the 19th and 20th centuries are highlighted.

204. Misra, Laxmi. *Education of Women in India 1921-1966.*
      Bombay: Macmillan, 1966, vii + 225 pp.

      This is a well-designed study of women's education--
      well-documented and with material arranged chrono-
      logically. Provisions for education in the five-year
      plans of Free India are included. Educational programs
      of the missions and governments are also discussed.
      Tables, plates (14) explaining the statewide enrollment,
      an extensive bibliography, and references make this
      publication extremely scholarly and useful.

205. Nag, Kalidas, and Lotika Ghose (eds.). *Bethune School
      and College Centenary Volume, 1849-1949.* Calcutta:
      Bethune Society of Education, 1950, 237 pp.

      The foreword is by the late Dr. Radhakrishnan, presi-
      dent of India. This centenary volume traces the history
      of early women's education by various Jesuit societies
      and ladies' organizations. It also documents the his-
      tory of social-educational movements and their contribu-
      tion to women's education. A report of a symposium
      held on the occasion and some articles in Bengali are
      also included. Photographs enhance this publication.

206. Ojha, P.N. "Education of North Indian Women Under the
      Great Moghuls, 1556-1707 A.D." Pp. 208-212 in *Indian
      History Congress* 20, 1957, Vallabh Vidyanagar, Gujarat,
      Proceedings, 20. Bombay: Indian History Congress,
      1958.

      During the 16th and 17th centuries, Hindu and Muslim
      women of the wealthy class were educated by private
      tutors. Women in public entertainment were highly
      accomplished, independent, and assertive.

207. Panandikar, Sulbha; Neera Desai; and Kamlini Bhansali
      (eds.). *Future Trends in Women's Higher Education
      and the Role of the S.N.D.T. Women's University: Report*

of the Round Table Discussion. Bombay: S.N.D.T.
Women's University, 1975, 170 pp.

A historical survey of the development of women's
higher education and the role of the S.N.D.T. Women's
University in promoting higher education among women
is highlighted in this work. The various courses
offered by the university and the number of female
students who have benefited from them are discussed.
The role of the university in the years ahead is
stressed in considering changing times and sex roles.

208. Patel, M.S. "Gandhiji on Women and Their Education."
      Pp. 233-242 in his *Educational Philosophy of Mahatma
      Gandhi.* Ahmedabad: Navjivan Publishing House, 1953.

      Gandhiji's thinking on Indian women, their education,
      and the role they could play in national development
      and as teachers is discussed at length. Gandhiji's
      approach to basic education is described. He was in
      favor of coeducation and wanted curriculum improvement.

209. Patel, Tara. "A Note on Some Aspects of Women Students
      of the Gujarat University." *Vidya*, Vol. 7, No. 2
      (Aug. 1964), pp. 31-39.

      This study tries to probe the vital questions of
      higher education among women in relation to their
      caste, economic strata of their parents, age at mar-
      riage among college students, and their general health.
      Findings reveal that most students still belong to
      upper-middle and middle-class families, although some
      females from the lower economic strata and lower-caste
      groups do enter the university. A sample of 800 female
      students studying in colleges affiliated with Gujarat
      University has been analyzed.

210. *Role of Women in Education in India: A Report of the
      National Seminar on the Roles of Women in Education
      in India Held from October 3rd to 5th, 1975, at the
      Lady Willingdon Training College.* Madras: Madras
      Society for the Promotion of Education in India,
      1976, 62 pp.

      Proceedings and papers presented at the Seminar on
      "Roles of Women in Education in India" and "The Chal-
      lenges in Education for Women" are given along with
      the summary of discussions of formal and nonformal
      education.

211. Sardar, G.B.; Shakuntala Mehta; and Neera Desai (eds.).
      Golden Jubilee Commemoration Volume, 1916-1966.
      Bombay: Shreemati Nathibai Damodar Thackersey Women's
      University, 1968, 6 + 203 + 38 + 32 + 115 pp.

      This is a collection of papers and articles on various
      aspects of women's education in India and abroad. Part
      III presents a demographic profile of female education
      in India with information pertaining to the S.N.D.T.
      Women's University. Part IV contains a bibliography,
      a list of dissertations and theses and biographical
      sketches of the contributors. Some articles in the
      Marathi language are included.

212. Saxena, Rajendra Kumar. *Education and Social Ameliora-*
      tion of Women: A Study of Rajasthan. Jaipur: Sanghi
      Prakashan, 1978, 244 pp.

      Social movements aimed at promoting female education
      are described. The call for eradicating sati and child
      marriage and laws prohibiting widow remarriage helped
      to further the cause of education. Unless women are
      educated, their status will not improve. This book
      covers the period from 1818 to 1935, by which time an
      awakening had already begun.

213. Sen, N.B. (ed.). *Development of Women's Education in*
      New India. New Delhi: New Book Society of India,
      1969, 331 pp.

      As the title suggests, the book concerns itself with
      the general aspect and varying facets of female educa-
      tion in India. For so many important personalities to
      focus attention on the same topic is rare; some quota-
      tions are worth mentioning in speeches and addresses.
      There are many tables as well as photographs of women
      writers.

214. Shah, Madhuri R. "Status and Education of Women in
      India." *Journal of Gujarat Research Society*, Vol.
      38-39, No. 4/1 (Oct. 1976-Jan. 1977), pp. 15-24.

      After reviewing the recommendations of education com-
      missions in regard to women's education, the writer
      deals with the literacy rate, enrollment in schools
      and colleges, the importance of education from the
      point of view of employment, and student expectations
      from education. The utility of education has to be con-
      ceded and impediments to it removed so that women can
      assert themselves and improve their status. Shah offers
      many comparative tables to substantiate her point.

215.   Sharma, Prabhu Datta. "Women's Education: A Curricular
       Model for India." *Education Quarterly*, Vol. 25
       (July 1973), pp. 12-15.

       The writer proposes three different models for edu-
       cating females. (1) For single women who wish careers
       and are willing to compete with men, the model should
       be identical to that of men. (2) For the career woman-
       cum-homemaker, the author suggests courses that are
       job-oriented but at the same time give women a back-
       ground in the natural as well as the social sciences.
       (3) For housewives, courses in practical and domestic
       areas are suggested. The writer thinks that little·
       thought has gone into structuring higher education for
       females and, therefore, more women are unemployed. The
       article tries to assess future needs.

216.   Sharma, Savitri. *Women Students in India: Status and
       Personality*. New Delhi: Concept Publishing Co.,
       1979, 172 pp.

       An empirical and extensive study based on the academic
       assumption that a significant relationship exists be-
       tween the social class and personality traits of the
       individual. The tools used are the Guilford-Zimmerman
       Temperament Survey and the Allport-Vernon-Lindzey Scale
       of Values on a sample of 300 female students at a
       women's college in Patna. Topics discussed are: paren-
       tal influence, upbringing, the absence of father or
       mother and its impact on personality traits. Figures
       and tables are interesting, but on the whole this is
       a superfluous study. The bibliography does not list
       a single Indian title.

217.   Shridevi, Sripati. "Women's Higher Education Since
       Independence." Pp. 205-210 in Dr. N.B. Sen (ed.).
       Development of Education in New India. New Delhi:
       New Book Society of India, 1966.

       This article discusses the effects of higher educa-
       tion on women's economic independence and use of leisure
       time with their family.

218.   Shukla, Suresh Chandra. "Perspectives on Women's Edu-
       cation." *Educational Forum*, Vol. 22, No. 1 (Jan.
       1981), pp. 11-19.

       Shukla stresses the need to extend women's education.
       Raising the literacy rate should be given priority.
       Differential treatment at home and sex-typing of educa-

tion will not help much. He does not favor curricula
which prepare women to play only a secondary role.
Equality in all walks of life should be promoted. This
paper was first presented at a seminar on Women's Education, Hawabagh Women's College, Jabalpur, in 1979.

219. Singh, K.P. "A Comparative Study of the Attitude of
      Working and Non-Working Women Towards Women's Educa-
      tion and Employment." *Interdiscipline*, Vol. 11, No.
      3 (1974), pp. 89-100.

      This article presents data collected from 311 working
      and nonworking women regarding their attitude toward
      women's education. Women in different fields have ex-
      pressed opinions as to the type of education that is
      appropriate for women. Nonworking women want to be
      economically independent. The author has shed some
      light on what would be suitable jobs for women.

220. *Socio-Economic Background of Married Women Students of
      the University and Their Educational Problems*. Re-
      search Project Co-Sponsored by the National Council
      of Educational Research and Training, New Delhi, and
      S.N.D.T. Women's University, Bombay, Dec. 1969, 349
      pp. (mimeographed).

      The views of 372 married women were ascertained through
      a questionnaire and discussed with reference to the
      women's socioeconomic background and motivation for
      education. Dual roles (studying and homemaking) and
      triple roles (working, homemaking, and studying) seem
      to be performed with definite objectives. Problems
      are common: very little time to study, strain, and
      little or no cooperation from other family members.

221. Srivastava, Vinita. "Professional Education and Atti-
      tudes to Female Employment: A Study of Married Working
      Women in Chandigarh." *Social Action*, Vol. 27, No. 1
      (1977), pp. 19-32.

      Data for this research was collected in 1972 at
      Chandigarh by door-to-door survey of institutions em-
      ploying a large number of educated women, e.g., hos-
      pitals, universities, government offices, etc. From
      456 women identified, 150 were selected. Occupational
      status of the husbands of these women was matched to
      that of 150 nonworking wives who were also studied.
      The attitude of working women toward their work was
      positive; they enjoyed the feeling of being able to

contribute to family income. Nonworking women felt
frustrated because their talents were not put to any
use and their desire for work was strong.

222. Tellis-Nayak, Jessie B. *Nonformal Education for Women:*
        The Grihini Training Programme. New Delhi: Indian
        Social Institute, 1980, 110 pp.

      In a country where illiteracy among women is increas-
      ing with time, nonformal education and training in
      homemaking can be provided. This book reviews such
      programs as may be relevant. As most girls get mar-
      ried, bear, and rear children, teaching of the three
      R's does not make sense. In Madhya Pradesh, Bihar,
      Uttar Pradesh, and Haryana, for the past 20 years,
      teaching of Grihini (homemaking) programs has been im-
      plemented through (1) the center approach where girls
      come from a certain geographical area, (2) the network
      approach where a center coordinates the activities of
      units, (3) mini-mobile, and (4) live-in approaches where
      the teams go and live in the villages rather than
      bringing the girls to other areas. Women may develop
      self-confidence by reading this book, but only time
      can prove whether such programs can initiate social
      change in rural areas.

223. Thackersey, Premlila V. *Education of Women: A Key to*
        Progress. New Delhi: Ministry of Education and Youth
        Services, Government of India, 1970, 96 pp.

      The author reviews the history of female education from
      1813 to post-independence India. The goals of education
      for women, future trends, and present problems are
      highlighted through a worldwide comparison by tables
      and graphs. The book reproduces the recommendations
      made by the Education Commission, 1964-66, which are
      useful for those who want to make a comparative study
      of female education.

224. Tulpule, Malti. "A Pilot Study of Adjustment of Pre-
        University Students of the S.N.D.T. Arts College for
        Women, Bombay." *S.N.D.T. Women's University Research*
        Journal (1976), pp. 96-105.

      200 Marathi-speaking entrants were administered the
      Marathi version of the Bell Adjustment Inventory.
      Several areas (home, health, social, and emotional) were
      explored. 58% of the girl students showed some mal-
      adjustment, but the areas of home and health indicated

good adjustment. Economic security and social status
contributed to better adjustment. The transition from
high school to university was difficult for the lower-
middle group, and last borns were found to be well
adjusted compared to the first borns.

225. Verma, M. "Socio-Economic Study of Undergraduate
      Girl Students." *Indian Journal of Social Work*, Vol.
      21, No. 3 (Dec. 1960), pp. 283-286.

      This article is based on data collected through a ques-
      tionnaire from 80 girls students of Agra University, who
      were to appear for their B.A. examination. The ques-
      tionnaire surveyed attutudes toward education, their
      future plans, interests, and leisure-time activities.
      This is an analytical and descriptive study.

226. Vreede-De Stuers, Cora. *Girl Students in Jaipur: A Study
      in Attitudes Towards Family Life, Marriage and Career*.
      New York: Humanities Press, 1970, 141 pp.

      203 girl students in Jaipur were interviewed in regard
      to their ideas on marriage, family life, and career
      planning. Most of them were found to be traditional,
      i.e., they believe in caste. On the other hand, they
      do not believe in the extended family and the practice
      of dowry. This is a useful study because of the
      general lack of such material, but the analysis is
      extremely unsophisticated.

227. Wasi, Muriel (ed.). *The Educated Woman in Indian
      Society Today*. New Delhi: Tata McGraw-Hill, 1971,
      287 pp.

      Contributions on various facets of educated women and
      the field of education are included in this book.
      The general conclusion is that although the number of
      educated women has increased in the past 30 years, no
      one really knows how to utilize the services of the
      educated woman of India for her own as well as the
      nation's advantage. The YWCA of India invited women
      educators, journalists, and scholars to express their
      views. This is an action-oriented study, and in the
      last chapter the editor provides a plan for the future
      and practical suggestions.

228. Wig, O.P. "Neglect of Female Education: A Risk for
      the Future of the Family Planning Programme in Con-
      trolling Fertility in India." *Social Change* (Sept.-
      Dec. 1976), pp. 22-27.

The birth-control policy can succeed to only a limited extent in the absence of an economic-social-cultural revolution, and society is not advancing at a rapid rate. The educational aspect is neglected by the policy makers. The behavioral model evolved by Freedman should be utilized in family planning (i.e., creating a norm for family size, controlling the infant mortality rate and the fertility rate through education). The program administrators will have to make vigorous efforts in order to succeed. There are many references in this much-studied article.

229. Young Women's Christian Association. *The Educated Woman in Indian Society Today*. Bombay: Tata McGraw-Hill Publication Company, 1971, 287 pp.

This work attempts to drive home the need for equality of opportunities for women.

V
LEGAL STATUS

Women enjoy the same legal status as men under the constitution of India. However, the translation of these rights
at an interpersonal or social level poses a grave problem.
Indian women are still discriminated against, ill-treated,
and held back. The law does not always protect them; mis-
creants escape even after murdering women, burning them alive,
and raping them. The Hindu Code Bill of 1956 has given women
property rights, rights of abortion, adoption, divorce, and
maintenance. But the courts may deny justice. What is needed,
therefore, is a social awakening and a resolution among women
not to suffer any injustice. Such social change can be
achieved only through proper education of women.

230. Ahmad, Bashir. "Status of Women and Settlement of Fam-
     ily Disputes Under Islamic Law." Pp. 186-191 in
     Tahir Mahmood (ed.). *Islamic Law in Modern India*.
     Bombay: N.N. Tripathi, 1972.

     This paper examines the role of legal institutions
     under Islam and the status of Muslim women. It has
     been suggested that the law should be modified in such
     a way as to give better protection to women. A draft
     of the proposed Muslim Family Disputes Settlement Act
     is given.

231. Almenas-Lipowsky, Angeles J. *The Position of Indian
     Women in the Light of Legal Reform: A Social Legal
     Study of the Legal Position of Indian Women as Inter-
     preted and Enforced by the Law Courts Compared and
     Related to Their Position in the Family and at Work.*
     Wiesbaden: Franz Steiner Verlag, 1975, 217 pp.
     (Beiträge zur Sudasienforschung, Sudasien Institut,
     Universität Heidelberg, 11.) (Also available at
     Branch Office, 3 Kasturba Gandhi Road, New Delhi.)

     The author finds that although under the law equal
     rights and privileges are granted to Indian women,
     both in the home and at work, actual practice leaves
     much to be desired. The author compares the relative

positions of men and women and recommends some protec-
tive legal measures at home and at work. Unless these
measures are strictly enforced, real equality cannot be
achieved. The author also points out the weakest point
of Indian administration.

232. Anand, Madhava, and Mirza Karim Husain. *Marriage and
the Dissolution of Marriage in Muslim Law: With a
Commentary on the Dissolution of Muslim Marriages
Act*. Lucknow: Eastern Book Company, 1950, 127 pp.

Textual sections on marriage, divorce, and support
according to the Muslim law are reproduced here with
explanatory notes. Muslim law is based on the Quran.
The laws are believed to have emanated from Allah and
it is the duty of Muslims to follow them.

233. Bannington, John A. "The Hindu Code Bill: The Proposed
Bill, Backed by Nehru but Opposed by Hindu Tradition-
alists, Would Codify and Modernise Hindu Law, Giving
Greater Rights to Women." *Far Eastern Survey*, Vol.
21, No. 17 (Dec. 1952), pp. 173-176.

The legal benefits (e.g., property rights) to Hindu
women if this bill is passed are the subject of this
article. Opposition to this bill from the orthodox
and religious sector is also discussed. This is a
short but pertinent article.

234. Burway, R.G. *Present Position of Hindu Women and the
Means of Ameliorating Their Lot*. Bombay: D.B.
Taraporevala Sons and Co., 1941, 29 pp.

Burway was an advocate at the Bombay High Court.
Originally published as an article in 1941 in the *Bombay
Law Journal*, with a foreword by B.G. Kher, then Chief
Minister of Bombay State, the booklet contains relevant
quotations from ancient scriptures pertaining to the
privileges and commentaries on various legislations,
along with marriage and divorce laws in the U.S.A.,
U.K., and Soviet Union. The appendix deals with love
marriages in India and throws light on their legal aspect.

235. Derret, J., and M. Duncan. *Hindu Law Past and Present:
Being an Account of the Controversy Which Preceded
the Enactment of the Hindu Code, the Text of the Code
as Enacted, and Some Comments Thereon*. Calcutta: A.
Mukherjee and Co., 1957, 408 pp.

        This book presents the actual code, topic by topic,
        along with a discussion of the controversy it created
        when it was proposed and the opposition from the
        conservative quarters of Hindu society. The
        arguments and the pros and cons are analyzed.
        Appendices give notes, references, and the full text of
        the bill.

236.   Derret, J., and M. Duncan. *Essays in Classical and
        Modern Hindu Law*. Vol. 4: *Current Problems and the
        Legacy of the Past*. Leiden: E.J. Brill, 1978, 454 pp.

        Articles on the criminal procedure code and rights
        of women are included in this final volume of collected
        papers. Hindu marriage, the deserted wife, and the
        rights of widows are discussed with the idea of pro-
        viding a legal explanation.

237.   Ehrenfels, U.R. von, and P.V. Velayudhan. "Legislation
        Against Matriliny." *Anthropologist*, Vol. 3, No. 1/2
        (1956), pp. 35-47.

        The authors compare matrilineal and patrilineal sys-
        tems in the context of the Hindu Succession Act of 1956
        and inheritance law. Women of the patrilineal parts
        of the country regard this Act as a panacea whereas
        women belonging to the matrilineal system consider it
        an encroachment on their rights. In fact, under a
        matrilineal system women enjoy more legal benefits than
        under a patrilineal system.

238.   Gajendragadkar, P.B. *The Hindu Code Bill*. Dharwar:
        Karnatak University, 1951, 52 pp.

        Gajendragadkar delivered these two lectures before
        the students of Karnatak University at the time the
        bill was discussed in the first parliament of Indepen-
        dent India. Gajendragadkar was a progressive jurist
        who advocated the bill.

239.   Gangrade, K.D. (ed.). *Social Legislation in India*.
        Delhi: Concept Publishing Company, 1978, Vol. I, 288
        pp; Vol. II, 259 pp.

        The dry subject matter is presented in nontechnical
        language in these volumes. Family and marriage, medical
        termination of pregnancy, maternity benefits, and im-
        moral traffic in women and girls--the legal provisions,
        deficiencies, and solutions--are discussed.

240. Gharpure, J.R. *Rights of Women Under the Hindu Law.*
      Bombay: N.M. Tripathi, 1943, vi + 165 pp.

      Originally prepared as the Sir Lallubhai A. Shah
      Memorial Lecture, the book finds that Indian women
      were equal to men during Vedic times, although this
      equality was later lost in regard to marriage, property,
      and inheritance. The book is very informative and
      cites some typical cases. The bibliography, subject
      index, and index of cases make this publication valuable.

241. *India Hindu Law Committee, Report.* New Delhi: Manager
      of Publications, Government of India, 1947, 183 pp.

      A committee was appointed in 1944 to draft the Hindu
      Law. The report of this committee is the substance of
      this book, which discusses the debatable points--mostly
      concerning women--based on expert opinions on various
      issues.

242. India (Republic). Committee on the Status of Women in
      India. "Women and the Law." Pp. 102-147 in its
      *Towards Equality: Report of the Committee on the
      Status of Women in India.* New Delhi: Department of
      Social Welfare, Ministry of Education and Social
      Welfare, Government of India, 1975.

      This report reviews the major legislative provisions
      pertaining to Indian women regarding polygamy, age at
      marriage, dowry, divorce, adoption, guardianship,
      maintenance, and inheritance. Many recommendations
      have been made with a view to removing disparities.

243. India (Republic). Planning Commission. *Social Legis-
      lation: Its Role in Social Welfare.* New Delhi: Plan-
      ning Commission, Government of India, 1956, 418 pp.

      Intended for the lay public, this book aims to edu-
      cate the masses about social welfare legislation.
      Sections include "women and law," "immoral traffic,"
      etc., and suggest improvements to existing legislation.
      India's first five-year plan has inspired this book as
      well as influenced legislation.

244. Kidwai, M.H. *Woman Under Different Social and Religious
      Laws: Buddhism, Judaism, Christianity, Islam.* Delhi:
      Seema Publications, 1976, 167 pp.

      The author traces women's status since the early Romans
      under various laws in different parts of the world. As

a Muslim, he concludes that women under Muslim law enjoy rights, dignity, and equality (a debatable point).
Women's legal status under Buddhism, Judaism, and
Christianity is also discussed with this bias; the
book is limited by this prejudice. Researchers should
therefore weigh the contents cautiously.

245.   Masani, Shakuntala. "Equal in Law, Unequal in Fact."
       Illustrated Weekly of India (3 June 1973), pp. 30-33.

       Constitutional guarantees of equal rights to women
       have proved inadequate. A struggle may be necessary
       to achieve the objective of social and economic
       equality. A national committee on the status of women
       was constituted in 1971 with this objective in view.
       But Masani laments that the dual role has increased
       women's burden, and, moreover, discrimination in jobs
       and promotions reflects the traditional mind. Social
       legislation has to be backed by a change in attitude
       among concerned people, and some sort of a social re-
       form movement must be launched. Women's organizations
       must propagate such an awareness. The article traces
       the history of social reform movements in brief. Some
       statistical information is also provided.

246.   Mehta, Ramanlal V. *A Thesis on the Legal Rights of
       Women Under the Different Communal Laws in Vogue in
       India.* Bombay: G.G. Bhat, 1933, 93 pp.

       Presented here in layman's language is an exhaustive
       picture of Indian women's legal rights and liabilities.
       The rights of divorce, judicial separation, remarriage,
       succession, and the general legal status of Hindu and
       Muslim women in British India are discussed. The essay
       originally won a prize in an essay competition sponsored
       by the Civil Marriage Association of Bombay.

247.   Minattur, Joseph. "Women and Law: Constitutional Rights
       and Continuing Inequalities." *Social Action*, Vol. 25,
       No. 3 (1975), pp. 292-301.

       The laws pertaining to child marriage, widow remar-
       riage, Hindu marriage, divorce, property, adoption,
       employment, education, and abortion are discussed with
       a view to the status of Indian women. Indian women are
       suffering in spite of their new constitutional rights.

248.   Mitter, Dwarkanath. *The Position of Women in Hindu Law.*
       Calcutta: University of Calcutta, 1913, 707 pp.

The book reviews the position of women according to
Hindu law in general and marriage and status of married
women, widows, courtesans, and dancing girls, in particular. For substantiation, the author quotes from
the ancient texts, describes inheritance law, and suggests some legislative and social measures to improve
the legal status of Hindu women. Interesting contemporary court cases are also cited.

249. Mukherjee, Bishwanath. "Awareness of Legal Rights Among
Married Women and Their Status." *Indian Anthropologist*, Vol. 5, No. 2 (1975), pp. 30-58.

This study, sponsored by the United Nations, collected
data by interviews from 1,872 ever-married women (1,470
rural and 402 urban) of reproductive age belonging to
Haryana, Tamil Nadu, and Meghalaya. The research study
attempted to establish the relationship between legal
rights, status, and educational and employment levels.
It was presumed that the higher the status, the greater
is the extent of women's knowledge of their various
constitutional rights. However, women were not well
informed, although urban women were much better informed
than the rural ones.

250. Nagaswami, R. "A 13th Century Sale Deed on Rights of
Women." Pp. 84-88 in his *Studies in Ancient Tamil
Law and Society*. Madras: Institute of Epigraphy,
State Department of Archaeology, Government of Tamil
Nadu, 1978.

Discussed here is a Tamil inscription that describes
the sale deed and the right of inheritance of 13th-
century women. The inscription suggests that right to
property was exercised by women, although transactions
were carried out by male members of their families.

251. People's Union for Civil Liberties. "Women and Their
Rights." *People's Union for Civil Liberties Bulletin*,
Vol. 2, No. 9 (Sept. 1982), 31 pp.

This issue is devoted to women and civil rights and
includes field reports received by specialists in the
field on subjects such as rape, brothels, the chipko
movements (in which women prevent forest contractors
from illegally felling trees), dowry atrocities, Muslim
women and the uniform civil code, and women and health.
Nowhere else can one find the data on rape which are
given here. The editor has compiled a list of actual

cases of dowry deaths from Jan. 9, 1982, to Sept. 20, 1982, with the names, causes, and modes of death. This is a must for researchers.

252. Prakash, (Dr.) Gyan. *Hindu Code*. Allahabad: Allahabad Law Agency, 1958, vii + 500 + cl pp.

This is a commentary on the Hindu Succession Act, the Hindu Adoption and Maintenance Act, the Hindu Marriage Act, the Minority and Guardianship Act, etc. As a jurist, Prakash has attempted to encompass everything that one should know on the subject and also has offered his comments. The table of cases, detailed footnotes, and references are very useful.

253. Ranade, Mahadeva Govind. "The Sutra and Smriti Texts on the Age of Hindu Marriage." Pp. 26-52 in his *Religious and Social Reform: A Collection of Essays and Speeches Composed by M.B. Kolasker*. Bombay: Gopal Narayan, 1902.

The traditional and orthodox ideas expressed in the scriptures are no longer relevant.

254. Rao, Shakuntala. *Women in the Sacred Laws*. Bombay: Bharatiya Vidya Bhavan, 1933, xiii + 193 pp.

Dharmashastra (codification of the sacred laws) is discussed, and the laws pertaining to women are described with evidence from the ancient scriptures. Also described are the laws as given by Manu, who is notorious for restricting the freedom of Hindu women. The last chapter explains the spirit behind certain laws. The foreword to this book is by K.M. Munshi who founded Bharatiya Vidya Bhavan and his open University Book Programme. This publication is a part of this programme.

255. Ray, Renuka. "The Background of Hindu Code Bill." *Pacific Affairs*, Vol. 25, No. 3 (1952), pp. 268-277.

Ray offers a feminist-like argument in favor of the Hindu Code Bill. Provisions of the bill are discussed. The bill had opponents even in the Indian National Congress, as well as in the other conservative and communal parties.

256. Sarkar, Lotika. "Law and Status of Women in India." Pp. 99-122 in *Law and the Status of Women: An International Symposium*. New York: Centre for Social

Development and Humanitarian Affairs, United Nations,
1977. (Reprinted in *Columbia Human Rights Law Review*, Vol. 8, No. 1 (1977), pp. 95-122.)

Sarkar reviews the legislative as well as the constitutional provisions for Indian women, in such matters
as health, employment, and inheritance. Although equal
status is granted by the preamble to the Constitution,
the law has so many loopholes that women are no closer
to equal status and equal opportunity, socially speak-
ing.

257. Sarkar, Rishindranath. *Synopsis of and Introductory
      Lecture on the History of Development of Hindu Law
      in British India.* Calcutta: R.N. Sarkar, 20-A, San-
      karitola East, 1932, 158 pp. (*Tagore Law Lectures*
      (15), 1932.)

The history of the development of Hindu law in British
India is itself a vast subject. In these lectures,
different topics are discussed at length while Sarkar
reviews the changes in the offing. In addition to different schools of Hindu law and their origin, the
author has tried to describe the East India Company
and the British sovereignty, the necessity of Hindu
law, the history of legislation, caste law or precedents, and causes which helped the growth of Hindu law.
Sarkar offers a comprehensive treatment of the subject.

258. Sarkar, (Dr.) U.C. *Epochs in Hindu Legal History.*
      Hoshiarpur: Vishveshvaranand Vedic Research Institute,
      1958, xvi + 440 pp.

Originally written as a thesis for the LL.D. degree
at Dacca University, this work has been revised by the
author to delve deeper into the nature, sources, and
changes of Hindu law. After a discussion of the sages
who structured these laws, the author states that the
laws must now be changed. The ancient rules should
not be taken as final. A table of cases, comments,
and index are added to an extremely readable and informative treatise.

259. Sivaramayya, B. "Equality of Sexes as a Human and Con-
      stitutional Right and the Muslim Law." Pp. 69-79 in
      Tahir, Mahmood (ed.). *Islamic Law in Modern India.*
      Bombay: N.M. Tripathy Private Ltd., 1972.

Muslim law does not grant equal status to women.
Sivaramayya advocates equality of sexes under the Muslim

personal law and reiterates that the adherence to secular principles will be a step in the right direction.

260. Tribhuvan, Jyotsna. *Law Relating to Women in India.*
      Ahmednagar: Author, Dr. Ambedkar Road, 1965, 112 pp.

      The author is a lawyer herself and has made a com-
      mendable effort to bring together all the legal provi-
      sions concerning women, e.g., marriage, divorce,
      property rights, succession, dowry, maternity benefits,
      and prevention of immoral traffic in women and girls,
      not only for Hindu women but also Muslims, Parsis,
      and Christians. She also briefly explains the offenses
      and penalties under the Child-Marriage Restraint Act
      and the Dowry Prohibition Act. Moreover, she suggests
      some ways to make these laws more effective and bene-
      ficial to women.

261. Verma, B.R. *Muslim Marriage and Dissolution.* Allahabad:
      Law Book Company, 1971, 358 pp.

      The author studies pure Muslim personal law relating
      to marriage and the Muslim marriage law and points out
      how both these laws affect the lives of Muslim women.
      He suggests some remedies.

262. Wadia, Avabai. "Women's Role in the New India." *Asiatic
      Review*, Vol. 48, No. 176 (1952), pp. 248-265.

      The writer reviews the constitutional as well as legis-
      lative rights of women. Women's work, interest in pub-
      lic life, and need for equal status are emphasized.

263. Yaqin, Anwarul, and Anwar Badar (eds.). *Protection of
      Women Under the Law: An Annotated Bibliography.* New
      Delhi: Deep and Deep Publications, 1982, 200 pp.

      The Chief Justice of India, Y.V. Chandrachud, states
      in the foreword to this book: "The editors have done a
      commendable job by bringing to the doorstep of the
      readers ready knowledge about the literature bearing
      on the protection of women under the law. The editors
      have also successfully identified the weak spots of the
      existing legal order and the blind spots of our social
      system which have contributed to the exploitation of
      women." The book includes literature dealing primarily
      with social, political, economic, educational, adminis-
      trative, industrial, moral, psychological, and other
      problems. This is a pioneering work covering material
      on court decisions from 1950 to July 1981, and laws

pertaining to polygamy, divorce, inheritance, maintenance, and rape, from a variety of law journals and
liberal magazines. There are 417 annotated entries
and author and title indexes of judicial decisions.

Medical Termination of Pregnancy Act
(Abortion)

Inspired by Japanese experiments to legalize abortion,
the Indian government considered such a law in order to control the increasing population. The strong reactions both
for and against are cited. In the following entries, the
law with its implications and attitudes is explained.

264. Mahajan, A. "Social Implications of Legislation of
      Abortion." *Indian Journal of Social Work*, Vol. 37,
      No. 1 (April 1976), pp. 31-38.

      The Medical Termination of Pregnancy Act, which came
      up for discussion in 1974, created much controversy,
      and the Shantilal Shah Committee was appointed to study
      the matter. Here the attitudes toward the law are
      studied by the quota-sampling technique, with 100 women
      selected for interviews. Their as well as their hus-
      bands' education, occupation, and economic status are
      considered. Women have a favorable attitude toward
      abortion but at the same time emphasize that qualified
      doctors should supervise such abortions.

265. Shah, M.H., and J.S. Agarwal. *Medical Termination of
      Pregnancy Programme, Gujarat 1973-74: An Overview*.
      Ahmedabad: Demographic and Evaluation Cell, State
      Family Planning Bureau, Directorate of Health Ser-
      vices (HS), Gujarat, 1974, 10 pp.

      This leaflet describes the progress on the program
      started under the Medical Termination of Pregnancy Act
      of 1971. Also discussed are the reasons for abortions
      and the sociocultural background of the women who de-
      sire them.

266. Singh, K.S., and R.K. Raizada. *Abortion Law in India:
      Past and Present*. Chandigarh: Family Planning Asso-
      ciation of India, Haryana Branch, 1976, 171 pp.

      The Medical Termination of Pregnancy Act was passed
      by the Indian Parliament in 1971, when abortion was a
      social and legal taboo, and in April 1972, it took

effect. This book studies a human problem in its historical perspective. Provisions of the Act with
reference to the Human Rights Charter of the United
Nations and comparison to the abortion laws in other
countries are helpful. Many quotations from the
sacred scriptures, modern law books, and journal articles are quite informative. Appendix 1 reproduces
the Act, with an explanation; other appendices describe
the notifications, the Act of Jammu and Kashmir.
There is a bibliography of books and journal articles
and an index. The volume is useful, and is the only
comprehensive book on the subject.

Adoption

     Adoption rights for women is a relatively new phenomenon.
The Hindu Code Bill granted women property rights; adoption
and maintenance rights therefore became necessary. A few
entries are listed in this subsection to explain the present
position.

267.   Gandhi, Ambalal Bhikhabhai. *The Law of Maintenance of*
         Wives, Children, and Parents in India. Bombay: Milan
         Law Publishers, 1975, 135 pp.

       The author cites critical and recent court cases to
       describe the laws relating to Hindus, Parsis, and Mus-
       lims regarding maintenance.

268.   Government of India, Ministry of Law. *The Hindu Adop-*
         tions and Maintenance Act, 1956 (Act No. 78 of 1956).
         Reprint. Delhi: Manager of Publications, 1959, 11 pp.

       Preliminary remarks and adoption and maintenance laws
       and their various provisions are reprinted here. Al-
       though called the Hindu Law, the law applies also to
       Buddhist, Jain, and Sikh populations. Muslim, Chris-
       tian, Parsi, and Jewish populations are not guided by
       this law, as they have their own religious laws.

269.   Kane, Pandurang Vaman. "Maintenance and Other Topics."
         Pp. 803-824 in his *History of Dharmashastra: Ancient*
         and Medieval Religious and Civil Law. Vol. 3, 2nd
         ed. Poona: Bhandarkar Oriental Research Institute,
         1973.

       Maintenance obligations of the householder are dis-
       cussed, and various textual injunctions with special

reference to widows and concubines are summarized. The author also comments upon the ancient laws and contemporary efforts to modify the maintenance laws.

Child Marriage

Child marriages were very common in the last century as early marriage prevented aggressors or attackers from kidnapping young girls. The infant mortality rate among male children was higher than among girls and so there were many child widows. During the British rule, the Indian social reformers took up this cause. The law restraining child marriages was passed, and the marriage age was raised to 14 for girls and 16 for boys in 1929. Since then the law has been further amended and now the age of marriage is 18 for girls and 20 for boys.

270. Heimsath, Charles H. "The Origin and Enactment of the
        Indian Age of Consent Bill 1891." *Journal of Asian
        Studies*, Vol. 21, No. 4 (1962), pp. 491-504.

        The writer of this informative article traces the
        issue of the Age of Consent Bill as expressed in the
        writings of the Malbari (an ardent 19th century social re-
        former and antagonist of infant marriages) and declares
        that all English-educated Indians agree about the need for
        this social reform. Moreover, he discusses the age of
        consent for widow remarriage and suggests reforms.

271. *India Age of Consent Committee Report, 1928-1929*. Cal-
        cutta: Central Publication Branch, Government of In-
        dia, 1929, 353 pp.

        This report recommends strongly that the age of con-
        sent be raised to 15 years. Information about the forma-
        tion of the Committee, the history of consent legisla-
        tion, existing conditions statewide, and opposition to
        this reform is provided. Recommendations and remedial
        measures along with statistical information make the
        report meaningful. There are numerous appendices.

272. India Home Department. *Papers Relating to Infant Mar-
        riage and Enforced Widowhood in India*. Calcutta:
        Home Department, Government of India, 1886, 303 pp.

        A very important document on the subject, as it con-
        tains B.M. Malbari's notes on infant marriage in In-
        dia and enforced widowhood. Malbari advocates some

specific legal rights for child widows. He collected
opinions from 150 local officials and others who suggested reforms. See also Behramji M. Malbari, comp.
Infant Marriage and Enforced Widowhood in India. Bombay: Voice of India Printing Press, 1887, 109 pp.

273. Kulkarni, G.V. *Child Marriage Restraint Act No. 19 of
      1929, with Amendments up to Date by Act No. 41 of
      1949, Act. No. 48 of 1952*. Ahmednagar: K. Prashashan,
      1953, 180 pp.

      The evolution of the Child Marriage Restraint Act of
      1929 is traced and the amendments carried out by the
      1949 and the 1952 Acts are included and explained in
      this legal textbook.

274. Shastry, L.S. (ed.). *India (Dominion) Laws, Statutes,
      Etc. The Child Marriage Restraint Act as Amended
      up to Date by Act XLI of 1949*. 2nd ed. Allahabad:
      Law Book Company, 1956, 121 pp.

      The complete Child Marriage Restraint Act with its
      subsections is reproduced here including the amendments
      passed in 1949. After the Hindu Code was passed in
      1956, some additional amendments were carried out, all
      of which are incorporated here.

275. Tek, Chand, and H.L. Saran (eds.). *The Child Marriage
      Restraint Act: Being an Exhaustive, Critical and up
      to Date Commentary on the Child Marriage Restraint
      Act, XIX of 1929, as Amended by the Child Marriage
      Restraint (Amendment) Act, VII of 1938, the Child
      Marriage Restraint (Second Amendment) Act, XIX of
      1938 and the Child Marriage Restraint (Amendment)
      Act, XLI of 1949*. 2nd ed. Calcutta: Eastern Law
      House, 1951, 128 pp.

      As the title indicates, this book deals with the
      Child Marriage Restraint Act of 1929, 1938, and 1949.
      The main emphasis is on legal rendering, but the edi-
      tors also offer critical comments.

                              Dowry

    The Dowry Prohibition Act of 1961 did not eliminate this
evil. Parents become victims of the dowry system as there
is no limit to greed. Only a few parents actually adhere
to the law. It was therefore felt by the National Committee

of Women that during the International Women's Year, 1976,
the law must be simplified. The committee appointed by the
Parliament to look into the matter and suggest modifications
has completed its hearings in all the states. The report is
awaited, although there is a general feeling that taking a
dowry payment should be made a punishable offense.

276. "Dowry Custom." *Viveka Kendra Patrika*, Vol. 2, No. 2
     (1973), 256 pp.

     This compilation of material reprinted from various
     sources is comprised of 63 articles, essays, short
     skits and stories, and the text of the Dowry Prohibi-
     tion Act of 1961 along with the findings of some surveys
     by social scientists. The reader is able to study the
     various materials in one place. The stated policy is
     to oppose dowry in any form.

277. Hinchcliffe, Doreen. "The Widow's Dower Debt in India."
     Islam and the Modern Age, Vol. 4, No. 3 (1973), pp.
     5-22.

     A summary of important court cases concerning dowry
     and Muslim women's inheritance in India is given in
     this well-documented article.

Infanticide and Sati

Murdering female children immediately after birth and
the burning of widows after the death of their husbands were
practices of the last century. British rulers and Indian
social reformers created an awareness of these evil customs,
and laws were passed to eradicate these inhuman activities.
The birth of a son is still welcomed and even in modern India
the female fetus is sometimes killed. Entries pertaining
to these aspects are grouped in this subsection.

278. Panigrahi, Lalita. *British Social Policy and Female
     Infanticide in India*. New Delhi: Munshiram Manoharlal,
     1972, 204 pp.

     This book discusses the East India Company's social
     policy on female infanticide in the western and northern
     parts of India. The author traces the history of and
     describes the consequences of the enactment of the
     Prevention of Female Infanticide Act, 1870. An impor-
     tant publication with a good bibliography on the sub-
     ject.

279. Saxena, R.K. *Social Reforms: Infanticide and Sati.*
      New Delhi: Trimurti Publications, 1975, 155 pp.

      The author examines the social systems propagating
      and the movements protesting the evils of female infan-
      ticide and sati in Rajasthan (Western India) during
      the first 50 years of the 19th century. The book is
      useful for historical-legal research.

                            Inheritance

      Women's right to inherit property was frowned upon from
the days of Manu, the ancient law giver, so much so, in
fact, that when the draft of the Hindu Code was discussed
in the Indian Parliament, the reactionary and conservative
members of Parliament and other religious leaders opposed
it to the death. When the bill became an act, some people
called it Nehru's (then Prime Minister) greatest single
achievement, as it was a victory over the orthodox forces of
Hindu society. The entries listed here describe the property
rights in matriarchal as well as patriarchal systems.
"Stridhana," as it is called, means women's exclusive right
over money, ornaments, or immovable property. The attitudes
toward property rights could be pro or con. Some people were
worried that daughters might now file suits against their
brothers in exercise of this right, but this has not occurred.
On the contrary, there are still cases of in-laws snatching
women's property.

280. Altekar, A.S. "The Daughter's Right of Inheritance."
      Pp. 217-223 in P. Sheshadri (ed.). *Har Bilas Sarda
      Commemoration Volume: Presented on the Occasion of
      His Completing Seventy Years.* Ajmer: Vedic Mantralaya,
      1937.

      Altekar describes the ancient law of inheritance with
      citations from Vedic literature and highlights the
      vicissitudes in the 20th century. This is an informa-
      tive and interesting article.

281. Altekar, A.S. "The History of the Widow's Right to
      Inheritance." *Journal of the Bihar and Orissa Re-
      search Society*, Vol. 24, No. 1/2 (1938), pp. 4-28.

      Widows did not inherit in ancient India. The ancient
      literature (i.e., Dharmasutra, 300 B.C.) does not men-
      tion this matter. But a sympathetic attitude did de-
      velop in the 18th century. Conservatives may not agree

to this even today, but laws have been liberalized in
independent India. The regional traditions may vary,
but the right to inherit is granted.

282. Bannerjee, Gooroodass. *The Hindu Law of Marriage and
      Stridhana: Being the Tagore Law Lectures for 1878*.
      Calcutta: S.K. Lahiri, 1923, 550 pp.

      Six lectures on marriage and six on Stridhana (woman's
      exclusive right to money, jewelry, etc., given to her
      at marriage) discuss the traditional Hindu marriage
      law with the help of ancient legal texts and con-
      temporary court cases and legislation describing the
      position before the new Hindu Code was conceived and
      passed in 1956.

283. Bhattacharya, N.N. "Matrilineal Inheritance in India."
      Pp. 63-71 in D.C. Sircar (ed.). *Social Life in An-
      cient India*. Calcutta: University of Calcutta, 1971.

      The southwestern and northeastern parts of India
      have a matriarchal pattern. Discussed here are the
      patterns of inheritance in these parts, which also
      prevail in other parts. Myths from the ancient epic
      Mahabharata are also cited to explain the origin.

284. Chaudhary, Roop L. *Hindu Woman's Right to Property:
      Past and Present*. Calcutta: Firma K.L. Mukhopadhyay,
      1961, 156 pp.

      The classical origins of Hindu women's limited rights
      to property are described. Their rights of alienation
      and of surrender and the Hindu Succession Act of 1956
      are described and discussed at length. A table of
      cases, a bibliography, an index, and references listed
      at the end of every chapter are very helpful.

285. Duff, Ruby. "The Property Rights of Women in the Sutra
      Period." *Modern Review*, Vol. 118, No. 3 (1965), pp.
      239-246.

      Based on ancient Dharmasutra texts, this article
      briefly describes the rights of women to various types
      of property at different stages of life.

286. *Hindu Women's Property Rights: Report of the Committee
      Appointed by His Highness the Maharaja of Baroda*.
      Baroda: Printed at Government Press, 1930, 213 pp.

      The Maharaja of Baroda was a very progressive person;
      having noticed the inequalities of inheritance laws and

realizing that the status of women could not be improved
unless these barriers were removed, he appointed a committee to examine the property rights of women under
Hindu law and suggest amendments. The evidence from
religious as well as contemporary sources enriches the
report. A specially prepared questionnaire is included.

287. Kane, Pandurang Vaman. "Stridhana." Pp. 770-802 in
     his *History of Dharmasutra: Ancient and Medieval Re-
     ligious and Civil Law*. Vol. 3. 2nd ed. Poona:
     Bhandarkar Oriental Research Institute, 1973.

     Stridhana means a woman's property, given to her
     by either parents or in-laws. In these 32 pages,
     the author explains the Hindu legal traditions and
     clarifies the meaning of "Stridhana," woman's control
     over it, and inheritance of it.

288. Madan, Atma Prakash. "Stridhana or Woman's Property
     in Indian Law: An Appraisal of Its Concept and Con-
     tents." *Vishveshvaranand Indological Journal*, Vol. 9,
     No. 1 (1971), pp. 85-108.

     In this article the author attempts to classify dif-
     ferent kinds of stridhana with the help of Sanskrit
     texts and also discusses some recent court cases.

289. Mukherjee, Prabhati. *Property Rights of Women as Re-
     corded in Kautilya Arthasastra and Manusmrti*. Cal-
     cutta: Our Book Company, 1947, 420 pp.

     Ambivalent attitudes regarding the property rights of
     women are the subject of this book. In his examination
     of these two ancient canonical books, the author high-
     lights the unhappy legal standing of women.

290. Narang, Sharda. "Women and Property." Pp. 309-311 in
     Shyamkumari Nehru, ed. *Our Cause: A Symposium by
     Indian Women*. Allahabad: Kitabistan, 1938.

     The writer gives a summary of Hindu, Islamic, Parsi,
     and Christian laws of inheritance for women. Hindu
     law is the most archaic according to the author, but
     the Islamic, Parsi, and Christian laws are not pro-
     gressive enough to favor women in any way.

291. Sirvya, Bhagvandas. *Hindu Women's Estate: Non-Technical
     Stridhana*. Calcutta: Butterworth, 1913, 418 pp.

Hindu women's property rights as described in traditional legal texts are documented in this book.   All
cases available up to the end of August 1913 are listed
and discussed.   This volume will be useful for researchers engaged in comparative studies.

292.   Sivaramayya, B. *Women's Right of Inheritance in India:
A Comparative Study of Equality and Protection.*
Madras: Madras Law Journal Office, 1973, 215 pp.

Sivaramayya compares the legal position of Hindu and
Muslim women regarding the laws of inheritance.   He
describes and discusses the Hindu Succession Act of
1956 and the law of inheritance according to Muslim
law as described in the *Quran*.   Also indicated briefly
are present trends and his suggestions for reaching
the goal of equality.

Marriage and Divorce

According to ancient Hindu scriptures, marriage is a
sacrament: once married, always married, but there are still
destitute women and separated couples.   Bigamy is also prevalent and often women are humiliated and insulted.   The medieval age and the Moghul rule denied women all rights.   During
British rule, an awareness of wrongdoing was created, and
rules remedying the situation were passed.   After independence, an equal-rights movement was launched.   In this section
are listed ancient laws as well as new laws regarding marriage and divorce with commentaries and critiques.

293.   Agrawala, Rajkumari. *Matrimonial Remedies Under Hindu
Law.* Bombay: N.N. Tripathy, 1974, 332 pp.

The book discusses the form, content, and potential
of the Law of Marital Relief to the Hindus of India.
Agrawala also studies in depth the restitution of
conjugal rights, judicial separation, divorce, nullity,
maintenance and alimony, desertion, cruelty, adultery,
impotence, and other such grounds for relief.   The pro-
cedure of claiming such relief is also discussed.

294.   Agrawala, Rajkumari. "Restitutions of Conjugal Rights
Under Hindu Law: A Plea for the Abolition of the
Remedy." *Journal of the Indian Law Institute*, Vol.
12, No. 2 (1970), pp. 257-268.

The author pleads for the removal of the provision in
the Hindu Marriage Act of 1955 under which the court

compels the husband and wife to cohabitate. Mere staying together may not establish harmony. Therefore,
legal intervention is not justified and should be
avoided. Also recommended here is reconciliation
through counseling.

295. Bagga, V. (ed.). *Studies in the Hindu Marriage and
      Special Marriage Act.* Under the auspices of the Indian
      Law Institute, New Delhi. Bombay: N.M. Tripathi,
      1978, 352 pp.

      This book reports the special seminars held to dis-
      cuss both these acts. Many papers examine critically
      various provisions, compare the acts, and suggest
      modifications.

296. Chaudhri, D.H. *India (Republic). Laws, Statutes, Etc.
      The Special Marriage Act: Act No. 43 of 1954, with
      an Exhaustive Commentary, Explanatory and Critical
      Notes, Case-Law, High Court and State Government
      Rules, Table of Cases, Index, Etc.* 2nd ed. Cal-
      cutta: Eastern Law House, 1958, 340 pp.

      The actual text and detailed interpretation of the
      civil marriage act are discussed. Intercaste marriages,
      civil marriages with the couple belonging to the same
      caste, and interreligious but solemnized marriages
      and their implications are examined. Throwing light
      on the law itself with the help of typical cases, this
      publication is a handy guide for any given problem.
      It can make decision-making easier.

297. Das, R.M. *Women in Manu and His Seven Commentators.*
      Bodh-Gaya: Kanchana Publications, 1962, xxii + 288 pp.

      Manusmruti occupies a unique position under the Hindu
      Dharmashastra. This book is a commentary on Manu's--
      the ancient lawgiver's--treatise. Manu was a very ortho-
      dox person who put many restrictions on the freedom of
      woman--as a daughter, sister, wife, mother, widow--in
      whatever role or status she may have. In this book, a
      commentary is offered and numerous quotations are
      cited. An index and glossary of Indian terms are also
      given.

298. Deolalkar, P.V. *Hindu Marriage Act, 1956 No. 25, As
      Amended Up To Date.* 2nd ed., Allahabad: Law Book
      Company, 1764, 347 pp.

The Act, commentary, some typical court cases, and
court rulings are listed. References to other marriage
laws are cited, creating a comparative study. As a
guide to precedents, it is a very useful book.

299. Desai, Kumud. *Indian Law of Marriage and Divorce*.
     3rd ed., Bombay: N.M. Tripathi, 1978, 576 pp.

     The Special Marriage Act 1954, the Hindu Marriage
     Act 1955, the Parsi Marriage and Divorce Act of 1936,
     the Indian Christian Marriage Act of 1872, and the In-
     dian Divorce Act of 1869 are included in this book.
     Various provisions, amendments, and relevant cases
     are discussed in detail. There is a reference to
     Muslim personal law.

300. Hussain, S. Jaffer. *Marriage Breakdown and Divorce
     Law Reform in Contemporary Society: A Comparative
     Study of USA, UK and India*. New Delhi: Concept
     Publishing Company, 1983, 240 pp.

     Divorce is not a matter for guilt but rather a re-
     sult of the breakdown of marriage, according to this
     publication. The author mirrors the legal developments
     in Anglo-American society and makes a strong case for
     reforms in the divorce law of India. As the former
     justice of the Supreme Court of India says in the fore-
     word: "Dr. Hussain's contribution, marked by well-
     arranged case-law, well-planned structure and well-
     argued thesis, is a welcome addition to the not-so-
     plentiful literature on comparative matrimonial law."
     A comparative, in-depth study of Indian Divorce Law,
     recommended reforms, and suggestions for a common
     secular civil code are the components of this book.
     An epilogue, notes, a bibliography, and an index are
     all useful.

301. Jailal. *Law of Marriage and Divorce in India*. Delhi:
     Metropolitan Book Company, 1956, xvi + 262 pp.

     The laws pertaining to marriage and divorce among
     four major communities (Hindus, Muslims, Parsis, and
     Christians) are described, discussed, and interpreted
     in four distinct sections. This book presents a com-
     parative picture of legal provisions.

302. Jhabvala, Noshirvan H. *Law of Marriage and Divorce in
     India*. Bombay: D.B. Taraporevala Sons and Co. Ltd.,
     n.d., 172 + 12 pp.

Published as a part of the Law for the Layman series,
this book will serve as a guide on matters such as
engagement, marriage, and divorce among Hindus, Muslims,
Parsis, and Christians. Various religious laws govern-
ing these communities are explained in detail. A 12-
page supplement, "Summary of the Special Marriage Act
of 1892," is attached at the end.

303. Kapadia, K.M. *Hindu Marriage and Divorce Bill (A Criti-
      cal Study)*. Bombay: Popular Book Depot, 1953, 27 pp.

The sections pertaining to the marriage and divorce
laws along with the proposed changes in the Hindu Code
Bill are objectively discussed in this brochure. Quoting
the findings of two M.A. theses (Gunial Desai's empirical
study on Gujarati women in Bombay city and B.L. Mankad's
study of Vadnagra Nagars of Kathiawar) regarding the
age at marriage, infant mortality, selection of partners, bigamy, and divorce, the writer makes some valuable
suggestions for the proposed bill.

304. Mukherjee, B.N. "Awareness of Legal Rights Among
      Married Women and Their Status." *Indian Anthropolo-
      gist*, Vol. 5, No. 2 (1975), pp. 30-38.

1,872 married women from Haryana, Tamil Nadu, and
Meghalaya states were interviewed with reference to
modernism, personal efficacy, attitudes toward small
families, and women's legal rights. The study reveals
that they don't seem to be much concerned about equal
wages for equal work or legal abortion. But even in
rural areas, women were aware of their right of inheritance.

305. Muller, Max F. (ed.). *The Laws of Manu, Sacred Books
      of East Series*. Vol. 25. Oxford: Clarendon Press,
      1886, cxxxviii + 60 pp.

Civil and criminal laws drafted by Manu pertaining to
women's lives are translated by Max Muller. The duties
of a woman as a daughter, sister, wife, mother, etc.,
are laid down. Laws pertaining to age at marriage,
gifts to be given to the daughter at the time of the
wedding inheritance, and widow remarriage are
also intended to affect women only, giving freedom to
men. The male chauvinistic attitude of Manu is reflected in the laws that he framed. Sanskrit couplets
in the original language and English translations with
comments are given exhaustively. Oriental alphabets

with English phonetics are also provided for scholars
who want to read the original text.

306. Qureshi, M.A. *Marriage and Matrimonial Remedies: A
Uniform Civil Code for India.* Delhi: Concept Publishing Company, 1978, 478 pp.

The author critically examines all the matrimonial
laws and compares their form, content, nature, and implications. He also discusses personal marriage laws
and suggests remedies for various marriage problems
in different communities while recommending a uniform
civil code in order to avoid complications.

307. Rees, J.D. "Meddling with Hindu Marriages." *Nineteenth
Century*, Vol. 28 (Oct. 1890), pp. 660-676.

This 16-page article discusses dispassionately the
ethics of British and legal intervention in regard to
the female age of marriage in India. Opinions of eminent persons are included, and many statistics are
cited.

308. Saharay, H.K. *Laws of Marriage and Divorce in India.*
Calcutta: Assam Book Depot, 1980, 40 + 18 + 151 pp.

This book describes the institution of marriage in
detail, viz. the Hindu Marriage Act, 1955; the Special
Marriage Act, 1892; the Indian Divorce Act; the Foreign
Marriage Act, 1969; the Muslim Marriage and Divorce
Law in India; and the Parsi Marriage and Divorce Act,
1936. Recent decisions of the Full Bench, Special
Bench, and Division Bench of different High Courts
have been added. Amendments proposed by the Law Commission of India are appended. A comprehensive index
and a table of cases add to the usefulness of this
volume.

309. Thomas, P. *Women and Marriage in India.* London: George
Allen and Unwin Ltd., 1939, 224 pp.

The author looks at the marriage system and family
patterns of India as they existed in 1939. He discusses women's traditional subjugation, low health
standards, and the position of child-wives and widows,
while indicating the new trends and liberal ideas cal-
culated to improve conditions for the downtrodden and
to raise the status of Indian women, which leaves much
to be desired.

Prostitution

In ancient India, prostitutes and courtesans were guided by religious laws. In modern India, in order to protect prostitutes and prevent illegal trafficking in women, some legal safeguards have been provided. Entries pertaining to the relevant act are listed here.

310. Husain, Mazhar. *Mazhar Husain's The Suppression of Immoral Traffic in Women and Girls Act, 1956: With Critical Commentary, Case Law and States' Rules.* 3rd ed. Revised and enlarged by Vijay Malik. Lucknow: Eastern Book Company, 1978, 210 pp. (1st ed., 1958).

      Texts, interpretations, and references to relevant cases make this revised edition valuable. A comparative study has been made of the provincial and federal Suppression Laws for the benefit of practicing lawyers.

311. Jaykar, R.B.K. "Prostitution and Immoral Traffic in India." Pp. 353-371 in India (Republic). Planning Commission. *Social Welfare in India.* Ed. Durgabai Deshmukh. New Delhi: Publication Division, Ministry of Information and Broadcasting, Government of India, 1955.

      Jaykar briefly reviews the various legislation of different states of India on prostitution and recommends an All-India Act. Because of the poor enforcement of present laws, the government is not able to regulate prostitution. Jaykar discusses the role of rescue homes in rehabilitating prostitutes. The importance of sex education in preventing venereal disease is stressed.

312. Kane, Pandurang Vaman. "Vesya." Pp. 637-639 in his *History of Dharmasastra: Ancient and Medieval Religious and Civil Law*, Vol. 2, Pt. 1, 2nd ed. Poona: Bhanderkar Oriental Research Institute, 1974 (1st ed., 1941; Government Oriental Series Class 13, 6).

      The author and scholar discusses the law of the ancient Hindus relating to courtesans, prostitutes, and concubines. Their right to maintenance is also described and interpreted.

313. Sternbach, Ludwik. "Legal Position of Prostitutes Ac-
      cording to Kautilya's Arthasastra." *Journal of
      American Oriental Society*, Vol. 71 (1951), pp. 25-
      60.

      The writer, referring to this ancient source, has
      described the legal position of prostitutes from the
      point of view of the state. He discusses the state-
      supported system of prostitution as it existed in
      ancient India and the subsequent enactments of laws.

                              Sati

      Sati (Suttee) or self-immolation of a widow on her
husband's funeral pyre was a common custom in the 19th century. British rulers found it barbaric, and Indian social
reformers agreed it was a very cruel practice. With the
help of the social reformers, Britishers created a public
reaction against the practice, and it was abolished in 1829.

314. "Abolition of Suttees: 1829 Regulation 17." *Asiatic
      Journal*, Vol. 2, No. 5 (1830), pp. 38-39.

      This brief article discusses the text of the Suttee
      Prohibition Act passed by the British government in
      1829, which declared the custom illegal in Bengal.

315. Boulger, Demetrius C. "The Abolition of Widow Burning"
      in his *Lord William Bentinck*. Oxford: Clarendon
      Press, 1892, 77-111 pp.

      The custom of burning widows alive that was prevalent
      in India in the nineteenth century is described in
      detail. Also listed are the causes that led Bentinck
      to prepare his famous minutes, which were instrumental
      in the passing of the anti-suttee enactment throughout
      British India. This article is a primary source of
      research as the full text of the minutes is reproduced.

316. "The Suttee Regulation," *Asiatic Journal*, Vol. 2, No.
      7, 1830, 134-40 pp.

      Eight hundred Hindus protested to William Bentinck,
      Governor-General of India, against abolition of widow
      sacrifices. Bentinck's reply defending the Government's
      policy, newspaper reports supporting Bentinck, and
      Bentinck's further correspondence are the contents of
      this article. The original documents are reproduced.

VI

SOCIAL PROBLEMS

In spite of new constitutional rights and the freedom to
participate in various spheres of sociopolitical life, Indian
women, by and large, face numerous problems: social inequality, social injustice, discrimination, infanticide, foeticide,
child marriage, dowry payments, divorce, sati, suicide, and
widowhood. Although infanticide and sati are illegal and
prohibited by law, foeticide is a new problem. Knowing the
sex of the child in advance is no doubt a boon from one
point of view. What is regrettable is the abuse of this
knowledge when the female foetus is killed. Child marriages
are illegal, but in rural India they still take place. The
system of dowry poses a grave problem; "dowry deaths" and
"dowry debts" are the new phrases that have been coined to
explain this evil practice.

In this section, the issues are listed alphabetically.
Some of the problems are things of the past, e.g., sati--
burning of a widow on the funeral pyre of her husband. During
British rule sati attracted the attention of the authorities,
and many scholars spoke out forcefully against this practice.
Some new problems have, however, surfaced, e.g., sex typing
of jobs, inequality, divorces, widow remarriages and the
problem of children from the previous marriage, rape and
crimes against women, suicide because of role conflicts,
etc. At the end of this section, some entries provide information about organizations that provide help to women.

317.   DeSouza, Alfred. "Day Care for the Urban Poor: A Pro-
       file of Women and Children." *Social Action*, Vol.
       29, No. 4 (1979), pp. 404-425.

       This research article should be an eyeopener about
       the situation of children in the creches, their migrant
       mothers, and their socioeconomic characteristics. The
       data was collected from 23 creches: the working women
       came to Delhi from different parts of the country, and
       most of them were married, illiterate, had 4 to 6
       children of different ages, and engaged in either fac-
       tory or construction work. Their husbands are engaged

in vocations like washing, masonry, painting, and petty
trades and are from low-income strata. Their children
naturally suffer from malnutrition and poor health.
The profiles presented with the help of demographic
analysis present a ghastly picture.

318. Gandhi, M.K. *Women and Social Injustice*. Ahmedabad:
Navjivan, 1954, 207 pp.

The historical aspect of injustice to women in
ancient India is depicted here. The book also contains letters to Gandhiji from women who sought his
advice on various social problems and Gandhiji's replies, originally published in *Young India*, which
Gandhiji edited. There is an index.

319. Mantab, B.C. *Studies*. Calcutta: W. Newman and Company, 1904, 91 pp.

This small book includes chapters on early marriage,
widow marriage, prostitution, and education of girls.
The author has written this book primarily to describe
the effect of British rule on certain classes in Bengal.
Although not an in-depth study, it reflects the thinking
of a certain class of people at the beginning of the
present century.

320. Shintri, Sarojini; C.R. Yaravintelimath; and S.L.
Shantakumari (eds.). *Woman: Her Problems and Her
Achievements*. Dharwar: Karnatak University, 1977,
128 pp.

This volume presents the proceedings of the symposium
organized to celebrate International Women's Year.
Topics include family planning, dowry, employment,
political rights, and removal of inequalities. Economic exploitation is also discussed and welfare programs are suggested.

321. Singh, D.R. "Current Trends and Forms of Crime Against
Women." *Indian Journal of Social Work*, Vol. 42, No. 1
(April 1981), pp. 33-40.

Singh attempts to determine the trends and forms of
crimes against women and the constitutional and legal
positions vis-à-vis offenses against women in this
article. The author observes that offenses against
"suppression of immoral traffic" are on the increase
in India. The incidence of rape is also increasing.

322. Singh, Renuka. *Oppression of Women by Women*. New
         Delhi: Data Centre, Vishwa Yuvak Kendra, 1980, 48 pp.

      This booklet discusses a very topical subject. In
      Delhi, a woman judge acquitted a husband who was al-
      leged to have burnt his bride, but sentenced the woman's
      mother-in-law and sister-in-law to life imprisonment.
      Adapted from the author's Ph.D. thesis on the position
      of Indian women with 40 case studies developed from
      interviews, the booklet focuses attention on the destruc-
      tible and the destroyer. That the case studies are told
      out of context reduces the utility of the data on an
      important theme.

323. Young Women's Christian Association. *A Place to Live:
         A Study on Housing for Women*. Bombay: Allied Publi-
         cation, 1975, viii + 136 pp.

      This study deals with the housing needs of students,
      working women, and the aged. Part I deals with the
      housing problems, and Part II discusses the nature of
      the study and data and statistical tables. The data
      were collected through interviews with 700 women in 10
      cities. The survey recommends a mixture of different
      types of accommodation for working women on one site.
      The role of voluntary agencies in providing such
      special facilities is defined.

                          Child Marriage

     Child marriage and age at marriage pose a grave problem.
There used to be many child widows because of the high incidence of death among male children. Thought was given to
the question of the right age for marriage after India
became independent. The country again was faced with a
population problem. Entries pertaining to some studies on
infant marriages and attitudes against them as well as age
of consent for marriage and recent trends are listed.

324. Agarwal, S.N. *Age at Marriage in India*. Allahabad:
         Kitab Mahal, 1962, 296 pp.

      Census data from 1891 to 1951 are studied here with
      statistical techniques. Findings include a slow in-
      crease in the mean age at marriage among women, from
      roughly age 13 to 15, while the mean age at marriage

for men has remained steady at 20. Data is analyzed by
state for religion, caste, sex, age, and year. Numerous
graphs and tables present a comparative picture.

325. Chaterjee, Heramba. "Position of Women as Reflected
in the Forms of Marriage." *Calcutta Review*, Vol. 145,
No. 1 (1957), pp. 67-72.

Manu the lawgiver listed eight forms of marriage.
In this brief article, the writer describes these eight
forms and their implications as far as the status of
women was concerned. Manu favored child marriages.
Brahm was the best form and Pishach was the lowest.

326. "Child Marriages Still Widespread." NSS Data Analysis
by *The Economic Times* Research Bureau, 20 Dec. 1971,
4 + 6 pp.

As part of the National Sample Survey, analyzing 1951
and 1961-65 census figures regarding age at marriage of
Hindu women, both rural and urban, the article concludes
that child marriages are still common, although differences do exist in different communities and regions.
Full of statistical data, graphs, and three tables,
this article is a much-studied one.

327. Dandekar, Kumudini. "Age at Marriage of Women." *Economic and Political Weekly*, Vol. 9, No. 22 (1 Jan.
1974), pp. 867-874.

Dandekar notes the change in age at marriage in different states and also in rural-urban areas. She also
compares age at marriage in neighboring countries,
e.g., Pakistan and Sri Lanka. She discusses the in-
effectiveness of the legislation and the factors responsible for it.

328. Fawcett, Millicent Garrett. "Infant Marriage in India."
Contemporary Review, Vol. 58 (Oct. 1890), pp. 712-720.

The writer stresses the need for legislation to stop
child marriages in India. She supports the position
of Hindu women writers. She also notes the statements
of women doctors. She has collected from newspaper reports some cases of murder and suicide of child wives
and argues vehemently against the practice.

329. Fuller, M.B. *The Wrongs of Indian Womanhood*. Edinburgh:
Oliphant Anderson and Ferrier, 1900, 302 pp.

Pandita Ramabai Saraswati wrote the introduction to
this book dealing with the social life of women and
their problems such as child marriage, sati, etc. The
underlying tone indicates that Christianity alone can
change society and customs.

330. Goyal, R.P. "Shifts in Age at Marriage in India Be-
      tween 1961 and 1971." *Demography India*, Vol. 4, No.
      2 (1975), pp. 336-344.

      In this analytical article, the writer concludes from
      the census data that the age at marriage for males and
      females among both urban and rural populations in all
      the states had risen during 1961-1971 from 16.1 to 17.2
      for women and 21.4 to 22.2 for men. Kerala is at the
      top and Madhya Pradesh at the bottom.

331. Gulati, Leela. "Age of Marriage of Women and Population
      Growth: The Kerala Experience." *Economic & Political
      Weekly*, Vol. 11, No. 31/33 (Aug. 1976), pp. 1225-
      1234.

      The population growth rate in Kerala does not seem
      to have been affected by the raising of the marriage
      age. Raising the marriage age should have helped to
      reduce the number of children, but due to the reduction
      in infant mortality, there were more children.

332. Gulati, Subhashchander. "Impact of Literacy, Urbanisa-
      tion and Sex-Ratio on Age at Marriage in India."
      Artha Vijnana, Vol. 11, No. 4 (1969), pp. 685-697.

      By using the census data of 1961 and adopting statis-
      tical technical methods, the author of this article
      concludes that because of a rise in literacy, age at
      marriage is increasing in both sexes.

333. Hirmani, A.B. "Age at Marriage in Two Villages of
      Marathawada." *Social Change*, Vol. 6, Nos. 3 & 4
      (Sept.-Dec. 1976), pp. 13-17.

      Boys and girls still marry before the legal age.
      The stipulated age for marriage is 18 for boys and 16
      for girls, but the law is not strictly observed by
      lower-class communities in the rural areas. This article
      studies 20% of the families from Golatgaon and Kolghar
      villages near Aurangabad. The author concludes that
      social change has not reached these villages because
      enforcement of the law is a problem.

334. Jain, P.K. "Marriage Age Patterns in India." *Artha Vijnana*, Vol. 11, No. 4 (1969), pp. 662-684.

     The author has studied the census data of 1961 and tabulated marriage age by sex, state, and urban-rural areas of residence. This is an analytical study with tables, but no conclusions are offered.

335. Kale, B.D. "Education and Age at Marriage of Females in India." *Journal of the Institute of Economic Research*, Vol. 4, No. 1 (1969), pp. 59-74.

     Education helps raise marriage age, concludes the author after analyzing the census data of 1961. There is a positive correlation between education and rise in the age at marriage. Educational planners should take note of this.

336. Mayo, Catherine. *The Women and Children of India.* New York: Child Welfare Committee of America, Inc., 1928, 13 pp.

     This leaflet offers crude criticisms of Indian marriage patterns, including child marriages and enforced widowhood at the age of 20-40, which are now part of the past in independent India. This leaflet was written at the urging of the British government primarily to malign India.

337. Rathbone, Eleanor F. *Child Marriage: The Indian Minotaur. An Object Lesson from the Past to the Future.* London: Allen and Unwin, 1934, 138 pp.

     The facts concerning child marriage, its repercussions, and the remedy are discussed at length. The author has obtained the opinions of different authorities for this publication.

338. Ryder, Emily Brainerd. *The Little Wives of India.* Philadelphia: Allen, Lane and Scott, 1903, 134 pp.

     The author criticizes the custom of child marriage in India. She has collected many anecdotes and opinions from popular sources, and traces the custom's historical origin and lists the reforms that have taken place so far. Photographs illustrate her points.

339. Sengupta, N. *Evolution of Hindu Marriage with Special Reference to Rituals, c. 1000 B.C.-A.D. 500.* Bombay: Popular Prakashan, 1965, 191 pp.

The evolution of Hindu marriage, the origin of child
marriage, various forms of marriage, intercaste marriage,
and widow remarriage which adversely affect the status
and position of Hindu women are described and explained
with a critical view.

340. Singh, Mrs K.P. "Women's Age at Marriage." *Socio-
     logical Bulletin*, Vol. 23, No. 2 (1974), pp. 236-244.

     The trends with regard to marriage over three genera-
     tions are observed in this empirical study. The age
     at marriage is definitely increasing, but not yet to
     the desired extent. Data for this research article
     were gathered from 325 women in Chandigarh. Daughters'
     marriages are still considered a parental responsibility
     that parents are very eager to discharge.

341. "A Terrible Memorial: Fifty-Five Lady Doctors, Mission-
     ary and Otherwise, Petition the Indian Government on
     the Subject of Child Marriage." *Medical Missionary
     Record*, Vol. 6, No. 12 (1891), pp. 271-272.

     This article is critical of the custom of child mar-
     riage then prevalent in India. The physical damage
     caused by adult husbands to their young brides during
     sexual intercourse is attested to by women doctors.
     This article is presented in the form of a petition.

342. "Trends in Marriage Age of Girls in India." *Artha
     Vijnana*, Vol. 13, No. 1 (1971), pp. 119-137.

     The author concludes that since 1941 fewer marriages
     have taken place in the age group of 10-14. The age
     at marriage is continuously rising; in some cases the
     age at marriage has been between 20 and 24.

                           Destitution

     The problem of destitute women in India is no doubt
serious; however, no attempt has been made to study the
problem on a systematic basis. Destitute women suffer from
a stigma, and they will not talk about their situation open-
ly and frankly, but a few entries have been located.

343. Bose, Ashish. *Aspects of Aging in India*. Delhi: In-
     stitute of Economic Growth. (This study was not ex-
     amined by the compiler personally. The annotation
     is based on a press report in *Times of India*, 28 Sept.
     1982.)

Bose, the noted demographer, concludes in this study
that the number of single-member households among aged
women is higher than for men in both rural and urban
areas, indicating distress and destitution among the
women. There are more widows than widowers in older
age groups. Bose thinks that life expectation at birth
is lower for women than for men in India. At the age
of 45 and above, however, the life expectation of
women is higher. The social custom of discouraging
women to remarry may be one of the factors accounting
for women's destitution. He suggests some measures to
relieve the sufferings of destitute women who do not
have anyone to look after them, such as health in-
surance, part-time jobs, etc.

344. Chowdhury, T.K. "Women Destitutes." *Survey*, Vol. 13,
     No. 182 (1973), pp. 36-43.

Destitution is defined as the socioeconomic condition
wherein a person is deprived of privileges and opportunities of any kind. The government of Bengal and
some private social voluntary organizations have taken
some steps to help destitute women by providing legal
aid and rehabilitation. The author describes the difficulties in getting exact facts and figures about
such women.

345. Kumar, Arvind. *A Study in the Ethics of the Banishment
     of Sita*. 2nd ed. New Delhi: Sarita Magazine, 1975,
     68 pp.

The author examines the episode of the desertion of
Sita by Rama and tells us that it indicates the inferior
status of women. He feels that Indian society even
today sometimes intentionally suppresses women and
humiliates them.

346. Kumar, V., and Shubha Singh. "Government Sponsored Hell-
     Holes for the Destitute." *Eve's Weekly*, 7-13 Aug.
     1982, pp. 12-15.

Nari Niketan in Delhi is managed by the Delhi administration. Originally established by a voluntary organization named Nari Raksha Samiti, it changed hands in
1979 and has become a hell-hole. The inquiry committee
appointed by the Supreme Court to study its conditions
revealed that the women destitutes were neglected;
women with serious health problems were not treated
and women with psychiatric problems are housed together

in the same premises. Women are starved, used as prostitutes, and many suffer from venereal diseases. This
article brings out these facts forcefully.

Dowry

In present-day India, especially in the northern part of
the country, the problem of dowry has become acute and
chronic. Dowry deaths and dowry debts have risen to alarming proportions. The activist feminist groups are trying to
pressure the government to prevent this torture and the suicides committed by young brides. "Women are not for burning"
and "Down with dowry" are the slogans used to stir the government machinery to help the cause. India's having until recently had a woman Prime Minister has not been of much assistance to the cause, many women feel. The Dowry Prohibition
Act itself has many loopholes, and no attempt is being made
to eliminate them.

347. Anandan, Sujata. "Marriage or Murder." *Illustrated
        Weekly of India*, 15-21 Aug. 1982, pp. 16-19.

        Greed for dowry leads to harassment and murder of
        brides and daughters-in-law. The author provides
        statistics to explain the seriousness of the dowry
        problem. The needs for stricter legislation and social
        awareness to change attitudes toward women are empha-
        sized.

348. Gangrade, K.D. "Evils of Dowry." *Social Change*, Vol.
        9, No. 3 (1979), pp. 24-30.

        The article points out the disadvantages of the dowry
        system, listing the unfortunate happenings as reported
        in newspapers and other references and sources, dis-
        cusses the anti-dowry movement and legislation, and
        reiterates the need for the social reform movement
        that Gandhi launched to create awareness about these
        evil customs and eradicate them. References will prove
        useful to researchers who want to probe further into
        the matter.

349. Hooja, Swarna L. "Dowry System Among Hindus in North
        India: A Case Study." *Indian Journal of Social Work*,
        Vol. 28, No. 4 (Jan. 1968), pp. 411-426.

        A questionnaire study of 498 Delhi families of Hindus
        and Sikhs regarding attitudes toward dowry. The re-

searcher has correlated results by age, sex, caste, marital status, education, and economic strata. Findings indicate that negative aspects of this evil custom should be publicized.

350. Hooja, Swarna L. *Dowry System in India: A Case Study.* Delhi: Asia Press, 1969, 236 pp.

This is a study of 498 Delhi families belonging to the Hindu and Sikh religions concerning the prevalence of dowry and their attitude toward this practice. The question of why people give dowry is examined. The researcher has correlated results by age, sex, caste, marital status, education, and economic strata. Findings indicate the negative aspects of this evil custom and suggest some measures to eradicate this practice. The volume is illustrated with many tables.

351. Nair, P.T. *Marriage and Dowry in India.* Calcutta: Minerva Publications, 1978, x + 205 pp.

The general characteristics of marriage in India, the custom of dowry, and various forms of marriages (i.e., barter, purchase, capture, etc.) are described with examples from specific communities. The taboos regarding certain types of marriages are explained. Indian marriage customs are varied and colorful among tribal people. These customs are also described. A glossary, bibliography, and index are included.

352. Ras, Prakasha, and V. Nandini Rao. "The Dowry System in Indian Marriages, Attitudes, Expectations and Practices." *International Journal of the Sociology of Family*, 10 (1) (Jan.-June 1980), pp. 99-113.

The authors of this research paper examine students' expectations of dowry, comparing persons with different educational backgrounds, attitudes, and feelings about the dowry. Dowry expectations were not consistent.

353. Swaminatha, K. *Bridal Duty: A Tax Proposal.* Mysore: Rao and Raghavan, 1967, 35 pp.

This pamphlet recommends proposals for gathering marriage statistics through marriage registration. The author even suggests a tax to be levied on marriage expenditure with a fixed ceiling in order to eradicate this social evil.

354. Thankappan, Nair P. *Marriage and Dowry in India.* Calcutta: Minerva, 1978, 205 pp.

Unfamiliar marriage practices prevalent in India are
described. The author discusses the various aspects
of marriage (i.e., economic, choice of a marriage part-
ner, marriage according to curious rules, mock marriages,
couvade, and defloration in Kerala). The place of dowry
and its lessening relevance are also discussed.

355. Vander Veen, Klaus W. *I Give Thee My Daughter: A Study
     of Marriage and Hierarchy Among the Anavil Brahmins
     of South Gujarat.* Assen: Van Giorcum, 1972, 272 pp.

     This report is the result of an investigation to
     study the marriage pattern of Anavil Brahmins of South
     Gujarat, among whom dowry is obligatory for the parents
     of daughters. The data discloses a marked ideological
     continuity in the general processes of social change.
     This is an ethnographic study, considering women's roles
     in hypergamous marriage networks. This work was trans-
     lated from the Dutch.

356. Verghese, Jamila. *Her Gold and Her Body.* Delhi: Usha
     Publications, 1979, 160 pp.

     Because of the dowry problem, Indian women feel in-
     secure and they face rejection. They are considered a
     liability from birth. The psychological repercussions
     of this evil are discussed.

Divorce

    Marital disharmony and family disorganization that cul-
minate in divorce are discussed in this subsection. The incidence of divorce is still not yet alarming, because in
lower-class communities, couples do not have resort to courts
of law.

357. Agarwal, A.K. "Patterns of Marital Disharmonies."
     Indian Journal of Psychiatry, Vol. 13, No. 3 (1971),
     pp. 185-193.

     Forty couples are observed in a clinical situation,
     and their maladjustment as well as interactional pat-
     terns are examined at length. The author has concen-
     trated mainly on the reasons for marital disharmony
     and on whether mental health problems are responsible
     for divorce or not.

358. Fonseca, Mabel B. "Family Disorganisation and Divorce
     in Indian Communities and 'Marital Separations'--Dis-

organisation as Seen Through an Agency." *Sociological Bulletin*, Vol. 12, No. 2 (1936), pp. 14-33; and Vol. 13, No. 1 (1964), pp. 47-60.

The court records of 894 couples who have sought help from the Bombay City Civil Court since 1954 are studied to determine their education, age, occupation, length of marriage, number of children, cause of marital dissatisfaction, etc. These data are analyzed in the first paper through tables. The second paper deals with desertion resulting from domestic discord and at the same time tries to present a sociological and economic profile of the court cases. This is an interesting study.

359. Guha, U. "Attitude of U.P. Village Women to Purdah and Divorce." *Bulletin of the Department of Anthropology, Government of India*, Vol. 3, No. 2 (1954), pp. 1-7.

A sample was taken from Jaunpur district in Uttar Pradesh, and Hindu and Muslim women from 13 villages were interviewed. Many women supported purdah. Those who objected expressed their preference for equality, but divorce was not favored by many.

360. Kelkar, M.P. *When Marriages Are in a Turmoil*. Nagpur: Vishwa Bharati Prakashan, 1976, 140 pp.

The author, a lawyer specializing in divorce cases, narrates 12 such cases with complete proceedings in such a way that all facets of the problem of divorce become clear.

361. Lam, M. Tata. "Divorce in India." Pp. 287-305 in Shyam Kumari Nehru (ed.). *Our Cause: A Symposium on Indian Women*. Allahabad: Kitabistan, 1938.

This article encompasses important features of Hindu, Islamic, Parsi, and Christian divorce laws. Citation of particular cases helps clarify problems.

362. Mehta, Rama. *Divorced Hindu Women*. Delhi: Vikas Publishing House, 1975, vi + 173 pp.

This study takes the readers into the world of separated (not divorced) women. Most of them are victims of the dowry system, some staying with their parents and others engaged in their professions. The book depicts their life styles, ideas about fidelity and chastity,

modernity and traditionality. The book suffers from
its interchangeable use of such distinct terms as
"divorce" and "separation," "modern" and "Western."
Eight case studies do not reveal anything. This is a
disappointing study.

363. Narain, Dhirendra. "Family Disorganisation in India."
      Pp. 81-106 in Dhirendra Narain (ed.). *Explorations
      in the Family and Other Essays: Professor K.M.
      Kapadia Commemoration Volume.* Bombay: Thacker and
      Company, 1975.

      This article includes various indicators of family
      disorganization and summarizes a nationwide demographic
      study of widowed, divorced, disabled, destitute, home-
      less, institutionalized, and unemployed men and women.
      The data are presented in a well-organized form, i.e.,
      by sex, state, and urban-rural areas. The 1961 census
      data are analyzed. Many tables illustrate the points.

364. Shasmal, Kartik Chandra. "Divorce and Its Causes Among
      the Bauris of West Bengal." *Bulletin of Cultural Re-
      search Institute, Calcutta*, Vol. 6, No. 1-2 (1967),
      pp. 73-77.

      286 marriages of this scheduled caste are surveyed
      in Hoogli District. 102 of the women and 90 of the men
      were married for the second time. More than half of
      the divorces were the consequence of child marriages
      in which the brides refused to stay with their husbands.
      Other causes of divorce were economic backwardness,
      ill health, and similar disabilities.

                Family Planning and Abortion Studies

     The population explosion has wiped out whatever economic
strides India has been able to make. Because of the inferior
status of women, population-control measures (legalized abortion, sterilization, intrauterine contraceptive devices, oral
contraceptives, etc.) were devised for women only. Advocates
of family planning appealed to women to adopt small-family
norms, as if the sole responsibility for limiting the size
of the family were theirs. In this subsection entries pertaining to fertility control are indicative of women's inferior status.

365. Bhatnagar, N.K. "Status of Women in Family Planning in
      India." *Journal of Family Welfare*, Vol. 28, No. 3
      (1973), pp. 21-28.

The writer considers the question of whether the
higher status of women will result in the increased
adoption of family planning methods. A higher level of
education, a higher age at marriage, and greater economic participation may lead to the acceptance of the
small-family norm.

366. Dandekar, Kumudini. "Trends of Fertility Behaviour
      Reflecting the Status of Women." *Social Change*, Vol.
      4, Nos. 3 & 4 (1974), pp. 36-51.

      This is a descriptive paper that tries to answer such
      questions as: Do women have the capacity to control
      their own reproductive behavior? What is the performance
      of Indian women in this regard? Dandekar examines
      various factors (e.g., sex ratio, age at marriage,
      education, and employment opportunity) which lead her
      to conclude that Indian women are not capable of con-
      trolling their reproductive behavior. She suggests
      compulsory sterilization after bearing two or three
      children as the only way to raise the economic status
      of women in India.

367. Kar, S.B. "Opinion Towards Induced Abortion Among
      Urban Women in Delhi." *Social Science and Medicine*,
      Vol. 6, No. 6 (1972), pp. 731-736.

      300 randomly selected women were interviewed. A
      majority of them approved of abortion under the follow-
      ing conditions--rape, possibility of deformed offspring,
      and unwed pregnancy. 80% approved of abortion for
      limiting family size and for economic reasons.

368. Mullick, Saroj, and K.S. Bhardwaj. (National Institute
      of Family Planning). "Attitudes of Indian Women
      Towards Abortion." *Indian Journal of Social Work*,
      Vol. 33, No. 4 (1973), pp. 317-332.

      This study correlates the attitudes of 615 women of
      Delhi belonging to various socioeconomic strata and
      age groups regarding abortion, number of pregnancies
      and living children, occupation, education, type of
      family, contraceptives used, expected number of chil-
      dren, ideal number of children, etc. 36% of the women
      considered abortion a sin and a crime whereas 32%
      favored it.

369. Rajyaguru, H.M. "Relative Status of Women and Family
      Planning." *The Indian Journal of Social Work*, Vol.
      42 (July 1981), pp. 141-148.

For the purpose of family planning, the status of
the wife seems to be relatively more important than
her husband's socioeconomic status.

370. Reddy, P.H. "Family Structure and Fertility." *Social
      Change* (March 1978), pp. 24-32.

      This is a fertility study conducted at a microlevel
      at which the demographer tries to analyze the relation-
      ship between characteristics of individual respondents
      --age, age at marriage, marital duration, education,
      occupation, income, etc. 5,200 households--400 each
      from the rural areas of Bangalore--have been studied
      with the help of census data. Reddy states that the
      sex ratio at birth is 107.7 males per 100 females.
      Fertility indices are illustrated through tables; fer-
      tility rates in different types of families vary--they
      are higher in extended families and higher in rural
      than in urban families. Activists have to consider
      ways and means of influencing members of the family
      other than the couple. This article contains a very
      rich review of earlier studies and many references.

                        Female Infanticide

     Female infanticide was a common practice in medieval and
Moghul India, particularly in some communities. Among the
Patidar community in Gujarat, it was practiced because of the
dowry system. A female child was considered a liability at
birth and therefore was murdered. The British considered
this a barbaric custom and a much-debated policy was formu-
lated to stop it. Ultimately a law was enacted as a way of
implementing social reforms.

371. Brown, John Cave. *Indian Infanticide: Its Origin,
      Progress and Suppression*. London: W.H. Allen, 1957,
      xiii + 234 pp.

      Indian infanticide, its character and motives, the
      efforts to suppress it by legal actions in various
      parts of India and through creating an awareness of the
      ghastly custom through public meetings and discussions,
      statistics of female infanticide and how it was put to
      an end, etc., are all described in depth. Although
      the custom is obsolete, the recorded history is always
      useful. Tables, an appendix, and footnotes are im-
      portant.

372.   Edwardes, S.M. "Infanticide and Child Murder." Pp.
       29-33 in his *Crime in India: A Brief Review of the
       More Important Offences Included in the Annual Crimi-
       nal Returns, with Chapters on Prostitution and Mis-
       cellaneous Matters*. London: Oxford University Press,
       1924.

       The writer notes the prevalence and causes of female
       infanticide and suggests measures to eradicate it.
       Although the incidence is relatively low, general
       negligence toward and rejection of female children
       still prevail.

373.   "Female Infanticide in Central and Western India."
       Calcutta Review, Vol. 1 (Aug. 1844), pp. 372-448.

       Observations in this long article are by British
       authorities who tried to treat the root cause of this
       evil. The article is based on official papers on infan-
       ticide in India from 1824, 1828, and 1843 and it ob-
       serves that the custom started with Rajputs. The ar-
       ticle is very valuable for its documentation of the
       historical aspects of this evil. Solutions are sug-
       gested. Statistics of the last century are reprinted.

374.   Mehta, Makrand J. "A Study of Female Infanticide
       Among the Kanbis of Gujarat." *Topic*, Dec. 1966, pp.
       21-26.

       In the state of Gujarat, Kanbis are famous on the
       agricultural front. Most of them are agriculturists,
       growing cash crops, although there are also traders.
       Among this community, until the 19th century, the
       cruel practice of killing female children existed.
       This article deals with the origins of this custom
       and gives incidence by district during the years 1846,
       1847, and 1848; the factors responsible for this evil
       custom; and the Government of India Act No. VIII of
       1870 for the preservation of female infants.

375.   Moor, Edward (ed.). *Hindu Infanticide: An Account of
       the Measures Adopted for Suppressing the Practice
       of the Systematic Murder by Their Parents of Female
       Infants, with Incidental Reference to Other Customs
       Peculiar to the Natives of India*. London: J. Johnson
       and Company, 1811, 312 pp. (This publication was not
       available for examination.)

376.   Nath, Vishwa. "Female Infanticide and the Lewa Kanbis
       of Gujarat in the Nineteenth Century." *Indian Economic*

& *Social History Review*, Vol. 10, No. 4 (1973), pp. 386-404.

Lewa Kanbis are a peasant people who mostly live in Gujarat. The author examines the custom of female infanticide and its relationship to hypergamy, polygamy, the lineage system, and other social institutions. This is a descriptive study based on government records.

377. Pakrasi, Kanti. "The Genesis of Female Infanticide." *Humanist Review*, Vol. 2, No. 7 (1970), pp. 255-284.

Referring to the act of killing "useless mouths" because of the "grinding pressures of circumstances," the author attributes infanticide to war and poverty. Discussing Malthus, McLennan, Carr-Saunders, and Krzywicki's observations regarding overpopulation, poverty, exogamy, etc., the writer blames Indian marriage customs. The 37 references noted at the end of the article will prove useful to scholars.

378. Pakrasi, Kanti. "On Female Infanticide in India." *Bulletin of the Cultural Research Institute*, Vol. 7, No. 3/4 (1968), pp. 33-48.

This sympathetic review of the practice of female infanticide in the late 19th and early 20th century among some communities delves deeply into the causes, incidence, and effects of the custom. The custom of giving dowry to the in-laws of the daughter and the fear of kidnapping of girls by invaders are the reasons suggested to explain the cruel and odd custom.

379. Panigrahi, Lalita. *British Social Policy and Female Infanticide in India*. New Delhi: Munshiram Manoharlal, 1972, 204 pp.

In addition to tracing the British discovery of the practice of female infanticide in India, this study highlights the social policy of the East India Company in Bombay, Rajputana, North-Western Provinces, and Punjab and the development of social legislation to prevent female infanticide by the Act of 1870. Tables and an excellent bibliography of many official and private sources are presented.

Prostitution

The history of prostitution, its causes, and the socio-economic, psychological problems faced by prostitutes are dis-

cussed as a grave problem to society. Rescuing and rehabilitating the victims becomes difficult as this requires time,
energy, and, above all, money. Religious prostitution in
the form of temple dancers, princely prostitution in the
form of courtesans, and commercial prostitution, are all
dealt with in the following entries. The elitist forms,
e.g., call girls, friendship treaties (contracts signed by
men with women who act as the men's mistresses but possess
no legal rights) are becoming common in the cities of modern
India. In whatever form, ignorant and immature women are
trapped, led to brothels, and sexually exploited. These
women suffer from poverty, ill-health and neglect in old age.
Prostitution thus becomes a social problem. The entries in
this subsection try to trace its genesis and its effect on
the sociopsychological health of society; some empirical
works attempt to study the problems and suggest remedial
measures.

380. Agnihotri, Vidyadhar. *Fallen Women: A Study with
      Special Reference to Kanpur*. Kanpur: Maharaja Print-
      ers, n.d., 99 pp.

      400 out of 1,600 prostitutes of Kanpur city were
      studied, with special reference to their problems.
      Poverty seems to be the main cause of prostitution.
      Many young girls were kidnapped and sold to brothels
      and thus pushed into "the oldest profession." Their
      socioeconomic background and standard of living are
      examined. The author suggests some measures to mini-
      mize this evil. Tables, case histories, and photographs
      document this study.

381. Aiyappan, Parvathi. "Prostitutes: Notes from a Rescue
      Home." Pp. 261-268 in Devaiki Jain, ed. *Indian
      Women*. New Delhi: Publications Division, Ministry of
      Information and Broadcasting, Government of India,
      1975.

      This article presents interviews with and detailed
      case studies of 4 women staying in the rescue home in
      Ernakulam, South India, which was established under the
      provisions of the Suppression of Immoral Traffic in
      Women and Girls Act.

382. Banerjee, G.R. *Sex Delinquent Women and Their Rehabili-
      tation*. Bombay: Tata Institute of Social Sciences,
      n.d., 142 pp.

      Sex delinquency of women in ancient as well as present-
      day India is the main subject of this report, which

deals with the causes and some facets of the problem.
Rehabilitation, in the light of available statistical
data collected from the institutions that provide shelter to such deviant women, is also discussed at length.
Two appendices listing homes for sex-delinquent women
and a select bibliography are given.

383. Basu, Kajal. "The Devdasis of Pune." *Sunday Observer*,
          4 July 1982.

      This article refers to the unhealthy conditions in
which "devdasis" (young women dedicated during puberty
to individual gods and goddesses) live and suffer from
leprosy and venereal diseases. It is presumed that
Poona city has about 5,000 prostitutes, of whom 3,000
are devdasis. They have organized themselves and have
demanded certain rights, e.g., their illegitimate
children should be accepted, free education should be
provided, etc.

384. Bullough, Vern, et al., eds. "Area Studies: India."
          Pp. 40-42 in their *A Bibliography of Prostitution*.
          New York: Garland Publishing, 1977 (Garland Reference
          Library of Social Science, 30) (unexamined by the
          compiler).

      This bibliography lists 44 pertinent entries.

385. Bureau of Psychological Research. *A Psycho-Social
          Study of the Institutionalised Victims of Immoral
          Traffic and Commercialised Vice in Madras City*.
          Madras: Bureau of Psychological Research, 1969.
          (This report is annotated from a review article be-
          cause the book itself was not examined by the compiler.)

      This is an official report of an intensive study of
prostitutes. Personality tests indicated the age
range of victims, their marital status, and why they
became prostitutes. All of them reported faith in
gods and goddesses. Most of them possess low I.Q.s,
and they suffer from anxiety and negativism. They did
not appear to be amoral. The study presents and in-
terprets many tables.

386. Chandran, Ramesh. "Should Prostitution be Banned?"
          Illustrated Weekly of India, Vol. 93, No. 48 (26 Nov.
          1972), pp. 8-15.

      The psychology of prostitution is considered in this
article. The various definitions along with the special

circumstances which lead women to this profession are
discussed. Legal regulations, sexual diseases, and
other health problems are discussed. This popular
article is illustrated with photographs.

387. Chaterjee, Santosh. *Devdasi Temple Dancer*. Calcutta:
      Book House, 1945, 128 pp.

In South India, the custom of temple dancers existed.
Parents dedicated their young daughters to the god's
services. The recruitment and training was done by
the trustees of the temple. These devdasis were not
allowed to marry; often they were used as prostitutes.
This book throws much light on the lifestyles and problems of these women and refers to the anti-devdasi
movement and the social change in the offing. Some
drawings of the hand gestures of temple dancers and excerpts from personal accounts enhance this publication.

388. Crooke, W. "Prostitution (Indian)." Pp. 406-408 in
      James Hastings, ed. *Encyclopaedia of Religion and
      Ethics*, Vol. 10. New York: Charles Scribner's Sons,
      1919.

This is a brief history of prostitution in India from
the Vedic age to the British period. References from
Hindu scriptures and Buddhist religious literature are
quoted and the customs of temple dancers are described.
Primary sources augment the other good source material.

389. Edwardes, S.M. "Prostitution in India." Pp. 71-88 in
      his *Crime in India: A Brief Review of the More Im-
      portant Offences Included in the Annual Criminal Re-
      turns, with Chapters on Prostitution and Miscellaneous
      Matters*. London: Oxford University Press, 1924.

Reviewed in this article are the traditions of devdasis (temple dancers) and courtesans in princely states.
The chief duty of devdasis and other sacred prostitutes
was dancing before the gods. Every region had a brand
of prostitutes, as described in this essay. The modern
commercial type of prostitution is also dealt with in
detail. Comparisons are offered between European and
Indian prostitution. The total number of rape cases in
1924 is given by region.

390. Gupta, Rabindranath. "From the Green Hills of Purola
      to the Brothels of Delhi and Meerut: A Study of the
      Immoral Trafficking in Women from the Purola Block of

Uttarkashi District (U.P.)." Pp. 37-52 in *Bonded Labour in India: A Shocking Tale of Slave Labour in Rural India*. Calcutta: Indian School of Social Sciences, 1974.

Women from lower-class communities in Purola district are exported as bonded laborers. Due to dire poverty they are easily entrapped and then sold to brothels from which there is no escape. *Bonded Labour* ... includes the proceedings of the 1974 Seminar on Cultural Action for Social Change. This worthwhile publication is an eyeopener written in powerful language.

391. Hasan, Amir. "Immoral Traffic Among Harijans of Rawain in Uttar Kashi District of Uttar Pradesh." *Social Welfare* (May 1973), pp. 13-15.

Abject poverty forcing women into prostitution is the subject of this empirical survey article. Women from 45 out of 1,000 Harijan (untouchable) families (125 women in all) were forced to become prostitutes. 62 villages of the Uttar Kashi District were affected. 5 tables analyze the problem of trafficking and the methods of traffickers. The author blames prostitution on poverty, indebtedness of the Harijans to landlords, and the socioeconomic hegemony exercised by the local high-caste people.

392. Henriques, Fernandes. "Classical India." Pp. 140-203 in his *Prostitution and Society, a Survey VI: Primitive, Classical and Oriental*. London: MacGibbon and Kee, 1962.

Ancient books of history, epics, Buddhist and Muslim texts, travelogues, etc., are referred to and quoted to give a complete historical review of forms of prostitution.

393. Jaykar, R.B.K. "Prostitution and Immoral Traffic in India." Pp. 353-371 in Durgabai Deshmukh, ed. *Social Welfare in India*. New Delhi: Publications Division, Ministry of Information and Broadcasting, Government of India, 1955.

Prostitution is discussed as a social problem. The author emphasizes the need for All-India legislation. The rescue homes and programs for rehabilitating fallen women are discussed. The need for sex education and problems pertaining to venereal diseases are stressed.

394. Kapur, Promilla. *The Life and World of Call-Girls,
      Etc. in India: A Socio-Psychological Study of Aristo-
      cratic Prostitutes.* New Delhi: Vikas, 1978, 368 pp.

      Clandestine prostitution is the main subject of this
      research study. Why do college girls, married women,
      working women, and even schoolgirls earn money by sell-
      ing sex? Dr. Kapur answers many such queries after
      interviewing 150 such women in Bombay, Calcutta, and
      Delhi. Citing case studies, the writer concludes that
      frustrations in first love affairs, greed, sexual
      harassment at the place of work, and promiscuous habits
      are some of the major contributing factors. Some of
      these women were lesbians. The author suggests some
      preventive measures.

395. Mamoria, C.B. "Prostitution in India." *Indian Journal
      of Social Work*, Vol. 17, No. 2 (Sept. 1959), pp.
      106-112.

      This article discusses the problem of prostitution
      from various angles, and presents statistics provided
      by the All India Association for Moral and Social Hy-
      giene on the number of brothels in different states.

396. Mark, Mary Gilen. *Falkland Road.* London: Knopf, 1981,
      112 pp.

      A close study of the red-light area of Bombay and
      the women's lifestyles. The author stayed with one of
      the owners of a brothel and probed deeply into this
      underworld life. She describes how the human flesh
      trade operates and the roles of pimps and policemen.
      The book is illustrated.

397. Mathur, A.S., and B.L. Gupta. *Prostitutes and Prosti-
      tution.* Agra: Ram Prasad and Sons, 1965, 255 pp.

      The chief informants for this study were rescued
      prostitutes staying in a protective home in U.P.,
      North India, and from the streets of Agra. Their re-
      ports were verified by interviewing doctors and re-
      searchers. The life histories of the 20 main in-
      formants are supplied in the appendix.

398. Misra, Prashanta. "What Is Wrong with Prostitution?"
      Surya India, Vol. 1, No. 4 (1977), pp. 53-57.

      This empirical article studies prostitutes from Bom-
      bay City. The writer feels that banning prostitution

will not solve the problem; treating prostitutes like
human beings and solving their health problems will
prove a better solution. Photographs are included.

399. Mukherjee, S.K. *Prostitution in India.* Calcutta: Das
      Gupta and Company, 1934, x + 528 pp.

      A brief history of prostitution, lifestyles in
      brothels, and the means of suppression are given in
      this book. Abduction and the flesh trade are also
      described. The information was collected by personal
      investigations and from governmental sources, associa-
      tion reports, and from people who are actively engaged
      in fighting the trafficking in women. The book is
      well-documented.

400. Promodkumar. "Prostitution: A Socio-Psychological
      Analysis." *Indian Journal of Social Work*, Vol. 21,
      No. 4 (March 1961), pp. 425-430.

      This study deals with licensed prostitutes of Baria
      and Gutula in North India. The author has tried to
      study their mental health and dissatisfactions and
      frustrations. Deprived of love, they suffer the pangs
      of an uncertain future and social condemnation.
      Societal disapproval is painful for them.

401. Punekar, S.D., and Kamla Rao. *A Study of Prostitutes
      in Bombay.* Revised 2nd ed. Bombay: Lalvani Publish-
      ing, 1967, 244 pp. (1st ed., Bombay: Allied Publish-
      ers, 1962.)

      This is a field study of 370 prostitutes and 75 kept
      women. Their socioeconomic backgrounds, lifestyles,
      and motivations for entering this profession are studied.
      A comparison between the devdasis (temple dancers) and
      prostitutes is made. A good bibliography and some
      typical case studies enrich this field study.

402. Raikar, Y.A. "Prostitution During the Yadava Period."
      Journal of the Oriental Institute of Baroda, Vol. 13,
      No. 2 (1963), pp. 124-133.

      The prostitution that existed during the 12th and
      14th centuries is described here with the help of
      Marathi Mahanubhava cult literature and the Jnanesvari.
      The text is based on literature rather than historical
      sources.

403. Raina, Bhushan. "Delhi's Singing Girls." *Illustrated*

Weekly of India, Vol. 93, No. 48 (26 Nov. 1972), pp. 16-17.

In this too-short article the writer introduces the readers to a small community of dancing and singing girls in Delhi, who also indulge in prostitution. Photographs are included.

404. Rampal, S.N. *Indian Women and Sex*. New Delhi: Printex, 1978, 178 pp.

A sociological study of the sexual behavior of Indian women. Data were compiled from personal observations and a questionnaire returned by Delhi doctors. Relationships between men and women in India, the ancient saint Vatsyanana's approach to sexuality, and opinions of urban middle-class women about prostitution are also analyzed. Typical case studies enrich this empirical work.

405. Rao, Ranga M., and J.V. Raghavender Rao. *The Prostitutes of Hyderabad: A Study of the Socio-Cultural Conditions of the Prostitutes of Hyderabad*. Hyderabad: Association of Moral and Social Hygiene in India, Andhra Pradesh Branch, 1970, 79 pp.

70 prostitutes and 30 singing and dancing girls are studied in this brief report. Their educational and income levels and attitudes toward their profession are studied and analyzed. Interpretations are drawn from the demographic tables. At the end, 10 short life histories are presented for in-depth study.

406. Sinha, S.N., and N.K. Basu. *History of Prostitution in India*. Calcutta: Bengal Social Hygiene Association, 1933, 229 pp.

This book provides a historical picture of prostitution in India. This is the first volume in a series by the Social Hygiene Association. The roots of prostitution are traced to the ancient Indian custom of temple dancers. Details about these dancers in various parts of India are given, and the work of the Bengal Social Hygiene Association in rescuing minor girls from the brothels and rehabilitating them is highlighted.

407. Number omitted.

408. Trivedi, Harshad R. *Scheduled Caste Women: Studies in Exploitation*. New Delhi: Concept Publishing, 1976, 256 pp.

This book defines and describes three types of prostitution (religious, clandestine, and professional).
Also included are profiles of scheduled caste women
from the 1971 census data, traffic in human flesh in
Madhya Pradesh, Uttar Pradesh, and case studies of
prostitutes. Four appendices reproduce lists of
governmental and nongovernmental helpers, census
tables, genealogies for the case studies, and survey
results.

Purdah

Purdah means "a veil"; women should hide themselves behind the veil and should not come out in public barefaced
or without proper covering. This custom came into practice
because of foreign invasions on the borders of India;
the invaders kidnapped women and harassed them sexually.
Initially only Muslim women observed the purdah, which was
slowly adopted by Hindu women as well. Different forms of
purdah came into existence e.g., covering the full face
with the sari, covering the head, shoulders, and bust with
a shawl, etc. But this system restricted movements and
caused sex segregation. It impeded progress and participation in socioeconomic activities, and hence a social protest
movement started against it. Scholars found it indicative
of arrested progress.

409. Hanswirth, Frieda (Mrs. Sarangadhar Das). *Purdah: The
       Status of Indian Women*. London: Kegan Paul, Trench,
       Trübner and Co., 1932, ix + 289 pp.

       A Swiss writer, after her marriage to a Hindu hus-
       band, Mrs. Das had the exceptional opportunity of seeing
       life in India from an unusual viewpoint and found new
       angles of approach to the complex question of the
       status of Indian women. She deals with the Mohammedan
       influence and custom of purdah prevalent at the advent
       of British rule. The movement against the custom and
       the determination to assert women's rights are also
       dealt with in detail, and biographical references are
       made to the persons who guided such educational as well
       as national political movements. There are a bibliog-
       raphy, tables, and index, as well as a brief and good
       biography of Sister Nivedita.

410. Jeffery, Patricia. *Frogs in a Well: Indian Women in
       Purdah*. New Delhi: Vikas Publishing House, 1979,

vii + 187 pp. (Illustrated version available from
Zed Press, 57 Caledonian Road, London NI 9DN, U.K.)

The author portrays the lives of Indian women in
purdah, which means seclusion and restricted participation in educational, social, and career opportunities. For her in-depth study the author has contacted
Muslim women. She discusses the difference in the
Purdah system between Hindu women and Muslim women.
Purdah restricts development; life revolves around
hearth, home, and other "womanly" activities. References at the end of every chapter, tables, bibliography,
index, and sketches of women involved in various activities are very relevant.

411. "Prabha" (pseudonym). *Purdah Women's Abode*. Bombay:
Popular Prakashan, 1962, 100 pp.

The book narrates important incidents from the real
life of a purdah woman. Kalpana narrates her sufferings and states that her life has been ruined by the
invisible cruelties of the purdah system. According
to the author, the purdah system is a social evil
which isolates women and excludes them from any useful
activities by segregating the sexes. It should be
abolished as soon as possible.

412. Shastri, Shakuntala Rao. "The Purdah." *Journal of the
Gangnatha Jha Research Institute*, Vol. 7, No. 2/4
(Feb.-Aug. 1950), pp. 109-124.

Segregation of sexes and forms of seclusion in South
Asia are explained with the help of historical sources.
Shastri stresses that the sexes were not segregated
in Vedic times. The custom took root only during the
Epic period and grew worse during the Buddhism, Jainism,
and Moghul periods. This very informative research
article cites references from ancient primary sources
and Sanskrit creative literature to substantiate the
points.

413. Urquhart, M. *Women of Bengal: A Study of Hindu Pardana-
sins of Calcutta*. Calcutta: Association Press,
1926, 165 pp. (also London: Student Christian Movement, 1926, 165 pp.).

The scope of this book is limited to the high-caste
women of Calcutta. It describes the home life and
religious beliefs of these women. Coming out barefaced in public in the first quarter of the present

century was unthinkable for these women, and their interests were confined to family life. However, the
influence of various social movements brought about a
change, and they participated in the freedom struggle.
The book also discusses the Bengali homes, furnishings,
family life, manners and customs, religious life, etc.
The book is illustrated.

Rape

The rape of women and young girls is a grave problem in
India. Women are not safe at their workplaces, homes,
prisons, or even at police headquarters. The attitude
toward women as sex objects and objects of exploitation is
primarily responsible for this situation. The incidence of
rape is rising, and every day nine cases are reported.
There may be many more such cases which go unreported. The
entries in this subsection lament these facts, but the sorry
state of affairs continues due to many loopholes in the law.
Recently an awareness has been created, but awareness and
sympathy alone cannot remedy the situation.

414. Narayanan, Gita. "Rape: The Shame of a Nation." *Illus-
     trated Weekly of India*, 15 June 1980, pp. 31-32.

     The majority of rape cases go unreported because of
     the victim's feelings of guilt and the stigma attached
     to the rape. The raped woman is humiliated and shamed.
     This article refers to some of the famous rape cases
     which stirred the women of India, gives a table of
     registered cases of rape in India, and illustrates the
     callous indifference of the government administration
     and politicians toward this problem.

415. Ramchandani, H.N. "Rape Victims: The Legal Odds."
     Femina, 4-17 June 1976, pp. 35, 39, 43.

     In this article, the legal definition of rape under
     the Indian Penal Code is given along with interpreta-
     tions of the clauses and subclauses. The author ex-
     plains the difficulties encountered in dealing with
     rape cases in the courts and in bringing the rapist to
     book. The police in many cases treat the complaint
     in a light-hearted manner; they sometimes jeer at the
     victim. Parents of the girl victims are reluctant to
     go to court, as it is difficult to identify the rapist,
     and the testimony of the victim is not considered
     enough evidence by the court. So the offenders are
     often acquitted.

416. Savera, Mira. "Lacunae in Rape Law." *Eve's Weekly*,
10-16 Dec. 1977, pp. 10-11.

Rape has become one of the central concerns of the
women's liberation movement all over the world, but
in India, in spite of a rise in the incidence of rape,
true concern is lacking. The rape laws are full of
loopholes, so offenders are not punished while victims
suffer socially and psychologically. Women's organizations are not raising their voices against this crime,
and they are doing nothing to bring the culprits to
punishment or to assist the victims. The author
criticizes the law (i.e., the Indian Penal Code) and
complains about the prevailing situation.

417. "Sexual Harassment of Working Women." *Femina*, 2-15
Dec. 1977, pp. 27, 31.

Femina reporters (Y.K. Sapru from Bombay, Brinda
Dutta from Calcutta, Promilla Kalhan from Delhi, Shashi
Deshpande from Banglore, and Girija Rajendran from the
film industry) filed case studies of rape victims and
the conditions of sexual exploitation. A very frank
discussion and actual case studies are the outstanding
facets of this eye-opening article.

                              Sati

Sati (or *suttee*), burning a widow on her husband's funeral pyre,
was another cruel and barbaric custom. Social reformers--
mostly men, along with British rulers--aroused the public
against this practice and a law prohibiting it was finally
passed. Lord Bentinck, Raja Rammohan Roy, and Ishwarchandra
Vidyasagar were responsible for this reform. Entries in this
subsection deal with the history of the custom, the starting
of the protest movement, and finally the law prohibiting it,
which allows a widow the right to live.

418. Andhare, Shridhar, and Yogesh Badhwar. "Do We Still
Burn Our Widows?" *Femina*, 23 Nov. 1973, pp. 24-27.

In 1973, a crowd of 70,000 gathered to witness the
self-immolation of a widow in Rajasthan. The authors
discuss the origin of the custom of sati and give a
graphic description of widow burning. Two colored and
one black-and-white photographs help project a realistic idea of this custom. Andhare is a curator of
paintings in Bombay's Prince of Wales Museum, and he

provides historical as well as cultural information
about sati. This is a very informative article,
quoting many sources.

419.   Ganguli, Narendranath. "A Note on Sati." *Bengal:
       Past and Present*, Vol. 70, No. 133 (1951), pp. 55-57.

       The writer recounts an actual case of a woman who
       followed sati in Howrah in 1828 in spite of public
       protest. A table lists cases that occurred in Bengal
       from 1815 to 1828.

420.   Griffiths, Percival. "Suttee." Pp. 216-225 in his
       The British Impact on India. London: Macdonald,
       1952.

       British rulers considered sati, or self-immolation,
       barbarous. The British policy on this issue and the
       historic decision are discussed. A brief review of
       ancient attitudes is also given. This is a good source
       of firsthand material on the subject, citing historical
       sources.

421.   "Humayun First to Ban Sati." *Indian Express*, 14 Jan.
       1981.

       Humayun, a Moghul King, was the first to invoke the
       prohibition of sati. According to the National Ar-
       chives and various travelogues (e.g., Berniers), the
       ban on sati in Moghul times did not lead to any violent
       protests or demonstrations by the Hindu priesthood.
       But the emperor revoked the ban out of fear of divine
       retribution, as is brought out at an exhibition held at
       the National Archives, Delhi. The article is illus-
       trated with an original painting.

422.   Kamath, M.V. "Sati: The Shame of a Nation." *Illus-
       trated Weekly of India*, Vol. CL, No. 15 (13 April
       1980), pp. 20-23.

       The author describes in detail recent sati cases,
       with photographs, outlines the historical background
       with statistical tables, and describes the efforts of
       social reformers and British rulers to outlaw this
       barbaric custom.

423.   Mehta, M.J. "The British Rule and the Practice of
       Sati in Gujarat." *Journal of Indian History*, Vol.
       XLIV, Pt. II, No. 131 (Aug. 1966), pp. 553-560.

The practice of sati was the major social issue with
which the British government was confronted. This
custom was glorified in Hindu tradition, and monuments
to widows were erected that exist even today. Many
cases are cited in this article. The British efforts
to rouse public opinion against sati and the legal
measures taken to curb this evil are described. References to the governmental sources or gazettes as well
as tables are very important.

424. Nandy, Ashis. "Sati: A Nineteenth Century Tale of
Women, Violence and Protest." Pp. 1-31 in his *At
the Edge of Psychology*. Delhi: Oxford University
Press, 1980.

The writer looks at the sati problem from a psychological viewpoint, reviews the happenings since the
legal abolition of sati in 1829, and refers to the
authoritarian attitude of Indian men toward women,
social change, and the feminine protest. The ideals
that Indian women cherish and changes that have been
brought about are also examined. Notes and relevant
references are listed at the end of the chapter.

425. Rajbans, Malavika. "Sati--A Burning Issue." *Femina*,
8-22 Jan. 1981, pp. 23-26.

"The custom of sati originates in the belief that
women are mere appendages of their husbands, but years
of social conditioning have also made women only too
keen to give in to social demands," writes Rajbans.
In this brief article she cites some cases, traces the
origin of the custom to Vishnu Smriti, and gathers the
opinions of some men on the problem.

426. Roy, Rammohan. *Translation of a Conference Between an
Advocate and an Opponent of the Practice of Burning
Widows Alive from the Original Bengali*. Calcutta,
1818 (reprinted in translation of several principal
books, passages, and texts of the Vedas and some con-
troversial works on Brahminical theology, 2nd ed.,
London: Parbury, Allen and Company, 1932, 28 pp.;
also in *The English Works of Raja Rammohan Roy*.
6th ed. Ed. Jogendra Chunder Ghose, Calcutta:
Srikant Roy, 1901, 28 pp.

The arguments of both sides on the matter of burning
widows alive are given in these works, citing textual
authorities. Rammohan Roy's argument is that mounting

the funeral pyre was optional according to Hindu scriptures and that a widow could instead lead a pious life.

427. Salvi, Gouri. "Sati: A Disturbing Revival." *Eve's
      Weekly*, 7-13 Feb. 1981, pp. 17-49.

      The writer refers to a registered organization in
      the capital city of India (Delhi), which every year
      commemorates a sati committed several hundred years
      ago by sending out invitations and running newspaper
      advertisements, thereby trying to revive the medieval
      practice. The writer laments this attitude and
      stresses the need for abolishing it.

428. "The Suttee and the Widow." *Asiatic Journal*, Vol. 23,
      No. 90 (1837), pp. 112-123.

      The customs of child marriage and widow burning and
      the ill treatment meted out to widows by Hindu society
      are criticized in this article.

429. Thomson, Edward. *Suttee: A Historical and Philosophical
      Enquiry into the Hindu Rite of Widow Burning*. Boston:
      Houghton Mifflin and Company, 1928, 165 pp. (also
      London: G. Allen and Unwin, 1928).

      A detailed account of the evil of sati by an ardent
      crusader. He deals in this book with the origin of
      sati, the prevalence of this rite, sati memorials,
      causes, and attempts to ban the custom by British as
      well as Indian social reformers. Some cases are ap-
      pended.

430. Venkatarama Sastri, T.R. "Vedic Attitudes to Sati."
      Journal of Oriental Research, Vol. 20, No. 1/4
      (1953), pp. 1-4.

      During Vedic times, Indian women enjoyed such near
      equality that a widow could even head a family. This
      article refers to Vedic phrases and verses and indicates
      that the symbolic sati rite was practiced.

431. Yule, Henry, and A.C. Burnell. "Suttee." Pp. 878-883
      in their *Hobson Jobson: A Glossary of Colloquial
      Anglo-Indian Words and Phrases and of Kindred Terms,
      Etymological, Historical, Geographical and Discursive*.
      2nd ed. (reprint of 1903 ed.). Delhi: Munshiram
      Manoharlal, 1968.

      This article is of great importance as far as the
      etymological aspect of sati is concerned. Quotations

from ancient, medieval, and contemporary sources and
firsthand reports are useful to researchers, who may
be at a loss to understand the complex Indian culture.

Suicide

The problem of suicide is reaching alarming proportions.
Although it is not sanctioned by Indian society--as it is in
Japan--and is considered a crime, many people try to end
their lives. Women especially end their lives because of
unbearable poverty, marital disharmony, quarrels with in-
laws, dowry demands, and insulting and torturing situations.
Family counselling units and free legal aid are not yet provided by women's organizations. Hence, women feel helpless
and find suicide the only way to free themselves from the
miseries of life. Entries in this section deal with causal
factors and incidence. The problem has often been analyzed
by specialists, but the solution is difficult if not im-
possible to find.

432. Garg, R.B.L. "Anatomy of Suicides." *Free Press*,
       31 Dec. 1981.

       India ranks third in the world as far as the suicide
       rate is concerned. Every day there are 9 recorded
       cases of suicide by women in India. (The vast majority
       of such suicides probably go unreported.) This article
       reviews the global situation and compares it with the
       Indian picture. Psychiatrists at King Edward Memorial
       Hospital, Bombay, conducted a study on the mental state
       of those who attempted suicide and concluded that mood
       and thought disorders were responsible. Family feuds,
       marital disharmony, property disputes, and loss of
       loved ones were also found to be contributory factors.
       The article notes that the Indian Penal Code considers
       an attempt at suicide a punishable crime, but even
       then women immolate themselves and swallow insecticide
       in order to save themselves from the miseries of life.

433. Malhotra, Nirmala. "48,428 Suicides a Year." *Femina*,
       24 Nov. 1972, pp. 25-47.

       The article refers to an empirical study conducted
       by the Bureau of Police Research and Development to
       determine the broad sociological trends of suicide.
       The incidence of suicide has been found to have in-
       creased in India since 1965. Quarrels with in-laws,
       marital discord, despair over incurable diseases,

insanity, frustrations due to failure in love affairs, and poverty are the main causes. The article gives a state-by-state breakdown of suicide rates and lists the factors leading to suicide attempts. Reliable statistics are given.

434. Pai, (Dr.) D.N. "Epidemiology of Accidents and Other Causes of Violence." *Journal of Gujarat Research Society* (1967), pp. 241-261.

Along with deaths by road accidents and homicides, suicides in major cities in India (Calcutta, Bombay, Banglore, Madras, and Poona) are studied in this well-documented article. The biological gradient of suicide, social environment, regional variations, occupation of suicides, and measures adopted for commiting suicide in Bombay city are studied. Tables of such factors as age, sex, etc., are given. Measures for preventing suicide among women are suggested. The author considers that stress and strain from joint families and depression are responsible for many suicides.

435. Parvathidevi, S., and A.V. Rao. "Premenstrual Phase and Suicidal Attempts." *Indian Journal of Psychiatry*, Vol. 14, No. 4 (1972), pp. 375-379.

115 women patients from Madurai, South India, were included in this study of attempted suicides. 72 menstruating suicide attempters were analyzed to determine reasons for suicidal behavior. 64% of the subjects attempted suicide in premenstrual and early menstrual phases.

436. Santhaaram, Jaya. "A Suicide Every 12 Minutes." *Eve's Weekly*, 10 April 1976, pp. 10-11.

The editor comments: "There is a time to live and a time to die. Yet some leap before their journey is complete to a fearful tragic destiny. Why?" Financial difficulties, marital unhappiness, job dissatisfaction, failures, disappointments, and physical handicaps are often reasons for suicide. Dowry also drives many brides to an unnatural death. The article refers to the group of Samaritans (in Bombay) who try to prevent suicide by guiding and counselling desperate people.

437. Thakur, Upendra. *The History of Suicide in India.* Delhi: Munshiram Manoharlal, 1963, xviii + 229 pp.

This book considers the history of widow sacrifice during the British regime and reviews the movement to

abolish it. Eight photographs of stones honoring
satis are given. A brief description of group suicide
by Rajasthani women, due to defeats in war and in order
to escape sexual dishonor, is also given here. This
custom was prevalent in medieval India and was prohibited by British legislation. A select bibliography
of original sources and an index are provided.

438. Verma, Paripurnanand. "Accidental Deaths and Suicides
in India." *Social Welfare*, Jan. 1970, pp. 14-15.

The suicide rate is increasing to an alarming extent.
This article offers state-by-state statistical information provided by the Central Bureau of Investigation,
Government of India, and concludes that although the
number of male suicides is greater than female, in some
states the opposite is true. Social disorganization
is responsible for these untimely deaths.

Widowhood

Child widows, who were not allowed to remarry in orthodox
Hindu society, had to lead a life of economic dependency and
consequent insecurity, exploitation, and humiliation. They
were not treated with dignity and their status was very low.
The pathetic conditions of these widows are described in
some of the following entries. Widow remarriage and the
right to inherit a husband's property were granted as constitutional rights. The social movement in favor of widow remarriage also helped the cause.

439. Banerji, Poreshnath. "The Remarriage of Hindu Widows."
Calcutta Review, 115 (July 1902), pp. 101-110.

The writer believes in the remarriage right of Hindu
widows. Widow remarriage will not cause neglect of
children from the previous marriage and will not add
to population pressures. Equal status is desirable.

440. Bose, A.B., and M.L.A. Sen. "Some Characteristics of
Widows in Rural Society." *Man in India*, Vol. 46,
No. 3 (July-Sept. 1966), pp. 226-232.

Widows in three districts--Jalore, Barmer, and
Siroli--are studied through interviews. Their age,
living conditions, and economic positions are surveyed.
In all, 349 widows and 198 widowers were selected at
random for research. Findings revealed that most of
the widows returned to their parental homes after the

death of their husbands and worked either in the households or on the farms. The younger widows without
children were permitted to remarry, and some widows
with children continued to stay with in-laws. This is
explained with the help of demographic data, tables,
and graphs.

441. Hunter, William Wilson. "The Hindu Child-Widow."
      Asiatic Quarterly Review, Vol. 2, No. 4 (1886), pp.
      241-282 (reprinted as *The Hindu Child Widow*. Bombay:
      Voice of India, 1887, 48 pp.

      The author is a firm believer in the remarriage of
      widows. He reviews the pitiable condition of child
      widows in the late nineteenth century and suggests some
      legislative reforms for remarriage to ameliorate their
      condition. He strongly criticizes the orthodox and
      conservative Brahminical element in Hindu society.

442. India (Republic). Central Bureau of Correctional Ser-
      vices. *Women and Girls in Moral and Social Danger*.
      New Delhi: Central Bureau of Correctional Services,
      Department of Social Welfare, Government of India,
      1971, 127 pp.

      This report reviews the facilities for women's wel-
      fare--institutional as well as noninstitutional--in
      the first three five-year plans. Data were collected
      through a questionnaire by welfare and social hygiene
      workers.

443. Muller, Max F. "Rukhmabai and Ramabai." *Nineteenth
      Century Studies*, 10 April 1975, pp. 235-244 (reprinted
      from *Indian Magazine*, Vol. 201 [Sept. 1887]).

      The plight of Indian women who did not conform to
      the system of prearranged marriages is described. Both
      the women of the title were rebels. The article
      describes the difficult conditions of widows in India.
      The writer suggested to British rulers that a home and
      school for child widows be established in order to im-
      prove their condition.

444. Naidu, Muthyalayya. "Widow Remarriage Movement in
      India." *Modern Review*, Vol. 118, No. 6 (1965), pp.
      490-492.

      This article briefly surveys the widow remarriage
      movement and the contribution of Ishwarchandra Vidyasagar
      and other reformers in Bengal, Bombay, Madras, Bihar,

Punjab, Uttar Pradesh, and Madhya Pradesh to this movement. Reference is also made to the British government's efforts to promote this cause through legislative
measures.

445. Pakrasi, Kanti. "A Study of Widowhood in India, 1951."
     Bulletin of the Cultural Research Institute, Calcutta,
     Vol. 5, No. 1-2 (1966), pp. 67-74 (reprinted as pp.
     370-381 in Pakrasi Kanti, et al. *Biosocial Studies
     in India: A Reading in Collected Papers, 1960-70.*
     Calcutta: Cultural Research Institute, 1976).

     Widowhood is considered a disruption of marriage, as
     is divorce. Are widows and divorcees comparable?
     Although divorced women form a relatively small group,
     the instability, insecurity, and emotional setbacks
     are the same as those experienced by divorcees. The
     author has examined widows demographically and indicates
     that in southwestern and central urban areas of the
     country they show greater disruption.

446. Pandita, Ramabai Sarasvati. *The High Caste Hindu
     Woman*. New York: F.H. Revell, 1901, 42 pp. (1st ed.,
     1887) (also, Pandita Ramabai. *The Widows' Trend*.
     An Australasian edition of *The High Caste Hindu Woman*.
     2nd ed. Melbourne: George Robertson and Company,
     1903, 195 pp. Reprint available, Westport, Conn.:
     Hyperion Press, 1976). Illustrated with author's
     photograph.

     Widowhood is lifelong slavery for high-caste Hindu
     women. If they are child widows, their condition is
     all the more pitiable. This book was originally
     written as a plea to American readers.

447. Vidyasagar, Ishvarchandra. *Marriage of Hindu Widows*.
     Calcutta: K.P. Bagehi & Co., 1976, 144 pp.

     Translated from the Bengali, this well-documented
     book contains an introduction by Aravinda Poddar and
     throws light on the historical aspect of the problem
     of remarriage of Hindu widows. Vidyasagar started the
     reform movement, and arguments both for and against
     continued for some time. Two articles on Vidyasagar
     and his work are appended. Quotations in Sanskrit
     from religious scriptures with English translations
     will be useful to Sanskrit scholars.

448. "Widowhood and Niyoga in the *Arthshastra & Manusmruti*."
     Our Heritage, Vol. 11, No. 1 (1963), pp. 1-11.

In Kautilya's *Arthshastra* three customs (remarriage,
levirate--the marriage of a childless widow to her
husband's younger brother in order to produce an heir--
and temporary living together in order to have an
heir) were permitted, while during the times of Manu
(the ancient lawgiver), none of these customs was
allowed or encouraged. This article mentions that
Manu prohibited remarriage and never believed in giving
widows any freedom in the matter.

Women's Welfare Institutions

There are some voluntary organizations as well as governmental agencies devoted to women's problems. Information
about them is given in the encyclopedia and catalogues listed
in the following items.

449. Badley, Mrs. M.A. "The National Association for Supply-
      ing Female Medical Aid to the Women of India." *Cal-
      cutta Review*, Vol. 85, No. 170 (1887), pp. 229-246.

      This article compares the work done before and after
      the National Association was established and explains
      the long-felt need for such an organization. It also
      describes the activities conducted to promote better
      health among Indian women.

450. Balfour, Margaret Ido, and Ruth Young. *The Work of
      Medical Women in India.* London: Oxford University
      Press, 1929, 201 pp.

      Medical problems of Indian women and the efforts of
      British and American women to solve these problems are
      described. Maps showing the location of hospitals are
      included.

451. Bombay (Presidency). *Women's Council Handbook of
      Women's Work, 1928-1929.* 2nd ed. Bombay: Women's
      Council, Government of Bombay, 1929, 87 pp. (1st ed.,
      1920).

      Women's welfare agencies in the Bombay presidency
      and their programs are listed in this directory.
      Fields of welfare work (e.g., health, child welfare,
      education, widow welfare work) are described. This
      is a relevant publication as far as the historical
      evolution of women's welfare work is concerned, although
      some of the organizations have changed their functions
      in response to new problems that have cropped up.

452. *Catalogue of Agencies Reaching Poorest Women in India.*
      New Delhi: Institute of Social Studies, 1981.

      This catalogue is the result of a study commissioned
      from the Institute by the Swedish International Develop-
      ment Authority. The objective was to identify organiza-
      tions that serve the underprivileged. Nearly 6,000
      agencies from 20 states receive aid from the Central
      Social Welfare Board (Government of India). This cata-
      logue attempts to focus attention on and analyze prob-
      lems relating to the interdependence of developing and
      developed countries.

453. Number omitted.

454. Cour, Ajeet, and Arpana Cour (eds.). *Directory of*
      Indian Women Today. New Delhi: India International
      Publications, 1976, 10 + 659 + xlviii + iliv pp.

      This directory lists numerous social welfare organiza-
      tions for women according to state, with addresses.
      Also provided are brief biographical sketches of women
      workers and their addresses along with some photographs.
      This is a useful publication.

455. *Encyclopaedia of Social Work in India.* Delhi: Publica-
      tion Division, Ministry of Information and Broad-
      casting, Government of India, 1968, Vol. I, xxxi +
      527 pp.; Vol. 2, xv + 688 pp.; Vol. 3, 12 + 297 pp.

      This is a valuable source of relevant information
      regarding women. 133 well-written articles and 212
      statistical tables definitely enhance the presentation.
      Some of the biographical sketches discuss personalities
      and the welfare work they have undertaken. A directory
      of various agencies working in the field of welfare,
      state, and federal legislation is given in the appen-
      dices.

456. Engineer and Mithan Choksi. "Seva Sadan and Other
      Social Work in Bombay." Pp. 43-50 in Evelyn C. Gedge
      and Mithan Choksi, eds. *Women in Modern India.* Bom-
      bay: D.B. Taraporewala Sons, 1929 (reprint, Westport,
      Conn.: Hyperion Press, 1976).

Seva Sadan, a women's welfare organization established by Ranade, does remarkable work in the fields
of education and employment.

457. India (Republic). Women's Welfare Division. *Women in*
      India: A Compendium of Programmes. New Delhi: Women's
      Welfare Division, Department of Social Welfare,
      Government of India, 1975, 118 pp.

      A survey of government and voluntary services with
      programs for women's welfare is offered in these pages.
      More specifically, welfare programs pertaining to edu-
      cation, health, family planning, employment, training,
      and rehabilitation are discussed. Tables, charts and
      photographs are included.

458. Lalitha, N.V. *Voluntary Work in India*. New Delhi:
      National Institute of Public Co-Operation and Child
      Development, 1975, 344 pp.

      This study of voluntary work in India is informative,
      and welfare agencies are likely to find it useful. It
      is based on a study of 390 voluntary welfare agencies
      and 856 volunteers in major cities of India. The main
      purpose of this study was to identify the policies of
      social welfare organizations toward voluntary work and
      the level of participation of volunteers in welfare
      programs. Women were interviewed to determine their
      problems.

459. Maclay, Susan Roth. "Women's Organisations in India:
      Voluntary Associations in a Developing Society."
      Ph.D. Dissertation, University of Virginia. Ann
      Arbor: Xerox University Microfilms, 1970, No. 70-
      4811.

460. Nilkanth, Vidyagauri Ramanbhai. "Recollections of
      Social Progress in Gujarat." Pp. 38-42 in Evelyn C.
      Gedge and Mithan Choksi, eds. *Women in Modern India*.
      Bombay: D.B. Taraporewala Sons, 1929 (reprint, West-
      port, Conn.: Hyperion Press, 1976).

      The writer reviews the social reform and women's
      welfare work carried out in Gujarat, especially in the
      field of education and widows' remarriage, etc.

461. Shyamlal. "Thakkar Bapa and the Kasturba Trust." Pp.
      245-252 in T.N. Jagadisan and Shyamlal, eds. *Thakkar*
      Bapa: Eightieth Birthday Commemoration Volume. Madras:
      Diocesan Press, 1949.

The Kasturba Trust was formed to work for women's and children's welfare in rural areas. The trust was created after her death; several centers were opened and programs were planned to suit the needs of the areas. Thakkar Bapa was a Gandhian social worker who spent his life in social welfare work and became one of the trustees of Kasturba Trust. This chapter deals with his work and provides information about the activities of the Trust.

VII

WOMEN'S MOVEMENT AND POLITICAL PARTICIPATION

Women's movements in India have worked in accord with the political and social reform movements. The All-India Women's Conference, the premier institution of its kind, was active not only in the pre-independence era but is still engaged in a variety of activities through various branches all over the country. Most of the national political parties in India have a women's wing. Women's wings of the leftist parties are active in raising feminist consciousness and driving women toward militant feminism. On the other hand, organizations such as the Self-Employed Women's Association and Jyoti Sangh are trying to raise the status of women through economic independence and social justice. Entries in this section explain the roles of Gandhiji and other social reformers. The plight of a large number of rural women was completely neglected until recently. But the national bodies of women and newspapers are now making a conscious effort to uplift them.

462. Asthana, P. *Women's Movement in India*. Delhi: Vikas Publishing House, 1974, 175 pp.

This book depicts the position of Indian women in ancient India and shows how the exposure to liberal western ideas gave birth to the women's movement. Short biographical sketches of leading reformers--both men and women--are also given. The participation of women in the struggle for independence helped to bring about a change in their outlook. It has inculcated in them the necessary will and determination to achieve the goal. The contribution of the All-India Women's Conference-- a pioneering national body--to the women's movement is highlighted. A select bibliography is provided.

463. Bagal, Jogesh C. "Women in India's Freedom Movement I & II." *Modern Review*, No. 93-94 (June-July 1953), pp. 463-473, 53-61

This very informative two-part article gives a detailed account of women's participation in the freedom movement. It is illustrated with photographs of such prominent women freedom fighters as Kadambini Ganguli (the first woman to speak from a Congress platform), Swaruakumari Devi, Sarla Devi, Sister Nivedita, Lilavati Mitra, Basanti Devi, Urmilal Devi, Mohini Devi, and Hemaprabha Majumdar.

464. Chakravarty, Renu. "New Perspective on the Women's Movement after Twenty-Five Years of Drift." *Link*, Vol. 15, No. 1 (15 Aug. 1972), pp. 177-181.

The author presents a historical overview of some prominent women's organizations such as the All-India Women's Conference, Mahila Atmaraksha Samiti in Bengal, the National Federation of Indian Women, Brahmo Samaj, Theosophists, and Gandhiji's contribution through the passive resistance movement. The work of the All-India Trade Union Congress and of various noncommunist trade unions, especially in organizing women workers, is also included.

465. Chakravarty, Renu. "The Women's Movement in India." Pp. 27-48 in Vimla Farooqui and Renu Chakravarty. *Communism and Women*. New Delhi: Communist Party of India, 1973.

Trends in the women's movement during the pre- and post-independence periods are reviewed. The role of the communist party in this movement is described, keeping in mind the broad political canvas.

466. Chattopadhyay, Kamaladevi. *The Awakening of Indian Women*. Madras, Everyman's Press, 1939, 78 pp.

Indian women's hopes, aims, and aspirations are described in this booklet. It also deals with women's movements, and the contribution of eminent women is illustrated with photographs.

467. Chattopadhayaya, Kamaladevi. *Indian Women's Battle for Freedom*. New Delhi: Abinav Publications, 1983, 134 pp.

The author was a freedom fighter who, after independence, continued to serve the country by working with rural women and encouraging their creativity through the Handicraft Board. She looks back into the history of social reforms and the resultant changes. The present generation of women has not contributed to the social gains that they enjoy today; on the contrary, they are completely ignorant of these movements. The author describes women's heritage, the social reform movement, and the role women of those days played in the demand for political rights, and discusses what remains to be achieved in the movement for equality. The author creates an awareness of what is still to be done by pointing out the lacunae. The volume is indexed.

468. Chitalia, K.J. *Directory of Women's Institutions*. Bombay Presidency, Pt. I, Bombay: Servants of India Society, 1936, vii + 71 + 5 pp.

This directory was prepared primarily for the benefit of women interested in the uplift and advancement of less-fortunate sisters. The women's movement has been restricted to urban areas, and unless it extends to rural areas, the necessary awakening will not take place. This directory lists many organizations along with their addresses, names of presidents and secretaries, membership, and the nature of the organization's activities--mainly educational, operating special libraries and offering industrial training. This very useful directory is the only one of its kind available.

469. Chitnis, Suma. *A Review of the Progress Made in India Towards Achievement of the Objectives of the International Women's Decade*. Bombay: Tata Institute of Social Sciences and Women's Studies Unit, S.N.D.T. Women's University, n.d., 141 pp. (mimeographed).

This paper, prepared for the regional Preparatory Conference for the U.N. Decade for Women, fulfills a specific assignment--to review and appraise women's progress in India. Early reforms, post-independence development resulting in equality in all fields, women's movements, educational facilities and progress, and political participation are reviewed. Many tables, a bibliography, and National Plans are in the appendix.

470. Cousins, Margaret E. *Indian Womanhood Today* (revised and enlarged). Allahabad: Kitabistan, 1947, 205 pp. (1st ed., 1941).

The relationship between the nationalist upsurge and the women's movement is described here. The political participation of Indian women and the changes it has brought about are recognized.

471. Desai, Neera. "Emergence and Development of Women's Organisations in India." In Kate Young (ed.). *Just One Big Happy Family: Women's Place in Development*. London: Routledge and Kegan Paul (forthcoming).

The writer examines the various socioeconomic factors leading to the emergence of Indian women's organizations and their development during the British Raj as well as in the free India.

472. Everett, Jana Matson. *Women and Social Change in India*. New Delhi: Heritage Publishers, 1979, 229 pp.

This research study traces the historical development of the women's movement in India from the late 19th to the mid-20th century. Differences between the women's movement in India and in the United States and the U.K. are pointed out.

473. Gandhi, Mohandas K. *To the Women*. Ed. Anand Hingorani. Ahmedabad: Navjivan, 1941, 247 pp. (also available in an abridged pocket series, Bombay: Bharatiya Vidya Bhavan, 1964, 120 pp.).

Gandhiji's speeches, replies to letters addressed to him on women's issues, and articles published in *Navjivan* and *Harijan Weekly* are included. Gandhiji had very rational and revolutionary ideas about women. The period covered is from 1918 to 1940.

474. Gandhi, Mohandas K. *Bapu's Letters to Mira 1924-1948*. Ahmedabad: Navjivan, 1949, 387 pp. (also available as *Gandhi's Letters to a Disciple*. London: Gollancz, 1951, 234 pp. and New York: Harper, 1950, 234 pp.).

This volume includes letters written to Mira (Miss Slade) and views on various issues--rural unemployment, industrialization, and the woman question.

475. *Gandhi On Emancipation of Women*. Delhi: National Federation of Indian Women, 1969, 29 pp.

Using those writings of Gandhi earlier published in *Young India*, *Harijan*, and his speeches, five prominent authors have tried to reexamine Gandhi's thinking about the women's movement, the position of women in family and society, women's education and role in political life, and women's right to property and economic independence. Primary references are quoted exhaustively.

476. Gidumal, Dayaram (Dayaram Gidumal Shahani). *The Status of Women in India, or A Handbook for Social Reformers*. Bombay: Fort Printing Press, 1889, 102 + 337 pp.

After a 102-page preface on the Symposium of Hindu Domestic Reformers and anti-reformers, this book documents the facts, causes, laws, opinions of government

officials, and proposed solutions concerning the
various social problems Indian womanhood faced in those
dark days. This book has great historical interest.

477. Heimsath, Charles H. *Indian Nationalism and Hindu So-
      cial Reform*. Princeton, N.J.: Princeton University
      Press, 1964, 379 pp.

      National and social reform movements were conducted
      side by side during World War I, when women's problems
      such as age at marriage and widow remarriage were much
      discussed. The author discusses the relationship be-
      tween national and social reform movements and con-
      cludes that both these movements have ultimately helped
      the cause of Indian women.

478. Jain, S.P., and V. Krishnamurthy. *Role of Women in
      Rural Development: A Study of Mahila Mandals*. Hydera-
      bad: National Institute of Rural Development, 1979,
      93 pp.

      This report evaluates 15 women's organizations and
      their contribution to rural development at the grass-
      roots level. These organizations work closely with
      women while trying to improve their economic and social
      status. Their general functioning, structure, and
      financial arrangements, and the activities they conduct
      are studied here from the field data collected from 5
      states (Gujarat, Jammu and Kashmir, Orissa, Punjab,
      and Tamil Nadu). 24 tables and a chapter on recommen-
      dations reveal the need for overhauling the structure,
      function, and orientation of the activities.

479. Kanhere, Sujata, and Mira Savera. *A Case Study on the
      Organising of Landless Tribal Women in Maharashtra,
      India*. Bangkok, Thailand: Asian and Pacific Centre
      for Women and Development, June 1980, 13 pp.

      Almost 51% of working women in India are agricultural
      workers, unorganized, unlettered, and oppressed. This
      is a field study of 150 villages in Dhulia District in
      Maharashtra where, in 1972, agricultural rural women
      from the tribal communities went to all liquor dens and
      broke the liquor pots. This particular act was part of
      a revolt against wife beating. How the women decided
      to do this and the nature of leadership and structure
      of the protest movement are analyzed in this brief re-
      port, which offers conclusions.

480. Mahindra, Indira. "Is This Liberation?" 6 articles in
      Eve's Weekly, Nos. 30, 31, 32, 34, 36, 37 (7 July-
      11 Sept. 1976), pp. 16-17, 11-13, 20-21, 20, 24,
      11-13, 14-15, 18, respectively.

A series of six articles on the liberation of Indian
women: "Marriage or Bonded Labour," "A Woman's Right
over Her Own Body," "Women Are Willing Victims," "Divided
and Ruled," "The Ma-bahen Syndrome," and "American Woman
and Her Cross." The first five articles conclude that
because of the existence of the double standard, Indian
women do not enjoy the fruits of liberation. Age-old
ideals are still employed to brainwash women into sacri-
ficing their identity and rights.

481. Mehta, Rekha, and K. Sardamoni. *Women and Rural Trans-
       formation: Two Studies*. New Delhi: Concept Publish-
       ing Company, 1983, xii + 176 pp.

Rekha Mehta critically examines governmental policies
on rural transformation and their impact on the socio-
economic lives of women. She found out that neither
the government-conducted Community Development Programs
nor the type of activities planned and carried out by
the women's organizations had changed anything, the first
being male oriented and the latter being some sort of
women's clubs which could have no impact whatsoever
either on development or transformation.
The second study, by Sardamoni, traces the various
historical changes and legislation in Kerala that dis-
turbed the matrilineal system there. Legislation on
land reform is carried out by insensitive and opportunis-
tic politicians who do not come from the matrilineal
tradition, so the changes they try to bring are not
approved of by the women. The findings of both these
field studies are presented analytically with the help
of tables and charts.

482. Mehta, Vimla. *Attitudes of Educated Women Towards
       Social Issues*. New Delhi: National Publishing House,
       1979, xvi + 127 pp.

The book presents the results of an empirical study
on the attitudes of women teachers and students toward
social issues of vital importance. These respondents
were tested on a five-point Likert-type scale on
traditionalism, caste, religion, education, marriage,
work, and politics. The respondents made relevant
suggestions in regard to academic and vocational courses
for adolescent girls. Utilizing psychometric techniques
and factorial analysis and presenting its findings in
tables and graphs, the study is scholarly as well as
relevant. An index and a bibliography are included.

483. Omvedt, Gail. *We Will Smash This Prison*. New Delhi:
      Orient Longman Limited, 1980, 189 pp.

      Peasant and ex-untouchable women are doubly exploited,
      both as workers and as women. Gail Omvedt studied them
      in the rural part of Maharashtra, and in this publica-
      tion she analyzes the anti-price-rise movement, rural
      women uniting to fight exploitation, college students,
      the anti-dowry struggle, and the Progressive Organiza-
      tion of women's activities. Indira Gandhi's leadership
      is dealt with at length and the emergency imposed by
      her is defended. A leftist viewpoint and attitudes are
      reflected in the presentation of case studies. A glos-
      sary of terms and bibliographical notes, mostly giving
      information on leftist organizations and persons, are
      provided.

484. Omvedt, Gail. "Caste, Class and Women's Liberation in
      India." *Bulletin of Concerned Asian Scholars*, Vol. 7,
      No. 1 (1975), pp. 43-48 (reprinted in Manorania
      Barnabas, S.K. Hulbe, and P.S. Jacobs, eds. *Challenges
      in Societies in Transition*. Delhi: Macmillan Company
      of India, 1978, pp. 238-252).

      The main points of this article are that Indian women
      have benefited from the nationalist and social reform
      movements; low-caste women now enjoy greater indepen-
      dence; socioeconomic inequalities hamper full liberation;
      and Western influence has affected the Indian women's
      movement.

485. Ray, Renuka. "Impressions of the Tenth Session of the
      All-India Women's Conference." *Modern Review*, Vol.
      59, No. 2 (1936), pp. 209-212.

      This conference was significant because it was hosted
      by the Maharani of Travancore, and Margaret Sanger attend-
      ed in order to promote the birth control movement. The
      resolutions adopted at this conference were pragmatic.

486. *A Report of National Workshop on Organising Self-Employed
      Women in India*. Ahmedabad: Self-Employed Women's
      Association, Sewa Reception Centre, 1981, 55 pp.

      This is a report of workshop deliberations of 10
      women's organizations which aim at organizing self-
      employed women, providing adequate training to them,
      and also marketing their products. Self-reliance is
      the aim of all 10 well-organized institutions, which
      have acquired the status of regular movements. The

participants associated with these organizations try
to impart to others their methodology and expertise.

487. Ryland, Shane. "The Theory and Impact of Gandhi's
      Feminism." *Feminine Sensibility and Characterisation
      in South Asian Literature*, Guest ed. Fritz Blackwell,
      Vol. 12, No. 3/4 (1977), pp. 131-144.

      This article reevaluates Gandhiji's views on feminism
      and concludes that he was a dedicated feminist, other-
      wise he would not have been able to drag women into
      politics so successfully. The article is very rich in
      reference citations.

488. *Social Scientist*, Special Number on Women. Vol. 4, No.
      4/5 (1975), 160 pp.

      This issue is a collection of articles by famous In-
      dian and Western authors. Some of the titles are:
      "Perspective on the Women's Movement," "Women's Libera-
      tion and Productive Activity," "Patriarchal Capitalism
      and Female-Headed Family," "Rural Origins of Women's
      Liberation in India," "Women Office Workers," "Problems
      of Working Women in Urban Areas," "Sex Discrimination
      in Work and Wages," etc.

489. Tandon, Kalpana, and V. Rukmini Rao. "Learning From
      and About Women's Organisations: An Explanatory Analy-
      sis in the Indian Context." *Convergence*, Vol. 13,
      No. 1-2 (1980), pp. 124-135.

      Women's organizations, their goals, educational ac-
      tivities, membership patterns, the nature and scope of
      administration of their programs, and their impacts
      are studied through 2 case studies. The levels of
      commitment and achievement are compared to see whether
      such organizations can act as pressure groups and be-
      come agents of change or not.

490. Thomas, P. "Indian Freedom Movement and Women's Emanci-
      pation and Women's Suffrage in India." Pp. 324-333
      and 333-337 in his *Indian Women Through the Ages*.
      Bombay: Asia Publishing House, 1964.

      The author briefly reviews in these sections the
      Indian freedom movement and women's emancipation during
      British rule. How the Indian National Congress, Brahmo
      Samaj, and other sociopolitical and progressive religious
      movements ultimately won the franchise for Indian women
      is narrated. The roles played by Swami Vivekanand and

Gandhiji are highlighted. Detailed accounts of women
coming out of domestic life and participating enthusiastically in the non-cooperation and civil disobedience
movements led by Gandhi are given.

491. Wadia, A.R. *The Ethics of Feminism: A Study of the
      Revolt of Women.* New Delhi: Asian Publication Ser-
      vices, 1977, 256 pp. (reprint of London: G. Allen and
      Unwin, 1923).

      Feminist movements of the West are briefly discussed
      as are the ways in which Indian womanhood may be influ-
      enced. The author touches upon the comparative positions
      of Hindu, Muslim, and Parsi women.

                    Political Participation of Women

     The political awakening of Indian women gained momentum
from some social reform movements. When Gandhiji called
women to participate in the struggle for India's independence,
they responded enthusiastically. They participated actively
in the freedom movement in subjugated India. After the at-
tainment of independence, women demonstrated their willingness
to shoulder all sorts of responsibilities. Whether in elections for the municipal corporation, the state legislature,
or Parliament, women came forward and participated in the
democratic process. Some of them became mayors, members of
legislative assemblies, ministers, chief ministers, state
governors, and ambassadors. In exercising their adult franchise, they displayed political consciousness; although many
women voters are illiterate, they vote judiciously and in
large numbers. After the Prime Minister declared a state of
emergency and suspended human rights, then subsequently held
elections in 1977, after lifting the emergency, women showed
their wrath by helping to defeat the government. Since the
1980 general elections, the ranks of women candidates have
thinned and women are becoming disinterested. This may be
only a temporary condition. The entries in this section depict women's participation in the freedom movement, voicing
women's problems in the assemblies and Parliament.

492. Aery, Raj Rani. "Women Legislative Elite in Rajasthan
      (1962-65): An Analysis of Intra-Legislative Performance
      Political Science Review, Vol. 6, No. 1, 1967,
      39-57 pp.

      The women legislaters' performance in three legislative
      assemblies is examined, and their socioeconomic profiles
      are presented in brief. The author finds that some

were vocal and others were silent. Those who spoke and
participated were compensated.

493. Agnew, Vijay. *Elite Women in Indian Politics*. Delhi:
      Vikas, 1979, 163 pp.

      This book is based on the author's doctoral disserta-
      tion at the University of Toronto. The author attempts
      to give an account of Indian women's political partici-
      pation during the last hundred years.

494. Agnew, Vijay. "A Review of the Literature of Women."
      Journal of Indian History, Vol. 55, No. 1-2 (1977),
      pp. 307-324.

      This essay reviews the history of urban Indian women
      during the 19th and 20th centuries. This very rich
      essay from the point of view of bibliographical
      references even cites unpublished papers. The analy-
      tical approach is best suited to the author.

495. Bagal, Jogeshchandra. "Women in India's Freedom Move-
      ment." *Modern Review*, June–July 1953, pp. 53-61.

      The part played by the women of Bengal is highlighted
      by describing the women who were active in the Indian
      National Congress and how they participated in the civil
      disobedience movement of Gandhiji. Bengal is known to
      have women participants in terrorist movements, and
      some women participated through educational organiza-
      tions as well as women's associations. These women,
      especially Sarojini Naidu, Sister Nivedita, Sarladevi,
      and others, are remembered in this article.

496. Baig, Tara Ali. *India's Woman Power*. New Delhi: S.
      Chand and Co., 1976, xiv + 301 pp.

      The author depicts the Indian women's movements in
      pre-independence days as well as in independent India.
      The awakening, liberation, change in traditional images,
      the birth of a daughter, her childhood and adolescence,
      career and professional life, legislation, technological
      advances, and the future of the family are discussed.
      Notes for each chapter, tables indicating percentages
      of women voters, lists of women elected to state legis-
      latures and parliament from 1952 to 1971, lists of women
      appointed as ministers, and legislation passed from
      1900 to 1947 and also in the post-independence period
      are given in seven appendices. A select bibliography
      and index are also included.

497. Billimoria, Mrs. R.N. "Women and the Bombay Municipal
      Elections, 1973." *Journal of Gujarat Research So-
      ciety*, Vol. 51, No. 4 (1975), pp. 20-31.

      This study analyzes 38 female candidates who partici-
      pated in municipal elections in 1973 and their party
      affiliations, political acumen, campaign experiences,
      financial resources, etc., through tables and analysis.
      Their views on polling arrangements and voters' atti-
      tudes toward them are also indicated. The question of
      special representation for women is dealt with.

498. Chhabra, Rani. "Bypassing Women for Political Office:
      An Unhealthy Trend Continues." *Femina*, 1-14 July
      1977, pp. 33-35.

      The opening sentence of this article is: "As Alice in
      Wonderland would have put it: 'It gets worser and
      worser.'" With every general election, campaigns are
      becoming riskier and more violent. The decline in
      values and the use of unscrupulous means for winning
      elections deter women from participating. In this ar-
      ticle, the author has tried to review every party situ-
      ation vis-à-vis women's political position in every
      state through two tables. One may wonder why she has
      not mentioned Indira Gandhi's Congress Party. Actually,
      the main culprit in this political game is the party's
      President, whose attitude toward women and the role
      that they can perform determines everything.

499. Desai, Padma, and Jagdish N. Bhagwati. "Women in Indian
      Elections." Pp. 165-199 in Jagdish N. Bhagvati, et
      al. *Electoral Politics in the Indian States: Three
      Disadvantaged Sectors.* Delhi: Manohar Book Service,
      1975.

      Female candidates and winners in the 1962 and 1967
      Lok Sabha and Legislative Assembly elections are studied,
      and interstate and interparty comparisons are given.
      Election results raise many questions. Women fighting
      for election from former princely states and tribal
      constituencies are considered disadvantaged groups by
      this writer.

500. *Gandhi and the Emancipation of Indian Women.* Hyderabad:
      Gandhi Sahitya Prachuranalayam, 1969, 29 pp.

      The ideas of Gandhiji on women are compiled in this
      booklet. Published in Gandhi's centenary year, its
      primary goal is to express the sense of gratitude of
      Indian women toward the great man. Written by various
      writers, the booklet deals with the relevance of Gandhi's
      ideas to the women's movement, position and status,

education and role in political life, women's right to
property, and economic independence. Extensive quotations from Gandhiji's speeches, and writings from *Young
India*, *Harijan*, and *Amrit Bazar Patrika* from 1918 to
1948 are included.

501. Gavankar, Rohini H. "Female Representation in Maharashtra State." *Maharashtra Legislative Journal*,
   Vol. 3 (Jan.-July 1973), pp. 26-34.

   This paper describes women's political participation
   in ancient and medieval India and laments the decline
   (50%) from 1957-62 to 1967-72. Ironically, after
   Indira Gandhi became Prime Minister in 1966, this decline was more apparent. This point is explained with
   graphics and tabular presentation. Other aspects of
   the problem such as lack of political consciousness,
   background of members, their party loyalties, and general style of functioning are also discussed at length.

502. Ghosh, Satyavrata. "Women Terrorists of India." *Illustrated Weekly of India*, Vol. 94, No. 4 (28 Jan. 1973),
   pp. 34-38.

   The editor notes in the preface: "they lived under-
   ground, made and threw bombs, shot British governors
   and spent the best years of their lives in prison."
   This is a brief review of the contribution to the freedom movement of such women and events, illustrated with
   photographs.

503. Gray, Mrs. R.M. "Women in Indian Politics." Pp. 156-
   165 in John Cumming, ed. *Political India, 1832-1932*.
   London: Oxford University Press, 1932.

   This article deals exhaustively with the recommendations of the Indian Franchise Committee, 1921, with regard to granting voting rights to women and shows how
   this step of the British government helped the women's
   movement in India. Indian women started to participate
   actively in local self-government as well as exercising
   their voting rights.

504. India (Republic). Information Services. *Women Legislators of India*. New Delhi, 1953, 30 pp., illustrated.

   This is a pictorial, informative booklet introducing
   women legislators after the first general elections in
   free India in 1953. This directory gives brief biographical information with photographs.

505. "India. The Emergency: A Needed Shock." *Time*, 27 Oct.
   1975, pp. 28-29.

Prime Minister Indira Gandhi declared an emergency
in India in June 1975 and suspended human rights in
order to oppress her political opponents. This critical
article finds fault with the fact that a leader of her
stature resorted to autocratic policy just to defend
her position. The act of putting all senior nationalist
leaders behind bars is criticized vehemently.

506. Jhaveri, Vithalbhai, K., and Soli S. Batliwala, eds.
      Jai-Hind: The Diary of a Rebel Daughter of India with
      the Rani of Jhansi Regiment. Bombay: Janmabhoomi
      Prakashan Mandir, 1945, 130 pp.

      This diary describes an anonymous Indian woman who
      joined Azad Hind Fauz, founded by Subhash Chandra Bose
      (a freedom fighter who believed in fighting the British
      Empire with all his might rather than following the
      nonviolent creed of Mahatma Gandhi). It traces the
      origin of the Indian National Army and the organization
      and plans to fight the British.

507. Juneja, Monica. *Women on the March in Delhi*. Alterna-
      tive News and Features, No. 5, April 1980, 256 pp.

      The author presents an account of a Delhi women's
      group which has been campaigning against violence to
      women with mass rallies, demonstrations, memoranda to
      the government, seminar reports and press notes. It
      also reports on some short skits performed on the
      streets of Delhi.

508. Katzenstein, Mary Fainsod. "Towards Equality? Cause
      and Consequence of the Political Prominence of Women
      in India." *Asian Survey*, Vol. 18, No. 5 (1928), pp.
      473-486.

      This article critically examines the role of women
      in politics. Do women hold high positions in political
      parties or in government? If so, what are the plausible
      reasons for their power and what is the social percep-
      tion of them? The writer concludes that (1) some elite
      women hold high rank because of historical advantages
      they had over common women, and (2) the impact is neg-
      ligible because these elite women have not troubled to
      improve the situation of other women, who even today
      enjoy only second-class citizenship.

509. Kaufman, Michael T. "Indira's Return, Personality and
      Power in India." *New York Times Magazine*, 23 March
      1980, pp. 40-43, 60, 64, 66, 69, 70, 72, 74.

The author describes Indira's return to power in 1980 as a result of the success of her strategies to topple the Janata Government and thus establish her rule of the second largest country (population-wise) in the world. The writer comments that Mrs. Gandhi's family history and her personal strength may be responsible for her ability to manipulate power.

510. Kaur, Manmohan. *Role of Women in the Freedom Movement, 1857-1947*. New Delhi: Sterling Publishers, 1968, 287 pp.

The year 1857, when the war of independence was unsuccessfully launched for the first time, was an important landmark. India did not win her freedom until 1947. Indian women's role throughout these 90 long years is traced from unpublished government records, correspondence, newspaper reports, Indian National Congress records, books, and articles--all the material is analyzed and documented. Reference is made to contributions of women fighters, forces responsible for the political awakening, growth of extremist women in Indian politics, Mrs. Annie Besant and Home Rule agitation, and the civil disobedience movements. An exhaustive bibliography of 121 titles and a glossary of terms are included. Even the footnotes provide detailed information.

511. Khera, P.N. "History of Female Franchise in India." Pp. 543-545 in *Indian History Congress 5*, 1941. Hyderabad: Proceedings 5, Printed at Osmania University Press and Asam Steam Press, 1943.

In this summary of the actual paper, the researcher has surveyed the role of Indian women in the nationalist movement. Lord Montague appointed a committee to look into women's rights that recommended granting voting rights to Indian women. The paper criticizes some of the provisions of the Government of India Act of 1935.

512. Kini, N.G.S. "Modernisation in India: Women's Voting Behaviour as Index." *Political Science Review*, Vol. 8, No. 1 (1969), pp. 12-22.

Women's voting behavior in the 1967 general elections in Nagpur West is studied in this article. This particular constituency is considered to be most alert and politically conscious. Results regarding motivation, party affiliations, and participation in voluntary associations belie the expectations of the writer.

513. Mazumdar, Vina (ed.). *Symbols of Power: Studies on
          the Political Status of Women in India.* New Delhi:
          Allied Publishers, 1979, xxiv + 373 pp.

      The editor has raised some questions in this volume
      (e.g., Was the demand for the vote for women an elitist
      measure? Why are more women getting elected to state
      assemblies and parliament from the states which were
      pockets of feudalism? What about the reservation of
      seats for women?) But she has not bothered to answer
      these questions; instead, she has presented tedious
      profiles of female voting behavior. Geraldine Forbes
      in her research paper describes the role of various
      women's organizations in capturing votes during the
      years 1917-1927; other papers analyze voting behavior
      or the decreasing rate of political participation by
      women. Right to vote is a symbol of power, but in the
      case of Indian women it remains an empty slogan.

514. Mehta, Usha. "Indian Women and Their Participation in
          Politics." *Social Change*, Vol. 8, No. 3 (Sept. 1978),
          pp. 31-34.

      The author gives a short history of women's franchise
      rights in the world and in India. In India, women
      started voting in 1917 and acquired political equality
      in 1952 when 37.1% of women cast their votes in the
      general election. In 1971, 60% voted, but in 1977 only
      54.91% voted in the elections. The author attempts to
      examine this decline, compares the number of women mem-
      bers in state assemblies with parliament at the center,
      and arrives at the painful conclusion that women are
      afraid to enter the political arena. Traditional social
      norms, lack of education and economic independence,
      male-oriented political parties, and the hostile atti-
      tudes of male rivals, some of whom do not hesitate to
      indulge in character assassination, are responsible for
      women's poor performance.

515. Mehta, Usha. "Women and the Elections." *Indian Journal
          of Political Science*, Vol. 23, No. 4 (1962), pp. 371-
          379.

      Indian women's franchise and candidates are viewed
      from the historical angle. The general elections of
      1957 and 1962 and the patterns of voting behavior are
      studied at length.

516. Menon, Laxmi N. "Political Rights of Women in India."

Pp. 83-103 in Appadorai, ed. *The Status of Women in South Asia*. Bombay: Orient Longmans, 1954.

The writer concludes that the social reform and nationalist movements roused Indian women to participate in the public as well as political life of the country with the necessary zeal and enthusiasm. By providing data regarding the number of women in political parties and legislatures in different states, the author wants to convey that female participation has increased.

517. Mies, Maria. "Indian Women and Leadership." *Bulletin of Concerned Asian Scholars*, Vol. 7, No. 1 (Jan.-March 1975), pp. 55-66.

In this research paper the writer differentiates between two types of female leaders: (1) those who were educated and came from the higher economic strata, who participated in national movements, and who sacrificed for the nation and (2) female leaders in the farmers' revolt who suffered economically and were governed by different ideals. The characteristics of these two types of female leaders are bound to be different, as the first type was motivated by Gandhiji's ideals of simplicity and sacrifice and the second group operated out of self-interest. The article offers an excellent analysis of the leadership role and potentials of women and discusses some implications for women political leaders everywhere.

518. Mies, Maria. "New Law Gives Gandhi Regime Power to Imprison Without Trial." *New York Times*, 29 Sept. 1975, pp. A1, A7.

The Internal Security Act, which empowered Indira Gandhi to imprison persons without a trial, is discussed in this brief newspaper article, which also comments on the challenges posed by secessionist activities and regional movements.

519. Minault, Gail (ed.). *The Extended Family: Women and Political Participation in India and Pakistan*. Delhi: Chanakya Prakshan, 1981, ix + 312 pp.

This book is the product of a conference on the history of women at Mt. Holyoke College, where the editor met a number of scholars doing research on women. The contents of this book, contributed by experts in various fields, range from social reform and women's

participation in political culture to women's movement
toward equality. This publication provides a comprehensive view of each subject. Extensive notes, tables,
and an index help toward a deeper understanding of the
subject.

520. Oturkar, R.V. "Part Played by Jijabai, The Mother of
     Shivaji, in the Foundation of the Maratha State."
     Indian History Congress 21, 1958, Trivandrum Pro-
     ceedings 21. Bombay: The Congress, 1959, pp. 361-364.

     This paper presents material drawn from historical
     sources explaining the active role of Jijabai in build-
     ing the Maratha State. Not only did she bring up Shivaji
     properly and in a determined way, she also influenced
     some of his policies. Also included in this brief ar-
     ticle are the names of Maratha women who were influen-
     tial.

521. Parulekar, N.B. "Indian Women as Noncooperators."
     Asia, Vol. 31, No. 1 (1931), pp. 22-27.

     Indian women emerged from the house and participated
     in marches, singing protest songs, making bonfires of
     foreign clothes, and picketing liquor shops. The ar-
     ticle is illustrated.

522. Rajgopal, T.S. "Political Expression or Ballot: Vote
     for Women's Movement." Pp. 125-153 in his *Indian
     Women in the New Age or Women in Young India*. Mysore:
     Jaya Stores, 1936.

     Giving a brief history of voting rights for women in
     other countries, the author traces the beginning of
     Indian women's participation in the Home Rule Movement
     led by Dr. Annie Besant during 1914-1917 and their
     onward march through the freedom struggle under the
     leadership of Gandhiji. This is a well-documented
     chapter on the Acts of Reform during the British Raj.

523. Sahgal, Nayantara. *A Voice for Freedom*. Delhi: Hind
     Pocket Books, 1977, 118 pp.

     This is a collection of Sahgal's writings on political
     themes and her interviews with leading politicians.
     The book is dedicated to many innocent, anonymous In-
     dians who suffered imprisonment, humiliation, and
     anguish during the Emergency imposed by Prime Minister
     Indira Gandhi from June 1976 to August 1977.

524.   Sahgal, Nayantara. *Indira Gandhi: Her Road to Power*. London and Sydney: Macdonald and Co., 1983, xv + 260 pp.

Published in a different form in India in 1978, after the Emergency, under the title *Indira Gandhi's Emergence and Style*, this work was expanded to accommodate more information about events after 1977 when political developments took an unforeseen turn. The Janata Government failed and Mrs. Gandhi emerged as an undisputed leader. The book contains information about political parties in India and the constitutional structure and will be of help to students interested in leadership qualities. A few photographs decorate the publication.

525.   Sahgal, Nayantara. *Indira Gandhi's Emergency and Style*. New Delhi, Vikas Publishing House, 1978, 215 pp.

This work originated from a paper contributed in March 1974 to a conference on Leadership in South Asia at the School of Oriental and Asian Studies, University of London. It was expanded and completed in 1976 under a Radcliffe Institute Scholarship so that the author could express her views about the style of government of Indira Gandhi. Documented with reference to the imposition of the emergency and the censorship of press and personal letters of relatives of the senior leaders, who were put behind the bars. Indexed.

526.   Sayeed, S.M. "Women's Participation in U.P. Politics: A Study of Political Attitudes and Performance of the Women Members of the U.P. Assembly." *Indian Journal of Political Science*, Vol. 32, No. 2 (1971), pp. 213–223.

This empirical study is based on interviews with 18 women who won mid-terms elections in 1969. Their socio-economic profiles, entry into politics, pre-assembly social and political activities, views on success or failure, financial resources to fight elections, political attitudes, and perception of their own roles as legislators are examined at great length.

527.   Sen, Mrinalini. *Knocking at the Door*. Calcutta: Living Age Press, 1954, 208 pp.

This book describes Indian women's awakening and participation in political movements. The writer has

helped to bring about this change through inspiring
writings and addresses. This book is of special significance as it contains letters of Mahatma Gandhi,
Sarojini Naidu, and Rabindranath Tagore written to the
author on various occasions.

528.   Sen, S. "Role of Women Legislators." *Parliamentary
       Studies*, Vol. 2, No. 6 (Nov. 1958), pp. 16-20.

The author traces the role of women during the freedom struggle and in the demand for enfranchisement of
women in British India. This is descriptive article
documenting earlier efforts.

529.   Shah Nawaz, Begam (Jahan Ara Shah Nawaz). "Indian Women
       and the New Constitution." *Asiatic Review*, Vol. 29,
       No. 99 (July 1933), pp. 433-445, with discussion, pp.
       446-458.

The Indian Franchise Committee recommended voting
rights for Indian women, but conditions laid down by
the British government acted as barriers and many women
did not benefit from this right. Elite women tried to
highlight this fact through speeches at various forums.
This article is a reprint of a speech delivered at the
East India Association. The speaker recommends maximum
enfranchisement.

530.   Singh, Diana Roy. *Warring Women of India*. Bombay:
       Colour Publications, 1973, 136 pp.

Short biographical sketches of such warring women as
Rani of Jhansi, Zebun-Nisa, Tarabai, Bahinabai, and
Mira, all of whom were bold and courageous, are given.
They either confronted foreign powers on battlefields
or fought against the traditional orthodox forces of
the Hindu Society, thereby asserting their independent
identity and chalking out their own path. Colorful
illustrations and sketches from the Victoria and Albert
Museum and the India Office Library, London, are included.

531.   Singh, Nalini. "Vignettes of Women M.P.s in the Last
       Five Lok Sabhas." *Femina*, 11-24 March 1977, pp. 27-
       39.

In the first three Parliaments, women leaders who
were elected as Members of Parliament came from politically active families. They were either daughters,
sisters, wives, or mothers of male politicians. In
this article brief biographies of such members are
given. This article sadly states that the number of
women nominated on party tickets is declining, as is

the percentage of women voters. In other words, women's
representation is declining.

532. Sirsikar, V.M. "Role of Women in the Campaign." Pp.
      93-95 in his *Political Behaviour in India: A Case
      Study of the 1962 General Elections*. Bombay: P.C.
      Manaktala and Sons, 1965.

      In this very brief article, the author notes the
      mutual lack of interest of political parties and women
      in the 1962 General Elections in Poona.

533. "The Status of Women: A Symposium on the Discriminated
      Section of Society." *Seminar*, No. 165 (May 1973),
      pp. 10-43.

      Seminar's special issue presents various problems of
      women. Their second-class status is reflected in almost
      every sphere--legal, educational, economic, and social.
      A select and relevant bibliography (mostly magazine
      articles) compiled by D.C. Sharma is of great help.

534. Travers, John. *Indian Women and War*. Bombay and
      Madras: Oxford University Press, 1918, 75 pp.

      Indian women's indirect participation in World War I
      is described in detail. An account of their activities
      to comfort Indian soldiers in the British Army is given.
      Illustrations, by M.V. Dhurandhar, of Chandbibi, Indian
      women packing provisions for Indian troops, and Jijabai
      playing a dice game with Shivaji are attractive.

535. Tripathi, Harsha J. "Changing Attitudes of Women in
      Post Independent India." *Journal of Gujarat Research
      Society*, Vol. 29, No. 2 (1967), pp. 92-97.

      This is the text of the lecture delivered at the
      Gujarat Research Workers' Conference at Vallabh Vidyan-
      agar in October 1966. The paper discusses Indian
      women's emancipation and their opportunities for
      varied careers while retaining their irrational atti-
      tude toward religion. Women's organizations must en-
      courage participation in national affairs. The func-
      tions of such organizations in the post-independence
      era are spelled out in detail.

VIII

WOMEN IN ART AND CULTURE

Painting and Sculpture

Several bibliographies on Indian art and sculpture in
which female forms are involved, general works pertaining to
the contributions of women to the art world, and works about
individual artists are included in this subsection. In
India most art forms have a religious basis; goddesses
appear regularly in sculpture and paintings. Generally,
religious and mythological stories have inspired unknown
artists. Frescoes or murals, of Ajanta caves, for instance,
are influenced by Buddhism, and the sculptures of Ellora
are inspired by Hinduism and Buddism. *Marg*, an art
magazine, publishes special issues on specific themes.

536. "Amrita Sher-Gil." Guest eds.: Geeta Kapur, Vivan
        Sundaram, and Gulam Mohammed Sheikh. *Marg*, Vol. 25,
        No. 2 (1972), 72 pp.

        This is a special issue of *Marg* about the famous
        artist Amrita Sher-Gil and her paintings. Her feminist
        and intense sensitivity is reflected in her female
        figures. A brief account of her life and work is
        given, and typical specimens of her art are reproduced
        as illustrations.

537. Appasamy, Jaya. "Modern Indian Women and the Visual
        Arts." *Indian Horizons*, Vol. 24, No. 4 (1975), pp.
        30-34.

        The problems of contemporary artists are discussed.
        Information about some artists, their media of ex-
        pression, and some plates of their work are given.

538. Chandra, Jagdish (comp.). *Bibliography of Indian Art,
        History and Archaeology, VI: Indian Art*. Delhi:
        Delhi Printers Prakashan, 1978, 316 pp.

        Art, architecture, sculpture, painting, handicrafts,
        and greater India are the six main sections into which
        this bibliography is divided. There are 8,329 entries,

many of which relate to the talents of women artists, folk arts, feminine handicrafts, images, and myths. This volume is the Dr. Anand K. Coomaraswamy Memorial volume; Dr. Coomaraswamy was very knowledgeable on this subject.

539. Dasgupta, Charuchandra. "Bibliography of Ancient Indian Terracotta Figurines." *Journal of the Asiatic Society of Bengal*, Letters 4 (1938), pp. 67-120 (a supplement to this bibliography is available in *Journal of the Asiatic Society of Bengal*, Letters 10, 1 (1944), pp. 61-75).

175 books and articles (up to 1937) are listed and annotated. This bibliography contains subject and location indexes. Many figurines are feminine figures, and some illustrations are included.

540. Desai, Devangana. *Erotic Sculpture of India: A Sociocultural Study*. New Delhi: Tata McGraw-Hill Publishing Company, 1975, 269 pp., 155 plates, maps and line drawings.

A survey of the erotic sculptures of South Asia from the 6th to the 15th centuries is made in this scholarly presentation. The enigmatic presence of sex in the religious art of a culture that glorified austerity, penance, and renunciation inspired the author to make this study, which combines various interest areas-- anthropology, comparative religion, sociology, art, and history. The book includes extensive quotations from the authentic reference sources, illustrations, and an index.

541. Ganguly, Ordhendra C. "On the Authenticity of the Feminine Portraits of the Moghul School." *Rupam*, No. 33/34 (Jan.-April 1928), pp. 11-15.

The article examines and questions the authenticity of the portraits of the Moghul School. Who modeled for these portraits? How did the artists manage in the face of seclusion and sex segregation? The writer concludes that the portraits are genuine as the resemblances are striking. These portraits could have been executed by women, and, thus, the queens and princesses might have acted as models.

542. Gode, P.K. "The Role of the Courtesan in the Early History of Indian Painting." *Annals of the Bhandarkar*

Oriental Research Institute, Vol. 22, No. 1-2 (1941),
pp. 24-37.

This is a descriptive article about the courtesans
from 800 B.C. to 500 B.C. and how they were encouraged
to cultivate art and painting. In recent years courtesans have turned to music, dance, and drama.

543. Khandalawala, Karl J. *Amrita Sher-Gil*. Bombay: New
       Book Co., 1944, 71 pp.

       Written by a connoisseur of Indian art, this publica-
       tion reviews the artist's life and art. 28 plates are
       reproduced. It is a beautiful production.

544. Marwan, Mala. "Women as Practitioners of Art." *Link*,
       Vol. 18, No. 1 (15 Aug. 1975), pp. 95-97.

       The writer describes the work of female artists from
       the ancient texts of Kautilya's *Arthashastra* and the
       great epic *Mahabharata*. Contemporary women artists,
       their expressive media, and their problems are also
       discussed.

545. Mehta, Rustam J. *Masterpieces of the Female Form in
       Indian Art*. Bombay: D.B. Taraporevala Sons, 1972,
       56 pp.

       The classical and medieval sculptures are interpreted
       and appreciated. 100 plates from the second century
       B.C. to the sixteenth-century A.D. illustrating various
       aspects are included in this work.

546. Mode, Heing. *Women in Indian Art*. Translated from the
       German (*Die Frau in der Indischen Kunst*) by Marianne
       Hersfeld; revised by D. Talbot Rice. New York: Mc-
       Graw-Hill Book Company, 1970, 51 pp.

       Indian art is connected with Indian femininity, and
       women themselves have contributed to the world of art.
       This important publication presents the holistic view
       from ancient to modern times. 118 plates are included.

547. Prasad, Ambika Divya. *The Women of Khajuraha*. Trans-
       lated from the Hindi. Ajaigarh: Sahitya Sadan,
       1964, 111 pp.

       This is a collection of poems, inspired by the erotic
       female sculptures of Khajuraha, which are situated in
       Madhya Pradesh. The book is illustrated and beautifully
       printed.

548. Rukminidevi (Rukminidevi Arundale). "Woman as Artist."
     Pp. 113-120 in Shyam Kumari Nehru, ed. *Our Cause:
     A Symposium by Indian Women*. Allahabad: Kitabistan,
     n.d.

     An artist's description of characteristics of creat-
     ive women is offered in this article. The imagination
     and sensitivity of creative women are expressed in
     literature, dance, music, painting, or sculpture.

549. *Sher-Gil*. New Delhi: Lalit Kala Akademi, 1965, 25 pp.
     (plates).

     This album contains 25 plates of Amrita Sher-Gil's
     paintings in black and white and color. The introduc-
     tion describes her childhood through the eyes of her
     playmates who became admirers of her work in adult
     life.

550. Soloman, Gladstone W.E. *Women of the Ajanta Caves*.
     Bombay: Times of India, 1937, 29 pp., illustrated.

     This small pamphlet, written by a former curator of
     the art section of the Prince of Wales Museum in Bombay,
     discusses the female figures in the murals and frescoes
     of the Ajanta caves, comparing Indian art forms with
     Van Gogh's or Gauguin's works. The author mentions
     that the Indian figures differ in that "Woman is here
     restored to us, wholly lovable, wholly beautiful and
     wholly untarnished."

551. Spink, Walter. "Female Figures in Ajanta to Ellora."
     Marg, Vol. 20, No. 2 (1967), pp. 32-37.

     Photographs of a few selected sculptures from Ellora
     and paintings from the Ajanta caves are interpreted.
     Depiction of the female form had reached a high point
     of development long before the mid-fifth century. The
     cave temples show these beautiful and artistic forms.

552. Srivastava, M.C.P. *Mother Goddess in Indian Art, Arch-
     aeology and Literature*. Delhi: Agam Kala Prakashan,
     1979, 231 pp.

     Through photographs and line drawings, Srivastava de-
     picts the history of the mother goddess from prehistoric
     times to the present.

553. Thakur Singh, S.G. *Painting of Indian Womanhood*. Am-
     ritsar: Thakur Singh School of Arts, 1971, 22 pp.
     (plates).

22 colored plates show women performing everyday activities (bathing, worshipping, decorating their bodies, etc.). These paintings were done during 1920-1930 in a traditional and realistic style.

554. Upadhyaya, Padma. *Female Images in the Museums of Uttar Pradesh and Their Social Background*. Varanasi: Chaukhambha Orientalia, 1978, 322 pp. (Chaukhambha Oriental Research Studies 8.)

Hindu, Jaina, and Buddhist traditional female images in the museums of Uttar Pradesh are illustrated in 32 plates, and descriptions of these sculptures are given as to period, artistic worth, their respective secular and nonsecular settings, and their social value.

555. Yazdani, G. "Women in Sculpture of the Deccan: An Artistic Study." *Annals of the Bhandarkar Oriental Research Institute*, Vol. 23, No. 1-4 (1942), pp. 678-686.

An assessment of the merits of Deccan sculpture in general and female figures in particular focuses on beauty of form, posture, and the expression of inner feelings, with the help of plates.

Dance

The are four major dances in India (Kathak, Bharat Natyam, Manipuri, and Kathakali). Women artists have mastered the first three; Kathakali is mainly performed by male artists. Entries in this section mainly deal with the various schools of dance and with some of the famous artists, their life, training, and eminence. (See also the section on film, as the Film Division of India has produced many films on the dances of India as well as on individual artists.)

556. Agrawal, Chandra P. "Sitara in Kathak." *New Quest*, Vol. 2 (Aug. 1977), pp. 47-49.

This article describes the Kathak style of dancing (storytelling through dance), its origin, and Sitara-devi's contribution in the form of innovative themes, movements, and choreography.

557. Ambrose, Kay. *Classical Dances and Costumes of India*. London: Adam and Charles Block, 1950, 95 pp.

This book describes the revival of Bharat Natyam (an ancient school of dance), its historical facets and

characteristics. Information about other classical
dances is included. Photographs and line drawings
decorate the book.

558. Banerji, Projesh. *The Folk-Dance of India*. Allahabad:
      Kitabistan, 1944, 129 pp.

      Male and female dance schools of India of prepartition
      days are described by state.

559. "Bharat Natyam." *Marg*, Vol. 10, No. 4 (1957), 58 pp.

      A special issue of this art magazine is devoted to
      the dance of Bharat Natyam. The spiritual aspect of the
      dance and music, the origin of the dance and various
      guru (teacher) genealogies, and dance forms and their
      relations to ancient sculptures are discussed with the
      help of relevant drawings and photographs. This is an
      exquisite issue.

560. Bhavnani, Enakshi. *The Dance in India: The Origin and
      History, the Art and Science of Dance in India--
      Classical, Folk and Tribal*. Bombay: D.B. Taraporevala
      Sons, 1965, 261 pp.

      The author has surveyed the main classical schools
      of dance and the folk dance forms of various states and
      illustrated them through idols, paintings, and sculp-
      tures from the temples. The author has used her imagina-
      tion to explain the divine origin of dance, music, and
      costumes and to examine the revival of these cultural
      traditions after India became independent. The book is
      enriched with many photographs, a glossary, and a good
      bibliography, and is designed for Western art lovers.

561. Number omitted.

562. Menon, Narayana. *Balasaraswati*. New Delhi: Inter-
      national Cultural Centre, 1963, 23 pp.

      An art expert writes about Balasaraswati's life and
      work, especially her contribution to the Abhinaya
      (acting) form of the Bharat Natyam style of dancing.
      Photographs of actual performances are included.

563. "Mohini Attam." Guest ed., Kanak Rele. *Marg*, Vol. 26,
      No. 2 (1973), 55 pp.

      Mohini Attam is a rare type of dance from South India
      which is about 300 to 600 years old. It is based on
      Bharat Natyam and Kathakali and is performed by women.

Dr. Kanak Rele has revived this form, and she is its
outstanding exponent. A performer, teacher, and
director of a dance school, she discusses origin and
history, myths and techniques, costumes and make-up,
music and choreography. Photographs provide a visual
feast.

564.   Narayan, Shovana. "Sadhna Bose: End of a Long Quest."
       Lipilka, Vol. 2, No. 3-4 (1973), pp. 29-35, 56.

Sadhna Bose was a famous dancer from Bengal and she
knew all four styles (Bharat Natyam, Kathakali, Kathak,
and Manipuri). She was innovative enough to adapt
certain features of Western classical dance into Indian
dances. She appeared in Indian films in the 1930s and
1940s.

565.   Ragini Devi. *Dance Dialects of India.* Delhi: Vikas
       Publications, 1972, 227 pp.

India has in general four kinds of dance in four parts
of the country and a variety of folk dances. Ragini
Devi discusses all dance forms and gives information
about the personalities in the field of performing arts
as well as devdasis. Many illustrations are included.

566.   Sarabhai, Mrinalini. *The Eight Nayikas: Heroines of
       the Classical Dance of India.* New York: Dance Per-
       spectives, 1965, 49 pp.

The old concept of eight heroines and their place in
the classical dances of India (i.e., how they can be
portrayed or interwoven in the dance forms) is explained. Ancient texts have been utilized for inter-
pretive purposes, and the illustrations personify the
heroines.

567.   Vanzile, Judy. *Dance in India: An Annotated Guide to
       Source Materials.* Providence, R.I.: Asian Music
       Publications, 1973, 129 pp. (Bibliographies and Re-
       search Aids, 3.)

839 English sources on dance are annotated in this
book. Sections on temple dancers and individual biographical sketches of the dancers of particular dance
forms are also given. This is a good source book.

568.   Vatsyayan, Kapila. "In the Performing Arts." Pp. 288-
       297 in Devki Jain (ed.). *Indian Women.* New Delhi:
       Publications Division, Ministry of Information and
       Broadcasting, Government of India, 1975.

The writer of this brief article indicates women's
contributions to dance, drama, and music as well as
historical description and depiction of present trends.

569. Vatsyayan, Kapila. *Traditions of Indian Folk Dance.*
      New Delhi: Indian Book Company, 1976, 280 pp.

      Regional folk dance forms are described, as are the
      context, the musical instruments, and gender of the
      performers. An extensive bibliography of ethnographic
      and other primary source material is given. Photographs
      are included.

570. Venkatachalam, Govindraj. *Dance in India.* Bombay:
      Nalanda Publications, n.d., 132 pp.

      Short biographical sketches of the famous classical
      dancers (Rukmani Devi, Shanta Rao, Balasuraswati,
      Sadhna Bose, Menaka, and Shrimati Hutheesing) are
      given. Brief information about the dance forms is also
      provided.

571. Venkatachalam, Govindraj. *Bharat Natyam: Srimati Shanta
      and Her Art.* Bangalore: Hosali Press, 1944, 102 pp.

      Shanta is one of the famous Bharat Natyam dancers
      who has earned fame at home as well as abroad. The
      book describes her style and dance forms. A list of
      her repertoire and a letter written in her praise by
      her own teacher are included, along with photographs.

Art Forms of Embroidery,
Hairstyles, Jewelry, Dress, and Alpana

Women of India have contributed to the above-listed art
forms since ancient times. Rural as well as urban women have
developed mirror embroidery, bead work, filigree in jewelry,
sari and Indian costumes, and Alpana--the decoration of
floors, walls, ceilings, and open verandahs with folk motifs--
which is the domain of females for the most part. Entries
pertaining to these fields, including some bibliographies and
illustrated books, are found here.

572. *Alpana.* New Delhi: Publications Division, Ministry
      of Information and Broadcasting, Government of India,
      1960, 40 pp.

      Alpana is the ancient art of floor decorating, first
      revived in full at Vishwa Bharati University established

by the Nobel Laureate Rabindranath Tagore. In this
brief monograph, its history, decline, and revival are
discussed. The techniques and various styles are also
described.

573. Bannerjea, Biren. "India, Ritual Designs: Note on Geo-
      metrical Ritual Designs in India." *Man*, Vol. 33, No.
      168 (1933), pp. 163-164.

      This brief article describes the creative expression
      of women in ritual design. On special occasions or
      during religious festivals, women express themselves
      in a variety of ways.

574. Bhanawat, Mahendra. *Mehandi Rang Rachi: Folkloric
      Study of Colourful Myrtle*. Udaipur: Bharatiya Lok-
      Kala Mandal, 1976, 64 pp.

      The women of India are fond of applying henna, the
      green-leafed herb which is used for coloring the palms
      and the soles of the feet, for festivals and special
      occasions. The history and cultivation of the plant,
      the methods of preparing wet paste, the styles and
      designs, are explained. Beautiful drawings and special
      songs sung by women while applying henna on palms and
      feet are given.

575. Brij Bhushan, Jamila. *Indian Jewelry, Ornaments and
      Decorative Designs*. 2nd ed. Bombay: Taraporevala
      Sons, 1964, 189 pp.

      Jewelry in ancient India was different than in the
      Muslim period. This fact is brought out beautifully
      by information on craftsmanship. An inventory of
      ancient and modern jewelry with pictures, drawings,
      and a bibliography of 97 items presents a comprehensive
      view of the subject.

576. Chandra, Jagdish (comp.). "Embroidery." Pp. 246-248
      in his *Bibliography of Indian Art, History and
      Archaeology*. Vol. VI, Indian Art. Delhi: Delhi
      Printers Prakashan, 1978.

      The history of embroidery traditions is surveyed in
      this brief article. 68 entries are listed.

577. Chandra, Suman. *Bibliography of Indian Arts and
      Crafts*. New Delhi: Office of the Registrar General,
      Ministry of Home Affairs, Government of India, 1967,
      71 pp. (Census of India, 1961, vi, pt. II, 2.)

More than 1,400 items are here classified according
to the medium used for expression. Sections on jewelry
and ornaments, dolls, and toys are important to women's
studies as are the accompanying commentaries.

578. Chattopadhayaya, Kamaladevi. *Indian Embroidery.* New
      Delhi: Wiley Eastern Ltd., 1977, 76 pp.

      Different states in India have their own styles of
      embroidery. The author has studied them intensively
      and makes here brief references to the distinct charac-
      teristics of each style of embroidery. Except in Jammu
      and Kashmir State, embroidery is the preserve of women.
      Illustrations in color as well as black and white in-
      crease the utility of this book.

579. Dongerkery, Kamala. *Jewelry and Personal Adornment in
      India.* New Delhi: Indian Council for Cultural Rela-
      tions, 1970, 77 pp.

      Jewelry from the Indus Valley civilization to modern
      times is the subject of this monograph. Folk and tribal
      jewelry is also included, along with many photographs
      and drawings.

580. Dongerkery, Kamala S. *The Romance of Indian Embroidery.*
      Bombay: Thacker and Company, 1951, 62 pp.

      This monograph deals with the traditional as well as
      sociocultural and aesthetic aspects of Indian embroidery.
      Illustrations are included.

581. Dongerkery, Kamala S. *The Indian Sari.* New Delhi: The
      All India Handicrafts Board, n.d., viii + 99 pp.; 65
      illustrations.

      The author describes the sari through 65 illustrations
      in color and black and white. The sari is worn in more
      than a dozen styles in many countries and still dominates
      the Indian scene despite the onslaught of Western dresses
      and costumes. It is one of India's handicrafts, through
      which different types of material used for weaving and
      a variety of techniques of weaving and printing are kept
      alive. The author has done a remarkable job of explain-
      ing the use of ancient sculpture. Even the way to wear
      a sari is demonstrated through photographs. A bibliog-
      raphy, glossary, and index are useful.

582. Durai, Mrs. H. Ghana. "Preliminary Note on Geometrical
      Diagrams from the Madras Presidency." *Man*, Vol. 29,
      No. 60 (1929), 77 pp.

White powder is used for decorating the thresholds
and courtyards of homes and temples. In this brief article, the writer provides 11 such designs.

583. Fabri, Charles. *Indian Dress: A Brief History.* New
        Delhi: Sangam, Orient Longman, 1977, 92 pp.

    Male and female Indian costumes from 150 B.C. to the
    19th century are illustrated with the help of 30 plates.
    An archaeological bias is visible.

584. Ghurya, G.S. *Indian Costumes.* Bombay: Popular Prakashan,
        1966, 302 pp.

    Male and female dresses are described from a socio-
    logical and historical viewpoint, from 1800 to the
    present. The book is arranged according to geographical
    area, which enhances its significance. Numerous valuable
    illustrations are provided.

585. Hendley, Thomas Holbein. "Indian Jewelry." *Journal
        of Indian Art and History*, Vol. 12, 95/107 (1909),
        189 pp.

    This is a beautiful publication dealing with men's
    and women's jewelry of the 19th century. Explanations
    are offered of historical factors, modes of wearing,
    modes of making, regional specialties, and antique value.
    Although the work is based on personal observation and
    published material, the author has seen to it that
    justice is done to the subject with 167 full-page plates
    in both color and black and white.

586. "Indian Jewelry." *Marg*, Vol. 17, No. 4 (1964), 59 pp.

    In this special issue of a prestigious art magazine,
    many facets of the subject from history to aesthetics,
    traditional motifs to assimilations of contemporary
    designs, and the jewelry industry, etc., are dealt with.

587. Nicholson, S. "Women's Clothes in the Cuddappa Dis-
        trict, South India." *Man*, Vol. 20, No. 72 (1920), pp.
        149-152.

    This is an ethnographic account of saris, how they
    were first worn, and the significance of different motifs
    in them. Weaving patterns have associations with par-
    ticular gods, temples, and specific socio-religious
    rituals. The article includes some drawings of tradition-
    al motifs, and laments that some of these motifs and
    patterns are fast vanishing.

588. "Painting with the Needle." Guest eds.: Kamaladevi
      Chattopadhayaya and Jasleen Damija. *Marg*, Vol. 17,
      No. 2 (1964), 72 pp.

      This is a special issue of *Marg* on embroidery. Both
      the editors are authorities on the subject, and the
      issue deals with the origin and development of embroidery
      in India, a survey of traditions in embroidery, and the
      place of embroidery in Indian crafts. The issue is en-
      livened by numerous illustrations.

589. Palchoudhuri, Ila. *Ancient Hair Styles of India*.
      Calcutta: Rupa, 1974, 44 pp.

      Drawings of 15 hairstyles for women inspired by temple
      sculptures are presented with relevant photographs and
      brief explanatory notes.

590. Purohit, Veena. *Indian Hair Styles*. Bombay: Commercial
      Printing Press, 1962, illustrated with 79 plates.

      In the foreword Kamaladevi Chattopadhayaya writes:
      "Among the attributes of beauty for women, hair has
      always ranked high in Indian tradition. It was truly
      the crowning glory. For all aspects of Indian expression
      --literature, pictures, frescoes, crafts--hair was a
      prominent and significant factor." This well-researched
      book also includes an article entitled "The Charm of
      Feminine Coiffure" by C. Sivaramamurti.

591. Saksena, Jogendra. "Mandana: The Heritage of the Rajas-
      thani Woman and Mandana Art: A Case of Preservation
      and Revival." *Shakti*, Vol. 1 (Jan. and March 1965),
      pp. 24-27, 31-35.

      Rural women's art on the front walls of their modest
      homes is the subject of this article. Some typical
      designs are passed generation to generation; simple
      folk motifs are preserved. A second article describes
      the factors responsible for the decline of this art and
      recommends some measures for saving it.

592. "A Select Bibliography on Indian Jewelry." *Cultural
      News from India*, Vol. 8, No. 516 (1967), pp. 49-53,
      43-47.

      80 briefly annotated references are included in this
      select bibliography.

Women in Literature

In addition to some general entries describing the contribution of women to Sanskrit literature and images of
women in Buddhist and Jain literature, the literary activities of Indian women authors and criticism of their work are
annotated. India can be proud of its women authors who write
in English, a foreign or second language for most of them.
Despite handicaps and lack of special facilities, they have
maintained their creative urge and earned fame. They depict
the Indian way of life, values, woman's place in society, the
dilemmas faced by Indian women, problems of identity, the
suffering in joint families in a man-made world, etc. Some
of these women authors have sacrificed their personal life
in order to preserve their artistic life. Authors such as
Anita Desai, Kamala Markandaya, Nayantara Sahgal, Ruth Prawer
Jhabvala (Indian only by marriage), Santha Rama Rao, and
others have attempted to deal with Indian women's aspirations
and frustrations. Mira, a poet of the medieval period, was a
rebel and defiant woman who protested against traditional
customs. She wrote in Hindi, but her devotional songs have
been translated into English. Such poets as Toru Dutt and
Sarojini Nadiu in pre-independence India were inspired by
nationalism, Gandhian thinking, and the new social order
Gandhiji was trying to usher in. Kamala Das and Amrita
Pritam are the symbols of feminine creativity today. Many
women write poetry in their mother tongue, which is not
translated into English. Only those writers whose works
are available in English translation are included here.

593. Abidi, S.Z.H. *Kamala Markandaya's "Nectar in a Sieve":
      A Critical Study*. Bareilly: Prakash Book Depot, 1976,
      127 pp.

      The author critically evaluates the plot, characters,
      and events in the novel *Nectar in a Sieve*.

594-598. Numbers omitted.

599. "Amrita Pritam." *Mahfil*, Vol. 5, No. 3 (1968-69),
      134 pp.

      This special issue of *Mahfil* deals with the life and
      works of Amrita Pritam. Along with a selection of her
      poems, short stories, and criticism, a bibliography of
      her Punjabi works is attached.

600. Ashapurna Devi. *A Bouquet of Modern Short Stories*.
      Translated from Bengali by Anima Bose. New Delhi:
      Pankaj Publications, 1978, 72 pp.

Ashapurna Devi is a famous writer in the Bengali language whose short stories depict women in rebellion. This translation captures her spontaneity of style. She has won many literary awards.

601. Asnani, Shyam M. "The Novels of Nayantara Sahgal." *Indian Literature*, Vol. 16, No. 1-2 (1973), pp. 36-69.

Nayantara Sahgal's four novels and her favorite theme of the man-woman relationship in these years of social transition are discussed in this article.

602. Asnani, Shyam M. "Jhabvala's Novels: A Thematic Study." *Journal of Indian Writings in English*, Vol. 2, No. 1 (1974), pp. 38-47.

Positive comments on Jhabvala's *Esmond in India* are offered in this brief article. The favorite theme of this Polish-born author married to a Zoroastrian is the conflict between traditional and modern values in India today.

603. Asnani, Shyam M. "Contribution of Women in Indo-English Novel." *Triveni*, Vol. 44, No. 2 (1975), pp. 45-52.

Women writers and their favorite subjects are surveyed in this well-written article. The quality of the works is also assessed.

604. Balse, Mayah. *Just a Matter of Mistresses*. Bombay: Jaico Books, 1972, 208 pp.

This satirical novel depicts the love life of the hero--Narayan--who is involved in a chain of funny events.

605. Balse, Mayah. *Indiscreet*. Delhi: Orient Paperbacks, 1977, 181 pp.

This novel deals with sensational themes.

606. Balse, Mayah. *The Singer*. Bombay: Jaico Publishing House, 1975, 178 pp.

This novel, the author's first, depicts the life of a crippled singer, her loneliness, and her craving for her own home and family. The world of popular music does not bring her the satisfaction and sense of fulfillment she craves.

607. Bandopadhayay, Pranav (ed.). *Women Poets of India: An*

Anthology of Indian Poetry. Calcutta: United Writers,
1977, 78 pp.

This is a very useful anthology of works of 18 major
women poets from the end of the 19th century to the
present. Moreover, it includes English translations
of some female poets who wrote in their mother tongues.

608. Belliappa, N. Meena. "East-West Encounter: Indian Women
       Writers of Fiction in English." *Literary Criterion*,
       Vol. 7, No. 3 (1966), pp. 18-27.

       Three major women writers and their writings (Kamala
       Markandaya, Santha Rama Rau, and Ruth Prawer Jhabvala)
       are discussed. The cordial relationships between cultures
       are depicted in their writings, but one possible reason
       they are able to probe the depths of relationships may
       be because they do not identify with the Indian culture.

609. Belliappa, Meena. *Anita Desai: A Study of Her Fiction*.
       Calcutta: Writer's Workshop, 1971, 52 pp.

       Desai's early short stories and first two novels are
       examined. Anita Desai describes social reality and the
       role of women in it. The run-down status of women is
       lamented. Illustrations in the form of excerpts from
       her writings are given.

610. Bharucha, Perin. *The Fire Worshippers*. Bombay: Strand
       Book Club, 1968, 216 pp.

       This is the only novel written by a Parsi (Zoroastrian)
       writer to depict the lifestyle of the Parsi community
       in general. A middle-class housewife, totally dis-
       satisfied with her married life, seeks a relationship
       with a young man from a well-known family; her involve-
       ment with him is the subject of the novel.

611. Bose, Anima. "Ashapurna Devi: Perspective on a Bengali
       Novelist." *Indian Literature*, Vol. 19, No. 3 (1976),
       pp. 80-95.

       Bose highlights Ashapurna Devi's unique themes and
       style in depicting Bengali women's life styles and
       problems. Ashapurna Devi has created an immortal charac-
       ter (Subaranlata) who is discussed at length in this
       article. The article, in interview format, is informa-
       tive.

612. Bose, A. "Sarojini Naidu." *Literary Criterion*, Vol.
       2, No. 3 (1955), pp. 1-8.

The author expresses regret that Sarojini Naidu decided to write in English; Bengali literature would have
been enriched by her contribution. Her style and imagery are also discussed in this brief article.

613. Chakladar, Haranchandra. "Early Indian Poetesses."
      Pp. 65-74 in *Sir Asutosh Memorial Volume: Part 2*.
      Patna: J.N. Samaddar, 1928.

      The contributions of eight brahmavadinis and female
      saints of the Rigvedic age, and biographical details about
      them, are discussed in this article. Those interested
      in knowing about the contributions of ancient saint
      poetesses will find this article very informative.

614. Chauhan, P.S. "Kamala Markandaya: Sense and Sensibili-
      ty." *Literary Criterion*, Vol. 12, No. 2/3 (1976),
      pp. 134-147.

      The cultural contrast between East and West is nicely
      brought out by Kamala Markandaya with a little sarcasm
      and interweaving of political events. She is one of
      India's finest writers writing in English, but has not
      been understood by her own people.

615. Coomaraswamy, Anand K. "The Eight *Nayikas*." *Journal
      of Indian Art & Industry*, Vol. 16, No. 128 (1914),
      pp. 99-112.

      Types of Nayikas are described with the help of
      ancient Sanskrit poetry in translation and paintings
      of the Pahadi school. The author of this article was
      a Buddhist monk and scholar of Indian philosophy and
      ancient literature.

616. Cousins, James H. "The Poetry of Sarojini Naidu."
      Pp. 247-277 in his *The Renaissance in India*. Madras:
      Ganesh and Co., 1918.

      The noted poet evaluates Sarojini's book of poetry
      Broken Wing, which reflects with feminine sensitivity
      women's trials and tribulations. The dependent role
      and low status of Indian women are naturally not relished
      by the great feminist poetess. The author thinks that
      her feminist views appear in Sarojini's poetry, but
      they have not affected the quality of her poems ad-
      versely.

617. Dalal, Nergis. *Minari*. Bombay: Pearl Publications,
      1967, 236 pp.

This novel depicts love and politics at a hill station of present-day Rajasthan.

618. Dalal, Nergis. *Never a Dull Moment*. Bombay: Orient Longmans, 1970, 120 pp.

Dalal has written under the penname "Aries" in *Indian Express*; this is a collection of her brief essays.

619. Dalal, Nergis. *The Sisters*. Delhi: Hind Pocket Books, 1973, 149 pp.

This popular novel depicts the conflicts between two daughters of an English mother and Parsi father. As a Parsi, the author knows her subject matter.

620. Dalal, Nergis. *The Inner Door*. New Delhi: Orient Paperbacks, 1975, 144 pp.

This beautiful novel depicts a not-so-common theme-- an Indian boy is attracted to a foreigner's money-making scheme, "yoga for sex." The locale is Rishikesh and the style is satirical.

621. Dalal, Nergis. *The Nude*. New Delhi: Orient Paperbacks, 1977, 158 pp.

This is a collection of Dalal's 16 short stories. Some of them are prize-winners in an All-India short story competition, organized by *Illustrated Weekly*.

622. Das, Harihar. *Life and Letters of Toru Dutt*. London: Oxford University Press, 1921, 364 pp.

This brief biographical sketch of Toru Dutt was compiled from her friend Mary Martin's reminiscent account and from 53 letters written by Toru Dutt to Mary Martin. Some excerpts from her writings are included, along with some photographs.

623. Das, Kamala. *Summer in Calcutta*. New Delhi: Rajender Paul, 1965, 64 pp.

This collection of 50 poems, her first, was well received because of the sexual themes.

624. Das, Kamala. *The Descendants*. Calcutta: Writer's Workshop, 1967, 35 pp.

In her second collection of poems, Das's imagery sparkles. The collection includes poems on love and death.

625. Das, Kamala. *The Old Playhouse and Other Poems*. Delhi: Orient Longmans, 1973, 54 pp.

    33 poems on love, nature, people, drama, and the seasons are included in this collection. Most of them are prose poems.

626. Das, Kamala. *Alphabet of Lust*. New Delhi: Orient Paperbacks, 1976, 147 pp.

    This novel depicts the life style of a middle-aged woman poet. Dissatisfied with her marriage, the heroine looks around for excitement and becomes involved in extramarital relationships with politicians, thereby receiving the patronage to satisfy her ambitions.

627. Das, Kamala. *A Doll for the Child Prostitute*. New Delhi: India Paperbacks, 1977, 104 pp.

    This is a collection of 11 short stories. The title story is about a prostitute and her tragic experiences. Subjects treated are personal relationships, distrust, cruelty, sickness, etc.

628. Dasgupta, Mary Ann (ed.). *Hers, Indian Perspectives: An Anthology of Poetry in English by Indian Women*. Calcutta: Writers' Workshop, 1978, 106 pp.

    Biographical notes of 30 famous and not-so-famous women poets and their poems are included in this publication. Bibliographical notes are also attached.

629. Desai, Anita. "Women Writers." *Quest*, Vol. 65 (April 1970), pp. 39-43.

    In ancient Indian drama there are 8 types of Nayikas or heroines. In this article, these types are described. The article also discusses oral literature, which, because of India's high illiteracy rate, is still a significant medium, especially among women. Indian women are not used to being alone, and the author blames lack of privacy for the paucity of women's writing. Women have also felt limited in their selection of themes. The writer compares Indian men and women authors and laments the limitations placed on women writers.

630. Desai, Anita. *Fire on the Mountain*. New York: Harper and Row, 1977, 145 pp.

This novel deals with an elderly woman who, feeling exhausted, withdraws from life, causing her relatives and friends to suffer.

631. Desai, Anita. *Clear Light of Day*. Bombay: Allied Publishers, 1980, 183 pp.

A novel presenting a large number of characters, a wide span of time, and very complex relationships handles the theme of prepartition riots and the turbulent months leading to the murder of Gandhiji. The novel centers around old Delhi, relates the story of two brothers and two sisters growing up together and experiencing romance, guilt, and tension.

632. Desai, Anita. *Cry, The Peacock*. London: Peter Owen, 1963, 188 pp.

This novel depicts the life of a lonely woman who is not happy with her surroundings or her marriage. Her inner life and conflicts are nicely brought out.

633. Desai, Anita. *Voices in the City*. London: Peter Owen, 1965, 265 pp.

This novel deals with the life of a married woman in a great metropolis, who feels lost in a mass society. Her married life does not seem to be happy.

634. Desai, Anita. *Bye-Bye Blackbird*. Delhi: Hind Pocket Books, 1971, 266 pp.

Indian immigrants in Britain and their identity problems are the themes around which the plot is woven. "Asians," as they are known there, have their frustrations and aspirations.

635. Desai, S.K. *Santha Rama Rau*. New Delhi: Arnold-Heinemann Publishers, 1976, 96 pp.

The author critically examines Santha Rama Rau's novels, dramas, travelogues, and biographies. Although educated, married, and settled abroad, Santha Rama Rau has been able to maintain her identity as an Indian.

636. DeSouza, Eunice. "The Blinds Drawn and the Air Conditioner On: The Novels of Ruth Prawer Jhabvala." *World Literature Written in English*, Vol. 17, No. 1 (1978), pp. 219-224.

The autobiographical narrative of Ruth Jhabvala is

critically viewed by the writer of this article. Her
stereotyped characters, biased (Western) view of Indian
life, and her value system are vehemently defended.

637. Dustoor, P.E. *Sarojini Naidu*. Mysore: Rao and Raghvan,
      1961, 54 pp.

      A short biography and a critical appreciation of
      Sarojini Naidu's poems are included in this series on
      Indian writers. In fact, after she met Gandhi in 1914
      and started actively participating in the freedom
      struggle, she did not write much.

638. Dutt, Toru. "Bianca or the Young Spanish Maiden."
      Bengal Magazine, Vol. 6, Jan.-April (1978), pp.
      264-75, 279-94, 325, 31, 371-81.

      The locale of this unfinished novel is England.
      The fragment contains some of Dutt's poetry.

639. Dutt, Toru. *Ancient Ballads and Legends of Hindustan*.
      C.K. Paul and Co., 1880, 374 pp.

      This is an English translation of those poems original-
      ly written in French. Govin Chunder Dutt has written
      a sort of memoir as a preface.

640. Dutt, Toru. *Ancient Ballads and Legends of Hindustan*.
      London: Kegan Paul, 1882, 139 pp.

      A collection of early poems on Sita and Savitri which
      Dutt wrote while in Europe. Edmund W. Gosse wrote
      the introduction.

641. Dwivedi, A.N. *Toru Dutt*. New Delhi: Arnold Heinemann,
      1977, 168 pp.

      The author tries to examine Toru Dutt's literary con-
      tributions and her role in the development of Indo-Angli-
      can literature. Her poems, essays, novels, letters, and
      translations are evaluated and praised.

642. Falk, Nancy. "An Image of Woman in Old Buddhist Litera-
      ture: The Daughters of Mara." Pp. 105-112 in Judith
      Plaskew and Joan Arnold (eds.). *Women and Religion*.
      Revised ed. Missoula, Mont.: Scholars Press, 1974.

      Negative attitudes toward women did exist in early
      Buddhist literature, but later there was a change. This
      article notes that Hindus changed their attitude toward
      women when ascetic observance conflicted with the con-
      cept of woman as a temptress in Hinduism as well as in

Buddhism. In both Hinduism and Buddhism, saints and monks wrote most of the early literature, and this hostility is visible.

643. Goetz, Hermann. *Mirabai: Her Life and Times*. Bombay: Bharatiya Vidya Bhavan, 1966, 45 pp.

This very scholarly publication critically examines the prevalent legends and anecdotes about the great poetess of medieval India. This work is documented with primary as well as secondary sources in the bibliography.

644. Gupta, A.N., and Satish Gupta. *Sarojini Naidu's Select Poems*. Bareilly: Prakash Book Depot, 1976, 230 pp.

This selection of Sarojini's poems is annotated so as to illustrate her sensitivity. Her experiences. her poetic career, and her participation in the freedom struggle are described. The themes dealt with in her poetry are critically discussed. A bibliography for further study is attached.

645. Gupta, Rameshwar. *Sarojini, the Poetess*. Delhi: Doaba House, 1975, 142 pp.

A brief biosketch coupled with the evaluation of Sarojini's poetic genius is presented here. Her main themes are also examined and elaborated upon. Modern critics differ from traditional critics in their evaluation of her poetry.

646. Harrex, S.C. "A Sense of Identity: The Early Novels of Kamala Markandaya." Pp. 245-261 in his *The Fire and the Offering: The English Language Novel of India, 1935-1970*. Calcutta: Writers Workshop, 1977.

The writer discusses the problem of identity as crystallized in Kamala Markandaya's novels. For many Indo-Anglican writers, this seems to be a popular subject. Kamala weaves this theme into philosophical and sociopolitical reality. Harrex gives many examples from her writing to substantiate his points.

647. Hartley, Lois. "R. Prawer Jhabvala: Novelist of Urban India." *Literature East and West*, Vol. 9, No. 3 (1965), pp. 265-273.

Characters and themes used in Jhabvala's novels are discussed. Jhabvala depicts North Indian urban life, people, and their manners, sometimes making use of mildly satirical language. Also discussed here is Jhabvala's interview with the famous author R.K. Narayan.

648. Hutheesingh, Krishna Nehru. *Shadows on the Wall*. Bom-
      bay: Katub, 1946, 105 pp. (also published New York:
      John Day, 1948).

      This is a collection of her short stories, mostly
      based on her reminiscences of the people she met in pri-
      son during the national movement for independence. She
      was the youngest sister of former Prime Minister of
      India, Jawaharlal Nehru.

649. Jain, J.C., and Margaret Walter, translator. *The Gift
      of Love and Other Ancient Indian Tales about Women*.
      Delhi: Bell Books, Vikas Publishing House, 1976,
      99 pp.

      From the 2nd to the 12th century, the Prakrit lan-
      guage was in vogue in India; nine stories about women
      in Prakrit are translated and compiled. The women range
      from virtuous wives to prostitutes, courtesans, and
      procuresses.

650. Jain, Jasbir. "The Novels of Kamala Markandaya."
      Indian Literature, Vol. 18, No. 2 (1975), pp. 36-47.

      East and West are guided by different sets of values.
      In Kamala Markandaya's novels, the conflict between
      two sets of values exists.

651. Jain, Jasbir. *Nayantara Sahgal*. New Delhi: Arnold
      Heinemann, 1978, 176 pp.

      Nayantara Sahgal is the very talented daughter of
      Madam Vijayalaxmi Pandit, who combines political jour-
      nalism with creative writing. Jain highlights the
      importance of Gandhian philosophy and the national
      movement for independence in her works. An extensive
      bibliography listing her creative as well as journalis-
      tic writing is given.

652. Jhabvala, R. Prawer. *Amrita*. New York: Norton, 1956.
      283 pp. (also published London: George Allen, 1955,
      under the title *To Whom She Will*).

      When India won her independence, the country was
      divided into Pakistan and India. The problems of Pun-
      jabi refugees coming into India and adjusting to the
      changed circumstances is the main subject of this novel.

653. Jhabvala, R. Prawer. *The Nature of Passion*. London:
      G. Allen and Unwin, 1956, 261 pp.

This novel depicts the life styles of the nouveau
riche of India, who measure everything in terms of
money. It is highly satirical.

654. Jhabvala, R. Prawer. *Esmond in India*. London: George
      Allen and Unwin, 1958, 256 pp.

      This novel concerns an Englishman who looks at every-
      thing from a British viewpoint and becomes disillusioned.

655. Jhabvala, R. Prawer. *Get Ready for Battle*. London:
      John Murray, 1962, 224 pp.

      This novel deals with the change in a marital rela-
      tionship when the wife becomes assertive.

656. Jhabvala, R. Prawer. *Like Birds, Like Fishes and Other
      Short Stories*. New York: W.W. Norton, 1964, 224 pp.

      The main thread of these short stories is intergenera-
      tional conflict. The confrontation between male and
      female and Indian and British is also depicted in some
      of the stories.

657. Jhabvala, R. Prawer. *A Backward Place*. New York: W.W.
      Norton, 1965, 255 pp.

      This novel depicts the superficial relationship be-
      tween human beings in the modern urban environment.
      The characters come from different backgrounds.

658. Jhabvala, R. Prawer. *The Householders: A Screen Play*.
      Delhi: Ramlochan Books, 1965, 168 pp.

      This screenplay is based on her novel of the same
      title (London: John Murray, 1960), and depicts life
      among newly married couples in a North Indian city.
      The film produced by Ivory Merchant productions
      earned acclaim for Jhabvala. Some still photographs
      from the film are reproduced.

659. Jhabvala, R. Prawer. *A Stronger Climate: Nine Stories*.
      London: John Murray, 1968, 214 pp.

      This collection of short stories mostly depicts the
      lives of foreigners in India, their culture shock, and
      their adjustments.

660. Jhabvala, R. Prawer. *Travelers*. New York: Harper and
      Row, 1973, 247 pp.

This novel depicts Western tourists who come to India
in search of their identities. Western materialism has
created only dissatisfaction, so Westerners visit India
in search of the meaning of life.

661. Jhabvala, R. Prawer. *Heat and Dust*. New York: Harper
and Row, 1976, 181 pp.

This novel presents the peculiar life styles of the
British in India. The author finds some similarities
between the Maharajahs and the common people of modern
India.

662. Jhabvala, R. Prawer. *How I Became a Holy Mother and
Other Short Stories*. New York: Harper and Row,
1976, 218 pp.

This collection of short stories portrays the Westernized, wealthy Indians. The title story deals with
the seduction of a Swami by a woman who becomes a holy
mother. The approach is highly satirical.

663. Khan, Izzat Yar. *Sarojini Naidu: The Poet*. New Delhi:
S. Chand and Company Ltd., 1983, vii + 276 pp.

This publication evaluates Sarojini Naidu as an Indo-
Anglican poet. The first four chapters recount her
social, political, and literary background and her
craft as a poetic artist; the remaining five are devoted to a special study of her poetical works *The
Golden Threshold* and *The Feather of the Dawn*. The
poems of Sarojini that were not published in any of
her four anthologies are dealt with in an appendix.
Many references are cited in the footnotes. A bibliography of books, journal articles, and radio talks on
the poet and an index are included.

664. Kohli, Devindra. *Virgin Whiteness: The Poetry of Kamala
Das*. Calcutta: Writers Workshop, 1968, 28 pp.

The author discusses the poems of Kamala Das. Is it
her rebelliousness, her impulsiveness, or her suscepti-
ble sexual nature that prompts the poet to deviate from
the established and accepted norms of society? The
author analyzes some of her poems.

665. Kohli, Devindra. *Kamala Das*. New Delhi: Arnold Heinemann, 1975, 128 pp.

Kamala Das has attracted critical attention because
of her subjective approach and the openness with which

she writes about sex. A bibliography of her writings
and of literary criticism of her works is offered.

666. Krishnaswamy, Shantha. *Glimpses of Women in India.*
     New Delhi: Ashish Publishing House, 1983, viii +
     375 pp.

     Originally written as a doctoral dissertation, this
     study places in a critical perspective the woman in
     modern Indian fiction in English between 1950 and 1980
     as reflected in the novels of six major writers. Three
     of the authors are women--Kamala Markandaya, Anita
     Desai, and Ruth Prawer Jhabvala. "The Indian woman--
     passive or aggressive, traditional or modern--serves
     to reflect the writers' sense of isolation, fear, be-
     wilderment, and emotional vulnerability," comments the
     author in the abstract. All three novelists discuss
     various problems in their novels (identity, sexual ex-
     ploitation, and the identity problem of foreign women
     married to Indian men and living in India). This is a
     very scholarly yet readable work.

667. Macauliffe, M. "Legend of Meerabai, the Rajput Poetess."
     Indian Antiquary, Vol. 32 (Aug. 1903), pp. 329-336.

     This is a biography of Meera, the great poetess who
     wrote devotional songs. She was a rebel, ascetic, and
     an ardent devotee of Lord Krishna. She defied her
     husband and in-laws and worshipped Krishna instead of
     the family deity Shiva. Some selected poems are in-
     cluded.

668. Machwe, Prabhakar. "Prominent Women Writers in Indian
     Literature after Independence." Pp. 145-149 in
     *Feminine Sensibility and Characterisation in South
     Asian Literature*, guest ed. Fritz Blackwell. *Journal
     of South Asian Literature*, Vol. 12, No. 3/4 (1977).

     The writer has listed quite a few women writers,
     poets, novelists, and short story writers of independent
     India. Women are being creative and working on the
     committees of literary societies in major languages.
     Women writers who have won the highest literary awards
     from Sahitya Akademi are listed in this article.

669. Macnicol, Margaret (ed.). *Poems by Indian Women:
     Selected and Rendered by Various Translators.* Cal-
     cutta: Association Press, 1923, 98 pp. (Heritage of
     India) (also published, London: Oxford University
     Press, 1923).

14 languages and 56 poetesses are represented in this anthology. The periods covered are Vedic, early Buddhist, medieval, and modern. A comprehensive introduction, chronology of the poetesses, and a list of translators by language are also given. A judicious choice has been made in this representative volume.

670. Malhotra, M.L. "A Writer of Promise: Anita Desai." Pp. 205-211 in his *Bridges of Literature: 23 Critical Essays in Literature*. Ajmar: Sunanda Publications, 1971.

The writer of this brief article maintains that Anita Desai depicts only inner turmoil, confusion of mind, and individualistic themes rather than broad issues of a sociopolitical nature. Her style, according to the writer, is introspective.

671. Markandaya, Kamala. *Nectar in a Sieve*. New York: John Day, 1954, 255 pp.

This very famous novel depicts the influence of modern technology on the economy and family life. The migration to urban centers for the sake of employment and its impact on general life patterns are not always positive factors. The story is narrated by a woman in order to bring out the pathetic qualities. Incidentally, this was the first of Markandaya's novels to be published, and it was well received.

672. Markandaya, Kamala. *Some Inner Fury*. London: Putnam, 1955, 286 pp.

Taking the 1942 Quit India Movement as a backdrop, the author describes a woman's tragic life. Written with rare sensitivity, the novel depicts the sometimes improbable life of a middle-class Indian.

673. Markandaya, Kamala. *A Silence of Desire*. New York: John Day, 1960, 253 pp.

This novel deals with a middle-class family's struggle with illness. The emotional involvement and strange concepts of spirituality create many dilemmas.

674. Markandaya, Kamala. *Possession*. New York: John Day, 1963, 249 pp.

The possessive instinct is very strong in the Western world; Eastern thought does not put much emphasis on possession. Thus, the theme of materialism vs. spiritualism attracts many Indo-Anglican writers. This novel is a story of faith vs. rationalism.

675. Markandaya, Kamala. *A Handful of Rice*. New York:
      John Day, 1966, 297 pp. (also published, London:
      H. Hamilton, 1966).

      Urban living conditions and patterns of life, and
      marriage as an institution, are the subjects of this
      novel. A very serious message is presented in this
      well-documented novel with boldness and vitality.

676. Markandaya, Kamala. *The Coffer Dams*. New York: John
      Day, 1969, 256 pp.

      The building of a dam in South India and its adverse
      impact on tribal life are depicted in this novel. The
      author does not like loss of simplicity.

677. Markandaya, Kamala. *The Nowhere Man*. New York: John
      Day, 1972, 312 pp.

      This novel concerns an Indian immigrant to England
      in the twenties, who suffers culture shock initially
      and then gradually accepts Western values to the extent
      of losing his identity. This loss and his subsequent
      feeling of guilt are the problems discussed in this
      novel.

678. Markandaya, Kamala. *Two Virgins*. New York: John Day,
      1973, 250 pp.

      This tragic novel depicts the loss of traditional
      values in a glamourous urban life style. It is the
      story of two sisters who are temperamentally poles
      apart. The elder becomes a victim of urban lures, goes
      astray, and brings suffering to the whole family.

679. Markandaya, Kamala. *Golden Honeycomb*. London: Chatto
      and Windus, 1977, 468 pp. (also available New York:
      Thomas Crowell, 1977, and Bombay: B.I. Publication,
      1977).

      This fascinating novel narrates the story of a high-
      born young man of a princely state who falls in love
      with two women from two different worlds.

680. Mathur, Ramesh. "Women in Hindu Society: Status and
      Image." Parts one through four. *Journal of Inter-
      cultural Studies*, pts. 1-4 (1974-1977), pp. 21-42,
      42-50, 56-66, 55-64.

      The third part discusses images of women in litera-
      ture, and the fourth part indicates some ideals of femi-
      nine beauty and physical charm in literature and art.
      Examples are quoted from the ancient scriptures.

681. Mehta, Hansa. "Literary Achievements of Indian Women."
     Pp. 78-102 in Evelyn C. Gedge and Mithan Choksi (eds.).
     *Women in Modern India: Fifteen Papers by Indian Women
     Writers*. Bombay: D.B. Taraporevala Sons, 1929 (re-
     printed, Westport, Conn.: Hyperion Press, 1976).

     Well-known poetesses of the Vedic age to the present,
     the works of Sarojini Naidu, some well-known Hindi
     writers, and Indian women who are influenced by Western
     civilization and write in English are all covered with
     excerpts from their writings in the original along with
     English translations.

682. Mukherjee, Bharati. *The Tiger's Daughter*. Boston:
     Houghton Mifflin Company, 1972, 210 pp.

     A Bengali woman's desperate efforts to cope with frus-
     tration and alienation are dealt with in this novel.

683. Mukherjee, Bharati. *Wife*. Boston: Houghton Mifflin
     Company, 1975, 213 pp.

     A middle-class Bengali woman and her conflicts are
     presented in this novel. The romanticized ideas about
     marriage conflict with the realities of life; unrealized
     aspirations create dissatisfaction in the heroine.

684. Mukherjee, Meenakshi. "The Theme of Displacement in
     Anita Desai and Kamala Markandaya." *World Literature
     Written in English*, Vol. 17, No. 1 (1978), pp. 225-
     233.

     The writer examines the recurrence of the theme of
     displacement in these two novelists' writings. Main
     characters are usually depicted as living outside of
     India--why? Mukherjee poses the question without
     trying to answer it.

685. Naidu, Sarojini. *The Bird of Time: Songs of Life,
     Death and the Spring*. London: William Heinemann,
     1914, 102 pp. (also published New York: John Lane
     Company, 1928.).

     Naidu's personality and poems are discussed. Her
     earlier poems had a girlish ecstasy while the later
     poetry has serious themes as is expressed in Edmund
     Gosse's introduction to this book. Songs of love,
     songs of springtime, and songs of life are included.
     The poetess's love of nature and life becomes apparent
     in this collection, which contains her portrait.

686. Naidu, Sarojini. *The Golden Threshold*. New York:
      John Lane Company, 1916, 98 pp. (also published Lon-
      don: William Heinemann, 1916).

      The introduction is by Arthur Symons. This is sup-
      posedly Naidu's first anthology.

687. Naidu, Sarojini. *The Broken Wing: Songs of Love,
      Death and Destiny 1915-1916*. London: William Heine-
      mann, 1917, 107 pp. (also published New York: John
      Lane Company, 1917).

      As the title suggests, songs on love, death, and
      destiny are collected in this anthology.

688. Naidu, Sarojini. *The Sceptred Flute: Songs of India*.
      New York: Dodd Mead and Company, 1917, 231 pp. (also
      published Allahabad: Kitabistan, 1958).

      Poems published earlier in *The Broken Wing*, *The Bird
      of Time*, and *The Golden Threshold* are included in this
      book of verse. The introduction is written by Joseph
      Auslander, who maintains that the poetess sings from
      her heart. Folk songs, an ode to the late Nizam of
      Hyderabad, the flowering year, a peacock, love, nature,
      and historical themes are some of her subjects.

689. Nandakumar, Prema. "Bharati Sarabhai's English Plays."
      Pp. 249-269 in M.K. Naik, S.K. Desai, and G.S. Amur
      (eds.). *Critical Essays on Indian Writing in English*.
      Dharwar: Karnatak University, 1968.

      The writer gives in these 20 pages a critical evalua-
      tion of Bharati Sarabhai's two plays, considering her
      themes and the techniques she adopted. The author pro-
      vides some excerpts from her dramas and gives summaries
      by way of illustrating the points.

690. Narvane, Vishwanath S. *Sarojini Naidu: An Introduc-
      tion to Her Life, Work and Poetry*. New Delhi: Orient
      Longmans, 1980, 160 pp.

      This publication is a modest tribute to the poetess
      for her outstanding contribution to the social and
      political life of the country. Her close association
      with political leaders, her interest in the women of
      India, and her talents and creativity are assessed in
      this book. This is a commemorative volume published
      on the centenary of her birth.

691. Nilsson, Usha S. *Mira Bai*. New Delhi: Sahitya Akademi,
      1969, 70 pp.

      Sahitya Akademi is a governmental body that promotes
      literature. This particular publication is a part of
      the series "Makers of Indian Literature," and it dis-
      cusses Mira's life, her dedication to God, and the
      essence of her poems. Also included is an English
      translation of 50 selected poems.

692. Paradkar, M.D. "Contributions of Women to Ancient and
      Medieval Sanskrit Literature." *Bharatiya Vidya*,
      Vol. 26, No. 1-4 (1966), pp. 29-33.

      Names of many female writers from Vedas to classical
      Sanskrit literature are given; their works are also
      mentioned.

692a. Pritam, Amrita. *Black Rose*. Translated from Punjabi
      by Charles Brasch. New Delhi: Nagmani, 1967, 31 pp.

      This collection of poems by Amrita Pritam, who is
      considered to be a rebel poet, reflects her rebellion
      against established values.

692b. Pritam, Amrita. *Two Faces of Eve*. Translated from
      Punjabi by G.S.P. Suri and Prabhakar Machwe. Delhi:
      Hind Pocket Books, 1971, 160 pp.

      This novel deals with marital relations and the con-
      flict created by extramarital affairs. A short story
      ("Aerial") dealing with the same subject is also in-
      cluded.

692c. Pritam, Amrita. *Existence and Other Poems*. Translated
      from Punjabi by Mahendra Kulasrestna. New Delhi:
      Nagmani, 1968, 33 pp.

      This collection of introspective poems deals with
      some political aspects.

692d. Pritam, Amrita. *That Man*. Translated from Punjabi by
      Krishna Gorowara. New Delhi: Sterling Publishers,
      1974, 104 pp.

      This novel touches upon the superstition and conflict
      of a mother who places her son at the service of Lord
      Shiva because Shiva had granted her the son and there-
      fore owned him. The son's own existence and the mother's
      feelings are depicted in a most touching manner.

692e. Pritam, Amrita. *A Line in Water*. Translated from Pun-
      jabi by Krishna Gorowara. New Delhi: Arnold Heinemann
      Publishers, 1975, 141 pp.

      This novel deals with an artist's desire to marry his
      student.

693. Rajgopalachari, C. *Avvaiar: A Great Tamil Poetess*.
      Bombay: Bharatiya Vidya Bhavan, 1971, 32 pp.

      55 poems with English translations are compiled in
      this booklet. Avvaiar is considered as an "Avatara" or
      incarnation of the goddess of learning (Saraswati) and
      almost worshipped. The appendix includes poetry in the
      original Tamil.

694. Rajyalakshmi, P.V. *The Lyric Spring: A Study of the
      Poetry of Sarojini Naidu*. New Delhi: Abhinav Publica-
      tions, 1977, 221 pp.

      This is a very important publication on Sarojini Naidu,
      dealing with the recurring themes and emotions in her
      poems. She was a lover of nature and had a special eye
      for nature. This publication contains a primary and
      secondary bibliography.

695. Rao, C. Vimala. "Women and Fiction." *Literary Cri-
      terion*, Vol. 7, No. 3 (1966), pp. 42-51.

      Fiction writing is popular with women writers. Women
      observe the society around them keenly and make poignant
      observations on it. Examples from Indian writings are
      given.

696. Rao, Krishna A.V. *Nayantara Sahgal: A Study of Her
      Fiction and Non-Fiction, 1954-1974*. Madras: M. Sesha-
      chalam, 1976, 98 pp.

      The author examines Nayantara's four novels and eval-
      uates the political themes, styles, etc. Also examined
      here are her nonfiction works during a 20-year span.
      She has become popular among the Indian authors writing
      in English.

697. Rao, Narayan, and Surya Kolar. "The New Harvest: The
      Indian Novel in English in the Post-Independence Era;
      Women at Work: Kamala Markandaya." Ph.D. Disserta-
      tion, Pennsylvania State University, 1968, 356 pp.
      (University Microfilms 69-14,559) (not examined by the
      compiler).

698. Rao, Ramachandra B. *The Novels of Mrs. Anita Desai: A Study.* New Delhi: Kalyani Publishers, 1977, 65 pp.

In this critical study on the Indo-Anglican novelist Anita Desai, Rao examines her novels, their themes, characterization, literary quality, and her rank among novelists who write in English. Anita Desai's favorite themes are loneliness and inner conflict.

699. Rau, Santha Rama. *Home to India.* New York: Harper, 1945, 236 pp.

The author visited India and her grandmother after spending her childhood years in England and wrote this book about her impressions and experiences.

700. Rau, Santha Rama. *Remember the House.* New York: Harper and Row, 1956, 241 pp.

This novel depicts the problem of identity for traditional Indians in Malbar and Westernized Indians in Bombay city. The East-West conflict of values has been beautifully brought out.

701. Rau, Santha Rama. *Gifts of Passage.* New York: Harper and Row, 1961, 223 pp.

This is a collection of the author's travelogues written over a period of time. They are in chronological order and are prefaced with some introductory remarks.

702. Ray, Lila. "Women Writers." Pp. 177-192 in Tara Ali Baig (ed.). *Women of India.* Delhi: Publications Division, Ministry of Information and Broadcasting, Government of India, 1958.

This chapter is devoted to women writers in ancient, medieval, and modern times. Women novelists, short story writers, poetesses in Hindi (the national language), English, and many regional languages are also included. Illustrations from their writings and photographs are given.

703. Rout, Savitri. *Women Pioneers in Oriya Literature.* Cuttack: Manorama Rout, 1971, 136 pp.

Famous women writers' brief sketches and their noteworthy works are reviewed. Some excerpts from folk literature are a welcome addition.

704. Sahgal, Nayantara. *A Time to Be Happy.* New York: Alfred

A. Knopf, 1958, 277 pp. (also published London: Victor
Gollancz, 1958; reprinted: Bombay: Jaico Publishing
House, 1963, in paperback and New Delhi: Sterling Pub-
lishers, 1975).

Nayantara's first novel, describing the urban life of
upper-middle-class families during the days of struggle
for Independence and the types of adjustment demanded
by the politically insecure situation.

705. Sahgal, Nayantara. *From Fear Set Free*. New York: W.W.
      Norton, 1970, 240 pp. (also published London: Victor
      Gollancz, 1970; Indian reprint is available from Hind
      Pocket Books).

      Writing in a reminiscent style, the author gives many
      anecdotes from her life in India and abroad, and also
      comments on contemporary life.

706. Sahgal, Nayantara (ed.). *Sunlight Surround You*. New
      Delhi: Orient Longmans, 1970, viii + 174 pp.; illus-
      trated.

      This is a collection and compilation of tributes paid
      to Smt. Vijaya Laxmi Pandit (the editor's mother) by
      her friends and wellwishers on the occasion of her 70th
      birthday.

707. Sahgal, Nayantara. *Freedom Movement in India*. New
      Delhi: National Council for Educational Research and
      Training, 1970, 125 pp.; illustrated.

      Primarily written for teenagers, this historical work
      traces the main events. Its profuse illustrations and
      simple and lucid style will appeal to boys and girls
      from 15-19, who will also find it very informative.

708. Sahgal, Nayantara. *Storm in Chandigarh*. New York:
      Norton, 1969, 251 pp.

      This novel depicts the trials and tribulations of
      married life for upper-class families of Chandigarh
      during the turbulent political situation after the par-
      tition of the country.

709. Sahgal, Nayantara. *This Time of Morning*. New York:
      W.W. Norton, 1970 (also published London: Victor)
      Gollancz, 1970; reprinted: Delhi: Hind Pocket Books,
      1970, 224 pp.).

      This novel depicts the life style of people in the
      foreign services and the disparity in their private

and public lives. The novel discusses politics and
bureaucracy rather than social life; the plot moves
very slowly.

710. Sahgal, Nayantara. *The Day in Shadow*. Delhi: Vikas
Publications, 1971, 236 pp. (also published New York:
W.W. Norton, 1972, and by London Magazine Editors,
1975).

This is an autobiographical novel that deals with the
problem of divorce in traditional Indian society, where
a woman has to suffer from prolonged litigation and
economic difficulties. Divorce is still looked down
upon, and often the husband creates many hardships.
First and foremost, woman is a person, the author
asserts. The declining standards of political behavior
after the country's independence are lamented.

711. Sahgal, Nayantara. *A Situation in New Delhi*. London:
Magazine Editions, 1977, 165 pp. (Indian reprint:
New Delhi: Himalaya Books).

The political uncertainty and problems in the field
of education are the main themes of this novel. The
hero can be identified with the late Prime Minister of
India, Pandit Jawaharlal Nehru (the author's maternal
uncle), who was a charismatic leader and a man of words
rather than action.

712. Sarabhai, Bharati. *The Well of the People*. Calcutta:
Visvabharati, 1943, 54 pp.

This is a play written to propagate Gandhian thought,
depicting the true story of a poor woman who saved
whatever she could in order to contribute toward a
community well. The play is well conceived and written.

713. Sarabhai, Bharati. *Two Women*. Bombay: Hind Kitabs,
1952, 121 pp.

The sociopolitical situation as it existed prior to
Independence is dealt with in this play, which also
depicts the conflict between tradition and modernity
and the confusion it creates.

714. Saradhi, K.P. "Three Indo-Anglian Women Poets: Gauri
Deshpande, Roshan Alkasi and Kamala Das." *Journal
of Indian Writing in English*, Vol. 2, No. 1 (1974),
pp. 29-35.

Three poetesses and their poetry, and their reactions

to life and living conditions, are described in this article. The range of their expressive abilities and their distinct sensitivities are also described.

715. Sengupta, Padmini. *Toru Dutt*. New Delhi: Sahitya Akademi, 1968, 94 pp.

Published as part of the series "Makers of Indian Literature," this biography describes the formative period of Toru's childhood and the process of becoming an author. Her lonely childhood, exposure to international culture, her friendship with Clarisse Bader, and her untimely death are described. Her literary talents are evaluated critically.

716. Sengupta, Padmini. *Sarojini Naidu: A Biography*. Bombay: Asia Publishing House, 1966, viii + 359 pp.

The first part deals with the childhood and adolescence of the poetess. How her imagination worked before her participation in the freedom struggle is also explained in this book. In addition to photographs and a few poems in her own handwriting, this biography contains a good bibliography and is indexed.

717. Sengupta, Sankar (ed.). *Women in Indian Folk Lore: A Short Survey of Their Social Status and Position: Linguistic and Religious Study*. Calcutta: Indian Publications, 1969, 327 pp.

Folklore traditions and the portrayal of women in various linguistic and religious groups are described in 26 brief essays. All major languages and folklore traditions depicting the status of women are covered, e.g., women in Jainism, Sikhism, Buddhism, Hinduism, Islam, and women in Telegu, Tamil, Malayalam, Kannada, Gujarati, Marathi, Oriya, Assamese, Rajasthani folklore and folk songs. This is a very representative publication.

718. Shahane, Vasant A. *Ruth Prawer Jhabvala*. New Delhi: Arnold Heinemann Publishers, 1976, 198 pp.

This book evaluates Mrs. Jhabvala's fiction, her experiences in India, and her method of reflecting these experiences through her creative efforts. She is contributing to an understanding of the Indian way of life or value.

719. Sharma, D.K. "The Creative Art of Nargis Dalal."

Journal of Indian Writing in English, Vol. 5, No. 1
(Jan. 1977), pp. 17-23.

This is a critical appreciation of the author. Her
locale is often a hill station; her characters are
not very convincing. Her publication has been
limited to date.

720. Shirwadkar, Meena. *Image of Woman in the Indo-Anglian
Novel*. Bombay: Sterling Publications, 1979, xii +
169 pp.

The author finds the image of woman in Indo-Anglian
novels to be complex and multifaceted. Anglo-Indian
writers could not do justice to the theme as they
were either missionaries or the wives of British officials in India. They had many limitations, of which
not knowing the language was only one. Indian women
were hidden behind the walls. Reviewing the image of
Indian women in some Anglo-Indian fiction, the author
highlights the fact that insiders are able to depict
the social changes without any bias. A bibliography,
notes, and index are appended.

721. Srinivasa, Iyengar K.R. "The Women Novelists." Pp.
435-477 in *Indian Writings in English*. 2nd revised
ed. New York: Asia Publishing House, 1973.

There are quite a few women writers who do their
creative writing in English. Their themes, styles,
and formats are described in a sympathetic manner.

722. Srivastava, Narsingh. "Some Indian Women Writers in
English." *Indian Literature*, Vol. 18, No. 4 (1975),
pp. 63-72.

Pre-independence and post-independence poetesses are
compared in this article. Toru Dutt was a fiery poetess
of pre-independent India. The themes of her poems were
quite different from those of present-day poetesses.
The author has tried to explain these characteristics
while evaluating the poems.

723. Talim, Meena. *Women in Early Buddhist Literature*.
Bombay: University of Bombay, 1972, 242 pp.

Life in Buddhist monasteries is depicted; women were
brought up to lead a simple life. Some comparisons to
women in Brahmanical epics and Jain literature and
travelogues are made.

724. Turnbull, H.G. Dalway (ed.). *Sarojini Naidu: Select
      Poems*. Bombay: Oxford University Press, 1930, 241 pp.

      The representative poems of Sarojini Naidu are edited
      in this collection by a noted professor. In order to
      attract Indian students to these poems, the editor
      offers extensive notes and interpretations of each
      poem as well as an index to notes. The poems
      selected are no doubt her best ones.

725. Verma, Mahadevi. *A Pilgrimage to the Himalayas and
      Other Silhouettes from Memory*. Translated from Hindi
      by Radhika Prasad Srivastava and Lillian Srivastava.
      London: Peter Owen, 1975, 127 pp. (UNESCO Collection
      of Representative Works, Indian Series).

      Mahadevi Verma is a prominent and prolific writer in
      the Hindi language. Belonging to the mystic school of
      Hindi poetry, her poems are reflective, her essays are
      written in a poetic style, memoirs and plays are
      written with intense feeling. Her sketches depict the
      India of 1930-1940. The translator's comments are also
      given. This is a truly representative work.

IX

PSYCHOLOGICAL STUDIES

Empirical studies pertaining to sex differences, adjustment, personality, and the studies assessing attitudes
toward values, social change, modernity, job preferences
and job satisfaction are included in this section. Research
articles written by Indian psychologists on sex differences
in intelligence, learning capacity, aptitude, level of aspirations, fear of failure or success, person perception,
cognition, bilateral transfer, self-concept and creativity
are also annotated in this section. At the beginning of the
chapter, some books which throw light on the development of
psychology and research in psychology are listed for the
benefit of scholars in the field of cross-cultural psychology.
In the general introductory subsection, some entries are
annotated for an understanding of the Indian psyche, personality formation, family interactions and attitude formation.

General Studies

726. Bokil, Kamla. "Mothers' Perception of Parent-Child Re-
     lationships of Adolescent Girls in Urban Indian
     Families." Ph.D. dissertation in Education. Uni-
     versity of Florida, 1966, 161 pp. (University Micro-
     films 67-12,913).

727. Carstairs, G. Morris. *The Twice Born: A Study of a
     Community of High Caste Hindus.* London: Hogarth
     Press, 1961, 343 pp.

     This is an anthropological and fieldwork study of
     personality formation in Hindus. Not directly related
     to women but contributes to an understanding of the
     Indian psyche.

728. Cottrell, A.W. Baker. "Interpersonal Dimensions of
     Cross Cultural Relations: Indian-Western Marriages

in India." Ph.D. dissertation in social psychology.
Michigan State University, 1970.

729. Number omitted.

730. Kale, Pratima. "The Career of Secondary School Teachers in Poona, India." Ph.D. dissertation in education. University of Wisconsin, 1970.

731. Kapur, Veena. "Social Character of Women in the
Changing Indian Society." Ph.D. dissertation in
psychology. Catholic University of America, 1973,
235 pp. (University Microfilms 73-21,633).

732. Murphy, Lois Barclay. "Roots of Tolerance and Tensions in Indian Child Development." In Garden Murphy's
*In the Minds of Men: The Study of Human Behaviour and
Social Tensions in India*. New York: Basic Books,
1953, pp. 46-58.

While not directly related to the rearing of daughters
in India, this sociopsychological article has some interesting points. While in Ahmedabad doing some survey
work at B.M. Institute of Child Development, Murphy
studied child-rearing practices. She found the acceptance of children in the Indian family pattern striking.
The article is useful as it views the patterns of child
rearing in India through Western eyes.

733. Rao, Velagapudi Nandini Prakasa. "Role Conflict of Employed Mothers in Hyderabad, India." Ph.D. dissertation in sociology. Mississippi State University,
1971, 124 pp. (University Microfilms 71-27,025).

734. Spratt, P. *Hindu Culture and Personality: A Psychoanalytic Study*. Bombay: Manaktalos, 1966, 400 pp.

Hindu culture and personality formation are discussed.
Such topics as mother fixation and the cults of goddesses, women as inferior beings and men as superior
beings, the Oedipus complex, and the identification of
sons with mothers, etc., are discussed at length. The
book represents a male point of view; women are depicted as having masochistic personalities. Indexed.

735. Straus, Murray A. "Husband-Wife Interaction in Nuclear
and Joint Households." Pp. 134-150 in Dhirendra
Narain (ed.). *Explorations in the Family and Other
Essays: Professor K.M. Kapadia Commemoration Volume*.
Bombay: Thacker and Company, 1975.

A study of the decision-making powers in the Indian
family. The ultimate authority is the husband.

736. Vaeshney, S. "Survey Attitudes of Selected Women
     Towards Education Beyond High School." Ph.D. disser-
     tation, Utah University, 1965.

Studies in Sex Differences

737. Ahuja, G.C. "Sex and Intelligence." *Journal of Educa-
     tion and Psychology*, Vol. 30, No. 4 (1973), pp. 228-
     229.

     12,375 boys and 8,130 girls from Bombay were given
     group intelligence tests. The differences in in-
     telligence scores of boys and girls were relatively
     small and insignificant; the slight superiority shown
     by either sex in some categories can be attributed to
     the environmental effects.

738. Anantharaman, R.N. "The Effects of Sex, Social Class
     and Rural-Urban Locality on Values." *Journal of
     Psychological Researches*, Vol. 24, No. 2 (1980), pp.
     112-114.

     200 graduate students (100 males and 100 females) of
     Madras University were given Allport and Vernon Lindsey's
     study of value test and socioeconomic scale by Kuppuswamy.
     Male students were found to have more practical values
     while women students were more aesthetic. Upper-class
     students were more religious and upper-class urban
     students had more aesthetic values than theoretical.

739. Deo, Pratibha, and Bangia V. "Sex-Differences in Self-
     Acceptance of Punjab University Students." *Psycho-
     logical Studies*, Vol. 13, No. 1 (1968), pp. 64-69.

     This study attempts to discover sex differences in
     self-acceptance. Perceived selves of girls exhibit
     emotional traits which they would not like to find in
     their ideal selves. Findings indicate that girls tend
     to have higher discrepancies in social character, in-
     telligence, and aesthetic traits. Girls' ideals are
     higher than boys'.

740. Desai, K.G. "A Study of Sex Difference in Achievement
     in School Subjects." *Journal of Gujarat Research
     Society*, Vol. 22 (1960), pp. 42-45.

     The examination results of V to XI grades from twelve
     coeducational schools (in all, 2,264 boys and 881 girls)
     of Ahmedabad city and other semiurban areas were studied.

Girls surpassed boys in most of the subjects, including
languages. Girls may have better study habits and
take their work more seriously than boys.

741. Devi, Girishbala. "A Study of Anxiety in Men and Women
      College Students." *Psychological Studies*, Vol. 14,
      No. 1 (1969), pp. 35-38.

      186 girls and 186 boys from undergraduate and gradu-
      ate colleges of Orissa ranging from 15 to 21 years of
      age were administered Sinha's Anxiety Scale (Indian
      adaptation of Taylor's Manifest Anxiety Scale). Girls
      scored higher than boys; the difference was significant.

742. Devi, Girishbala. "A Study of Sex Differences in Re-
      action to Frustrating Situations." *Psychological
      Studies*, Vol. 12, No. 1 (1967), pp. 17-24.

      220 male and female students (110 each) from 16 to 24
      years of age belonging to middle-class socioeconomic
      strata were exposed to ten different frustrating situ-
      ations. Female students appeared to regress and resort
      to withdrawal behavior, while male students were found
      to be more aggressive. However, on other types of
      reactions (suppressed aggression, anxiety, adjustment,
      self-aggression and rationalization), the difference
      between boys and girls was not significant.

743. Dhaliwal, G.S., and G. Kaur. "Problems of Adolescents."
      Progress of Education, Vol. 55, No. 3 (1980), pp.
      62-66.

      Sixth and eighth grade boys (150) and girls (150) from
      two government secondary schools of Delhi formed the
      sample. They were asked to write on whatever problems
      that they have relating to their body, home, school,
      or anything in the world. 150 boys wrote 781 problems,
      150 girls wrote 736 (an average of 5 for both sexes).
      Both boys and girls were more worried about their
      health and physical development, social and psycho-
      logical relations, and adjustment to school work.
      They were not worried about curricula, teaching methods,
      or their future education or vocation.

744. Dixit, C.R., and M.B. Mathur. "Loving and Punishing
      Parental Behaviour and Masculine-Feminine Development
      in School Girls." *Journal of Psychological Researches*,
      Vol. 17, No. 2 (1973), pp. 47-49.

      100 girls from Jodhpur (Rajasthan) were tested on the

parent-child relationship scale (Mollie Smart) and the
masculine-feminine group. Girls from a loving-father
group scored higher on the masculinity scale, and girls
from a punishing-father group scored lower. Results
indicated that the masculine development of girls was
related to the father's love.

745. Dixit, Ramesh C. "Sex Role Consciousness Among Vil-
      lage Children of Upper and Lower Caste Groups."
      Journal of Indian Academy of Applied Psychology,
      Vol. 5, No. 1 (1968), pp. 32-36.

      The author studied three- to five-year-old children
      of upper- and lower-caste groups and concluded that
      sex-role consciousness was common among upper-caste
      children. Accordingly upper-caste girls were more
      feminine than lower-caste girls.

746. Dixit, Ramesh C., and P.L. Vishnoi. "Mother-Daughter
      Relationship as a Factor in Masculine-Feminine De-
      velopment." *Indian Journal of Applied Psychology*,
      Vol. 12, No. 1 (1975), pp. 17-18.

      275 junior college girl students of 13-17 years of
      Jodhpur (Rajasthan) city were administered a Hindi
      adaptation of the Masculinity-Femininity Scale taken
      from MMPI. The girls tended to score higher on "loving"
      than "punishing." The loving behavior of the mother
      was related to the feminine development in girls, and
      punishing behavior of the mother was related to their
      masculine development.

747. Number omitted.

748. Kapoor, S.D. "The Personality Differences Between
      the Sexes." *Psychological Studies*, Vol. 9, No. 2
      (1964), pp. 124-129.

      100 male and 100 female collegians of Varanasi were
      given the 16 personality factors questionnaire (Form B).
      Male students scored higher on dominance and sophisti-
      cation, while female students scored higher on inner
      relaxation and acceptance. Boys had slightly greater
      general intelligence, enthusiasm, and higher superego
      strength. Girls showed timidity and insecurity. The
      average male was more sociable, easygoing, dominant,
      aggressive, and shrewd; personality profiles of the
      sexes differed greatly.

749. Mohanty, G. "Sex Differences in Shifts and Rigidity
      in Level of Aspiration Experiments." *Journal of
      Psychological Researches*, Vol. 22, No. 1 (1978), pp.
      18-20.

      144 male and 144 female students of second-year B.A.
      and B.Sc. classes from higher, middle, and lower
      socioeconomic strata and high, middle, and low achievers
      (48 each) were selected and given Kuppuswamy's S.E.S.
      Scale, Class, and Performance Chart and Rotter's level
      of aspiration board and symbol digit substitution test.
      Female subjects indicated flexibility in their level
      of aspiration by increasing their levels with success
      and lowering their levels with failure in comparison
      with their male counterparts.

750. Number omitted.

751. Natraj, P. "A Study on Sex Differences in Neuroticism
      Among College Students." *Journal of Psychological
      Researches*, Vol. 10, No. 1, pp. 43-48.

      400 college students (260 girls of 17 years on an
      average and 140 boys of 18-24 years) were given the
      Maudsley Medical Questionnaire. Results show neither
      any association between sex and neuroticism nor any
      significant difference between the two sexes in
      neuroticism.

752. Ojha, H., and R.I.P Singh. "Sex Differences in
      Dependence Proneness and Prestige Suggestibility."
      Manas, Vol. 19, No. 1, 1972, pp. 12-15.

      100 male and 100 female undergraduate students of
      Bhagalpur University were tested on a Dependence
      Proneness Scale (5-point scale) which contained 20
      items describing initiating behaviors. The same
      subjects were utilized in a prestige suggestibility
      study. The females exhibited greater degrees of
      suggestibility and dependency. In this case, both
      are positively correlated.

753. Pandey, Uma Dutta, and Ranjit Prasad Singh. "The
      Effect of Sex and Culture on Achievement Motivation,
      Religious Beliefs and Religious Practices." *Journal
      of Psychological Researches*, Vol. 15, No. 2 (1970),
      pp. 49-52.

      84 aboriginal and non-aboriginal boys and girls (21
      each) of 10th and 11th grades from Lohargada (Bihar)
      were administered a religious belief scale, a religious

practices scale, and an achievement motivation scale
(adapted from Bending). There was significant correla-
tion between achievement motivation and academic achievement and also between religious beliefs and religious
practices. There were no significant sex differences.

754. Pathak, Ram Deo. "Sex Differences Among School Children
in the Areas of Adjustment." *Psychological Studies*,
Vol. 15, No. 2 (1970), pp. 120-122.

   200 boys and 200 girls (9th graders) from Jabalpur
   city were administered Saxena's Personality Adjustment
   test. Differences in health, social, and emotional
   adjustment between boys and girls were found, but in
   regard to home and school adjustment no difference was
   noticed. The inter-correlation between the five areas
   was found to be positive.

755. Sah, A.P. *Perceptual Suggestibility as a Function
of Age, Sex and Education.* Indian Journal of
Experimental Psychology, Vol. 7, No. 2, 1973,
pp. 56-60.

   90 boys and 90 girls from Meerut City from 8
   to 17 years old were tested on perceptual
   suggestibility. Results indicated that children
   were more suggestible than adolescents and girls
   were more suggestible than boys. Education helped
   reduce suggestibility among children.

756. Saiyadain, Mirza, and B.B. Siddiqui. "Sex Differences
in Colour Scales to Emotional Situations." *Indian
Journal of Applied Psychology*, Vol. 6, No. 2 (1969),
pp. 62-68.

   Six (red, green, yellow, orange, blue, and violet)
   silhouettes of human faces and eight statements regarding four emotional situations (strong positive,
   strong negative, mild positive, mild negative) were
   prepared. Pairs of silhouettes along with a statement
   written on the blackboard were presented to 100 undergraduate students of St. Xavier's College, Ahmedabad.
   Both sexes ranked red strong positive and green strong
   negative. Both sexes agreed on the ranking of mild
   positive and mild negative colors and extreme positive
   and negative emotions. In short, no sex differences
   were noticed.

757. Sehgal, K. "The Impact of Sex and Academic Discipline
on the Level of Knowledge of Current Affairs."
Progress of Education, Vol. 53, No. 12 (1979), pp.
223-227 and 233.

150 boys and 150 girls belonging to five different
disciplines--law, education, languages, sciences, and
social sciences--were randomly selected from Kurukshetra
University and administered a structured questionnaire.
Analysis of variance was done three ways--sex, achievement and academic discipline. Results indicated that
sex did affect the knowledge of current affairs but not
their own academic disciplines. No significant sex
differences were noticed.

758.   Singh, I.S. "The Role of Sex and Age of Perceiver in
       Person Perception." *Journal of Psychological Re-
       searches*, Vol. 24, No. 1 (1980), pp. 21-28.

       120 male and female graduate students were randomly
       selected from the faculty of Social Sciences at Benaras
       Hindu University for this study. Subjects were divided
       into 4 groups (age groups 17-18 and 21-23 years and
       male and female). A stimulus person aged 28 who was
       good-looking and well built was selected. A semantic
       differential scale was used to record the perceptual
       reactions. Conclusions are (1) sex is a critical
       factor and (2) so is age.

759.   Singh, Udai Pratap. "The Self Concept of Both Criminal
       Males and Females: A Comparative Study." *Psycho-
       logical Studies*, Vol. 15, No. 2 (1970), pp. 101-107.

       Subjective self-concept (what I think of myself),
       objective self-concept (what others think of me) and
       social conflict index (a discrepancy between the sub-
       jective and objective self-concept) of the male and
       female criminal were measured. Tests developed by the
       author were used on 100 male and 82 female prisoners
       in the Bhagalpur Central Jail. The socioeconomic con-
       ditions, place of residence, marital status, education,
       and age of the two groups were comparable. Female
       criminals had lower subjective and objective self-
       concepts as compared to males. It was also observed
       that criminals perceive themselves as rejected by
       society and therefore feel hostile toward society.

760.   Singh, Udai Pratap. "Comparative Study of Attitudes
       of Male and Female Criminals Toward Their Family,
       Parents and Authority." *Journal of the Indian Academy
       of Applied Psychology*, Vol. 9, No. 1 (1972), pp. 18-
       21.

       82 female prisoners and 100 male criminals from
       Bhagalpur Central Jail were matched on their economic
       conditions, residence, marital status, education and

age and administered a Likert-type 5-point scale con-
sisting of 40 items relating to family, parents, and
authority. They differed considerably in their attitudes toward family (female criminals were favorably
inclined toward their family). Female criminals also
favored their parents. Regarding attitudes toward
authority, male criminals displayed negative ones and
females positive.

761. Sinha, J.K. "Anxiety in Male and Female Adolescents."
      Manas, Vol. 22, No. 1 (1975), pp. 13-15.

      100 XI graders of 13-19 years (50 boys and 50 girls)
      took a comprehensive test of anxiety (Sinha and
      Krishnan, 1971). The groups did not differ significant-
      ly in terms of anxiety.

762. Srivastava, D.N., and J.N. Prasad. "Sex Difference and
      Bilateral Transfer in Eye-Hand Co-ordination Under
      Habitual Interference." *Psychological Researches*,
      Vol. 2, No. 1-2 (1967), pp. 5-8.

      59 male and 50 female subjects engaged in clerical
      work (age range 20-29 years) were tested on electrical
      mirror tracing apparatus. Females were found to be
      more dextrous with the right hand, while males were
      found superior in eye-hand coordination.

763. Srivastava, R.K., and K.D. Kapoor. "Personality Dif-
      ferences Between Male and Female Tharus." *Indian
      Journal of Personality and Human Development*, Vol. 1,
      No. 2 (1977), pp. 34-41.

      Tharus are tribal people residing in the northern
      part of India. 100 males and 130 females were tested
      with a Hindi adaptation of Cattell's 16 PF. Tharus
      males were found to be more humble, sober, conservative,
      and practical than females. On 4 personality factors
      (i.e., E.F.M. and L1) males were found to be different
      from females.

764. Srivastava, R.K., N.K. Saksena, and K.D. Kapoor. "Per-
      sonality Profiles of Rural Men and Women: A Compara-
      tive Study." *Journal of Personality and Human De-
      velopment*, Vol. 2, No. 1 and 2 (1979), pp. 31-39.

      100 men and 100 women of 20-25 years residing in the
      rural area of North India. The Hindi adaptation of
      Cattell's 16 PF was administered. Rural men were found
      to be significantly different on six factors: A,G,H,M,N,
      and Q1.

765. Vasudeva, Promilla. "Sex Differences Among Post-
      Graduate Students in Their Response Style." *Manas*,
      Vol. 19, No. 1 (1972), pp. 17-20.

      Sex differences in reactions and responses to a
      social attitude scale are the subject of this research.
      Sample consisted of 593 female and 523 male graduate
      students of Punjab University. The scale consisted of
      120 statements covering different social issues in the
      areas of education, marriage, technology, religion,
      women's status, and tradition. Since the social train-
      ing of the two sexes is different, the sex differences
      in the response styles are marked. Males made extreme
      responses more frequently while females were modest.

766. Verma, K., and J.N. Sinha. "Sex Differences and Edu-
      cational Level in the Influence of Prestige Suggestion
      on Secure and Insecure Persons." *Psychological
      Studies*, Vol. 14, No. 2 (1969), pp. 140-142.

      The purpose of this study was to find out the dif-
      ference between the influence of prestige suggestion
      on secure and that on insecure men and women. Maslow's
      inventory to identify secure and insecure persons was
      applied to 150 liberal arts students of Punjab Uni-
      versity. In the second and third phase, 3 lists--1.
      twelve slogans of national significance, 2. twelve
      names of the Indian leaders of repute, and 3. twelve
      slogans paired with the names of twelve leaders
      (givers of the slogans)--were used with an interval of
      10 days. The findings indicate that secure persons
      did not change their opinion and attitude under the
      influence of prestige suggestion, while insecure
      persons did. No sex differences were noticed.

            Studies in Childhood, Childrearing Practices

767. Gupta, Bimalenda. "Upbringing of an Indian Child." Pp.
      187-200 in Baidya Nath Varma, ed. *Contemporary India*.
      Bombay: Asia Publishing House, 1964, pp. 187-200.

      The data for this research are drawn from the research
      studies and the group discussion sessions at B.M. Insti-
      tute of Psychology and Child Development, Ahmedabad.
      Children in India are exposed to a varied environment
      since India is a country with diverse cultures. The
      prenatal-postnatal care, childhood experiences in joint
      families, and adolescent experiences in Hindu and
      Muslim families are discussed at length. A bibliog-

raphy at the end of this chapter is of great help.

768. Kakar, Sudhir. *Mother and Infants in The Inner World: A Psychoanalytic Study of Childhood and Society in India.* Delhi: Oxford University Press, 1978, pp. 52-112.

A psychoanalytic interpretation of the interaction and intimate relationship between mothers and infants in the Indian context is offered in this chapter. Also examined here are the intrapsychic forces and socio-cultural influences which form the personality. How a Hindu male is raised and how his identity is formed are discussed as are mother-daughter relationships.

769. Khalkdina, Margaret. "The Upbringing of a Girl." Pp. 87-97 in Devki Jain, ed. *Indian Women.* New Delhi: Publications Division, Ministry of Information and Broadcasting.

The birth of a daughter is still not a welcome event, and her upbringing has many constraints and fewer positive reinforcements. She goes through different roles--a disciplined daughter, a submissive daughter-in-law, and so on. She is taught to perform all the rituals and transmit them to her future progeny. Always caught between tradition and the changing values brought by industrialization, urbanization, and modernization, women face serious problems.

770. Minturn, Leigh, and William W. Lambert. *Mothers of Six Cultures: Antecedents of Child Rearing.* New York: John Wiley, 1964, 351 pp.

The Rajput mothers of Khalapur are studied in this field work study. Emotional coldness is a consistent personality trait of these mothers. They discourage emotional outbursts in their own children. These mothers do not spend much time with their children and allow grandmothers and elders to take care of them while the mothers cook and do some domestic chores. Obedience, peer group relationships, and aggressive behaviors are also examined.

771. Nandy, Ashis. "Woman vs. Womanliness in India: An Essay in Social and Political Psychology." *Psychoanalytic Review*, Vol. 63, No. 2 (1976), pp. 301-315 (reprinted in B.R. Nanda, ed. *Indian Women: From Purdah to Modernity.* New Delhi: Vikas Publishing House, 1976, pp. 146-160; also included in *At the Edge of Psychology.* Delhi: Oxford University Press, 1980, pp. 32-46).

The ancient family structure and cultural values are changing today and the concept of femininity is examined and evaluated. The writer has emphasized mother-son relationships, the cult of Kali in Bengal, and the changes that have come about because of the reform movements in India. The author discusses the relationship between creativity and womanliness and stresses equality in marriage as necessary for the emancipation of women. Important notes are at the end of the chapter.

772.   Roy, Manisha. "The Oedipus Complex and the Bengali Family in India: A Study of Father-Daughter Relations in Bengal." Pp. 123-134 in Thomas R. Williams, ed. *Psychological Anthropology*. The Hague: Mouton, 1975.

Freud's theory of the Oedipus complex is applied to Indian culture. While describing the life style of a Bengali family, the author discusses the social life of a Bengali girl. The status of a Bengali male and the pampering of a son are also described. When a girl comes of age, marriage, joint family living, repression, the attachment to the father, and other dynamics are explained. The author concludes that a Bengali wife does not experience a total emotional relationship with either her son or her husband. And, therefore, attachment to a guru, who is completely acceptable in terms of familial, cultural, and social standards, begins. Thus the Oedipus complex generated in her early childhood, maintained and perpetuated in her adolescence, and prolonged in her youth is at last fulfilled in her relationship with a guru, who combines the roles of father, son, brother, and god.

Adjustment Problems

773.   Bal, Sharayu. "A Psycho-Economic Survey of Married Women-Teachers (Secondary Schools) with Children (Age Group 1-15 Years)." *Journal of S.N.D.T. Women's University*, No. 2 (1969), pp. 34-68.

75 high school teachers from Poona City were given a questionnaire prepared by the author to investigate their triple roles as mothers, teachers, and homemakers. How do the teachers actually feel about these roles and do they experience any role conflict? Women teachers work to supplement family income; they are healthy; their children have no serious health problems and have acquired good habits; and these women participate in the social activities.

774. Kannan, C.T. *Intercaste and Inter-Community Marriages in India.* Bombay: Allied Publishers, 1963, x, 236 pp.

    200 intercaste marriages are studied through a questionnaire that was originally a Ph.D. dissertation at the University of Bombay. Social and personal factors of intercaste marriages, courting, caste and language, reactions of natal families, and the adjustment problems of inter-religious marriages form the chapters. The questionnaire reproduced in the appendix contains a bibliography, index, and many tables.

775. Ramadevi, B. "Adjustment Problems of Married and Unmarried Women Teachers." *Journal of Psychological Researches*, Vol. 4 (1960), pp. 65-69.

    75 married and 65 unmarried women, ranging from the ages of 20 to 40 were asked to respond to personality and attitude questionnaires. There was no difference between the two groups in neuroticism. 30-39 were found to be the most crucial years in the lives of unmarried women, which was not true for married women.

Character Disorders

776. Shanmugam, T.E. "Sex Delinquency and Emotional Instability in Women." *Indian Journal of Social Work*, Vol. 17, No. 1 (1956), pp. 30-43.

    40 sexually delinquent women in the Rescue Home and Vigilance Home in Madras City and 36 normal women were matched according to socioeconomic and educational levels as well as general intelligence. A personality inventory devised by the researcher was used. Both groups of women were found to be hypersensitive and excitable while sexually delinquent women manifested paranoid and neuresthenic symptoms and suffered from sleep disorders.

777. Shanmugam, T.E. "Sex Delinquent Women and Their Fantasies." *Journal of Psychological Researches*, Vol. 19, No. 2 (1958), pp. 17-23.

    50 delinquent girls 12 to 16 years of age referred to the Juvenile Guidance Bureau in Madras and 30 normal girls of the same age group were compared on Murray's Thematic Apperception Test. The recurring problems were ones of family relationships, anxiety, aggression, separation, rejection, love, and sex in delinquent girls while among normal girls family relationships, aggression, love and sex problems were also common.

Depression and economic concerns were more prominent in
the latter group.

778. Sinha, A.K. "Psychology and Non-Psychology College
      Women, A Comparison on Some Personality Traits."
      Psychological Studies, Vol. 13, No. 2 (1968), pp.
      94-97.

      College women who are psychology students are com-
      pared with other-major women students on anxiety, in-
      security, and neuroticism by a Hindi version of Taylor's
      Manifest Anxiety Scale, Maslow's Security-Insecurity
      Inventory, and Eysenck's Neuroticism Scale. The two
      groups did not differ significantly.

                       Problems of Aging

779. Vatuk, Sylvia. "The Aging Woman in India: Self-Percep-
      tions and Changing Roles." Pp. 287-309 in Alfred
      De Souza, ed. *Women in Contemporary India and South
      Asia*. Delhi: Manohar Book Services, 1980.

      In this anthropological field project the author
      describes the life-cycle of women in the Delhi and
      Rayapur area. When a woman's son gets married, that
      marks the beginning of old age. Some childless women
      are studied. In order to maintain the same prestige
      and prepare for old age, a change in self-perception
      becomes necessary. Detachment from worldly concerns,
      rest, minimal participation in household duties, care
      of animals, grandchildren, and participation in religious
      activities are the accepted norms and values for elderly
      women. This research paper also emphasizes their de-
      tachment from sexual activities.

                       Attitude Studies

780. Bal Sharyu, and S.J. Vanarase. "Attitude of College
      Girls Towards Marriage: A Study." *Journal of S.N.D.T.
      Women's University*, No. 1 (1966), pp. 19-31.

      Forty-eight psychology students at Poona College were
      administered a questionnaire consisting of 32 items to
      gauge their attitudes toward marriage, choice of mate,
      style of marriage, ceremony, conjugal relations, and
      happy married life. The majority of girls indicated
      that when selecting life partners, they will look for
      education, health, and intellectual makeup. In regard
      to love or the arranged marriage, most of them indicated

they wanted their parents' consent and support. The writers concluded that young college girls today are still in line with the traditional ideas about marriage and married life.

781. Banerjee, Debabrata, Tapan Basumallik, and Srilekha Banerjee. "A Study in the Attitudes of Unemployed Women." *Indian Journal of Psychology*, Vol. 48, pt. 2 (1973), pp. 69-72.

Unemployment is viewed as a sociopathological problem in this research article. 50 employed and 50 unemployed women were tested to measure their attitudes toward government, morality, religion, and society. The unemployed women as a group did not differ in the above four areas significantly.

782. Deshpande, C.G. *On Intercaste Marriage: An Empirical Research*. Poona: Uma Publication, 1972, 164 pp.

75 Maharashtrain couples with a solemnized intercaste marriage are studied in regard to their personality, attitudes, mate selection, adjustment, etc. The legal aspect of sanctions for such marriages in ancient scriptures, the social acceptance of intercaste marriages, conflicts, complexes and defenses, and personality characteristics of the couples are studied in depth. A bibliography is provided at the beginning of the book. Indexed.

783. Guharaj, Aysha, and S.C. Gupta. "Attitude Survey of Married Women Regarding Family Planning at Urban Health Centre, Alambagh, Lucknow." *Indian Journal of Public Health*, Vol. 12, No. 3 (1968), pp. 165-171.

94 married women were interviewed regarding their income, education, type of family, husbands' occupation, number of children, awareness of birth control measures and whether they used them. Many were found to be aware of these measures, but they were hesitant about using them. Education and socioeconomic factors were negatively correlated as far as the use of contraceptives was concerned.

784. Mittal, V.K. "Personality Differences Among Conservative and Progressive Ladies." *Research Journal of Philosophy and Social Sciences*, Vol. 2, No. 1 (1965), pp. 125-128.

A questionnaire was given to 50 women to measure the

personality differences between conservatives and pro-
gressives. The researchers conclude that there is a
positive relationship between conservatism and neuroticism and a negative relationship between conservatism
and self-sufficiency. Conservative women were more in-
troverted, dependent, submissive, and neurotic.

785. Natraj, P. "Mental Pictures of College Girls of Hindus,
     Muslims, and Christians." *Indian Journal of Social
     Work*, Vol. 26, No. 3 (1965), pp. 287-292.

     120 girl students from a women's college in Banglore
     City are examined regarding attitudes toward members
     of three religious groups. Obviously, the perception
     about one's own group is positive. Hindus and Muslims
     view Christians favorably, but Muslims and Christians
     perceive the Hindus less favorably.

786. Natraj, P. "Social Distance Within and Between Castes
     and Religious Groups of College Girls." *Journal of
     Social Psychology*, Vol. 65, No. 1 (1965), pp. 135-140.

     Social distance between Hindu, Muslim, and Christian
     girls of a women's college is measured. Attitudes toward
     food habits, marriage, friendship, residential proximity,
     and citizenship are examined.

787. Pandit, Harshida. "Students' Attitudes Towards Movies."
     Journal of S.N.D.T. Women's University, No. 1 (1966),
     pp. 144-152.

     114 girl undergraduate psychology majors of S.N.D.T.
     Arts College were administered Thurstone's "attitudes
     towards movies" scale. The findings indicate that most
     of the students are positively inclined towards movies.
     However, a few students believe that the movies have a
     negative influence on young minds.

788. Ramadevi, B. Adjustment Problems of Married and Un-
     married Woman Teachers." *Journal of Psychological
     Researches*. Vol. 4, No. 2, 1960, pp. 65-68.

     Two questionnaires to study emotional stability
     and attitudes towards teaching were based on
     Thurstone and Woodworth's Scales. Results revealed
     no difference in neuroticism between the married
     and unmarried groups. Marriage was not a con-
     tributory factor towards personal adjustment. The
     study also indicated that the thirties were the
     most critical period for unmarried women.

789. Ramadevi, B. "Indian Woman and Her Attitude to Tradi-
      tional Values." *Journal of Psychological Researches*,
      Vol. 7, No. 1 (May 1963), pp. 72-78.

      The article emphasizes the Indian woman's enviable
      position in the sacred scriptures. Feminine virtues
      and the concept of ideal womanhood in traditional litera-
      ture are lauded to such an extent that in contrast the
      present generation of women sound very traditional and
      unreceptive to changing times.

                    Research on Adolescent Girls

790. Christian, J.A. "A Study of Anxiety Among University
      Girl Students." *Journal of Institute of Educational
      Research*, Vol. 2, No. 2 (1978), pp. 32-36.

      500 adolescent girl students at Sardar Patel Univer-
      sity were administered Badami's Self-Analysis Question-
      naire for measuring anxiety and the Ladder Rating Scale
      for measuring perception by Cantrill and Hadley. They
      were also given a T.A.T. for measuring need for achieve-
      ment, fear of failure, and hope of success. The girls
      who had a high need for achievement reflected anxiety.
      Anxiety has a one-to-one relationship with personal
      hopes, aspirations, and achievement.

791. Gupta, M., and P. Gupta. "Adolescent Problems at Early
      and Late Adolescence." *Journal of the Institute of
      Educational Research*, Vol. 3, No. 3 (1979), pp. 8-11.

      500 urban adolescent girls of college age, i.e., 14-18
      years, were randomly selected from Lucknow city. They
      were given an Indian adaptation of the Mooney Problem
      Check List. The younger group was more concerned about
      social-recreational activities and personal relation-
      ships.

792. Lyle, Mary S., Mattie Pattison, and Haribhai G. Patel.
      Problems of Adolescent Girls in Gujarat State. Baroda:
      Faculty of Home Science, M.S. University of Baroda,
      1966, 60 pp.

      This study was conducted with the help of the Ford
      Foundation in order to identify the problems of high-
      school girls. A problem check list was given to 857
      girls in the 9th and 10th grades at various schools in
      the Gujarat State. The sample consisted of rural as
      well as urban girls. Areas of problems were health and

physical development, home and family, peer relations,
morals and religion, money and future, sex, marriage,
and personality. Economic problems, peer relations,
and the future worried the girls belonging to the
upper-age group while the girls belonging to the lower-
age groups worried about health and physical development,
sex, and relationships with boys, study, etc. The research report has many tables. A questionnaire is appended.

793. Natraj, P. "The Adjustment of Adolescent College
      Girls." *Psychological Studies*, Vol. 13, No. 1 (1968),
      pp. 60-64.

      300 college girls with a mean age of 18.3 years--185
      adjusted and 53 maladjusted students--were administered
      Bell's Adjustment Inventory. It was observed that ex-
      cept for the final-year students, adjustment was un-
      satisfactory. The adjusted and maladjusted groups
      differed widely.

794. Patel, Haribhai G. "Problems of Adolescent Girls in
      an Indian Village." *Journal of Gujarat Research
      Society*, Vol. 26, No. 1 (1964), pp. 57-64.

      After reviewing some of the masters' theses at the
      University at Baroda and the University of Delhi, Patel
      conducted a research project at the department of home
      science in which 30 adolescent girls of a village near
      Baroda were given a problem checklist to identify their
      problems. Data are analyzed according to caste and
      fathers' occupation. Individual problems, health,
      home, peer relations, morals, money and future, sex
      and marriage and personality were the areas studied.
      Adolescent girls who did not attend school had more
      problems. Adolescent girls of 17 had problems in almost
      all the areas.

795. Srivastava, P.K., S.N. Sinha, and U.C. Jain. "Some
      Correlates of Alienation Among Indian Female Students."
      Indian Journal of Psychology, Vol. 46, No. 4 (1971),
      pp. 395-398.

      Though the concept of alienation is based on the
      writings of Marx and Durkheim, the investigators explored
      the abortive nature of alienation among female students
      through a semistructured projective test, Sack's Sen-
      tence Completion Test. 40 female undergraduate students
      of Rajasthan University were administered the test.
      The findings indicate that nebulous fears compel the
      students to develop alienating tendencies in many areas.

796. Sudha, B.G., and L.V. Tirtha. "Problems of Adolescent
      Girls in Relation to Their Community and Religion."
      Journal of the Institute of Educational Research,
      Vol. 2, No. 1 (1978), pp. 35-40.

      1,400 Hindu, Muslim, and Christian girls were selected
      for this study. They were administered a problem inven-
      tory, socioeconomic status scale, and a parental expec-
      tation scale. Many problems faced by adolescent girls
      are the products of their sociocultural backgrounds.
      Many of the adolescent girls from this sample felt
      worried, emotionally unstable, and anxiety-ridden.

X

EMINENT WOMEN

Eminent women of India of all ages and from all walks of
life and in all areas--religion, education, art, literature,
politics, and social welfare are included in this section.
Some directories, Who's Who's, commemoration volumes, and
biographical dictionaries are listed in this section. Biographies and autobiographies, letters, diaries of famous women
are listed and annotated. One can be proud of these women,
who have sacrificed their time and worked tirelessly against
all odds for the amelioration of their less-fortunate sisters.
They have inspired today's women to work for such a noble
cause.

797. Abbas, Khwaja Ahmed. *Indira Gandhi: Return of the Red
      Rose*. Bombay: Popular Prakashan, 1966, 189 pp.

      This eulogizing and biased biography was published
      when Indira Gandhi became Prime Minister after the sudden
      death of Lalbahadur Shastri before she could prove her
      worth and do anything solid for the country. It in-
      cludes many photographs and an interview with John
      Kenneth Galbraith.

798. Abbott, Justin E. (translator). *Bahinabai: A Transla-
      tion of Her Autobiography and Verses*. Poona: Scottish
      Mission Industries, 1929, 301 pp. (Poet Saints of
      Maharashtra.)

      The autobiographical narrative of her childhood and
      some philosophical verses of this saintly personality
      are translated. She was troubled by the nature of
      womanhood, a problem which has found expression in her
      verses. 473 poems have been translated into English
      from Marathi originals. A glossary is included.

799. Akkamahadevi, *Vacanas of Akkamahadevi*, translated from
      Kannada by Armando Menezes and S.M. Angadi. Dharwar:
      Manohar Appasaheb Adke, 1973, 173 pp.

      315 poems originally written in Kannada are presented

with English translations. They are mostly devotional poems, praising gods and their graces. Indexed.

800. Alexander, Mithrapuram K. *Indira Gandhi: An Illustrated Biography*. New Delhi: New Light Publishers, 1968, 204 pp. (also *Madame Gandhi: A Political Biography*. North Guiney, Mass.: Christopher Publishing House, 1969, 226 pp.).

Attention is paid to her public life--how she came into the limelight and shed her shyness and how she was groomed for public life by her father. The Indian edition has many photographs.

801. Andrews, Robert Hardy. *A Lamp for India: The Story of Madame Pandit*. Englewood Cliffs, N.J.: Prentice-Hall, 1967, 406 pp. (also London: Arthur Barker).

A political and appreciative biography, describing her manifold roles as a freedom fighter, writer, ambassador to the United States, General Secretary of the United Nations, ambassador to the U.S.S.R., and High Commissioner at U.K. No matter what role she was performing, India's prestige was her main concern. Many photographs.

802. Arora, Jagdish. *Indira Gandhi: Harbinger of Peace*. Lucknow: Puri Publishers, 1976, 174 pp.

Published during the internal emergency which Indira Gandhi imposed on India. This biography has described her daily activities, the nature of her leadership, her economic policies and twenty-point program, emergency and suspension of fundamental rights. Some photographs are given. Written as propaganda.

803. Athavale, Parvati. *My Story: The Autobiography of a Hindu Widow*. Translated from Marathi by Hustin & Abbott. London: G.P. Putnam's Sons, 1930, 149 pp.

This is an autobiography of a Hindu widow, who got married at the age of 5 and became a widow at 12. She struggled to get herself educated. A rebel, she did not display any signs of widowhood, worked as a professor at D.K. Karve's Widow's Home near Pune, and spent a life of dedication to the cause of widows. A very inspiring account. Some photographs.

804. Atma-prana, P. *Sister Nivedita of Ramakrishna-Vivekananda*. Calcutta: Sister Nivedita Girls School, 1961, 297 pp.

The book describes the life of Sister Nivedita or
Margaret Nobel--her birth, childhood, and encounter
with Swami Vivekananda. Her dedicated, selfless service to the people of India is highlighted. A hand-
written letter is reproduced.

805. Baig, Tara Ali. *Sarojini Naidu*. New Delhi: Publications Division, Ministry of Information and Broadcasting, Government of India, 1974, 175 pp. (Builders
of Modern India Series.)

A biography based on friends', relatives', and co-
participants' accounts of the freedom struggle. The
book concentrates on her political life and gives an
inspiring and intimate rendering. Not much factual
information is gathered by the oral history method.

806. Banerji, Brajendranath. "Some Original Sources for a
Biography of Begam Sumroo in India." Indian Historical
Records Commission, 6th meeting, 10-11 Jan. 1924,
Madras: Proceedings 6. Calcutta: Central Publication
Branch, Government of India, 1924, pp. 96-99.

A very good listing of published and unpublished
sources in three languages (English, Marathi, and
Persian) regarding Begam Sumroo, who was born Muslim,
embraced Christianity, and played a significant role
in the politics of the eighteenth century. Portrait
of the Begam included.

807. Banerji, Brajendranath. *Begam Samru*. Calcutta: M.C.
Sarkar, 1925, 228 pp.

Full-length biography of Begam Samru, who played an
important role in politics in the eighteenth century.
Based on English, Marathi, and Persian source materials,
this is a well-researched publication. Illustrated,
with many documents reproduced in appendices.

808. Bankey, Behari. *Bhakta Mira*. 2nd ed. Bombay: Bharatiya
Vidya Bhavan, 1971, 190 pp. (1st ed., *The Story of
Mirabai*. Gorakhpur: Ghanshyamdas Jalan, 1937, 150 pp.).

Life sketch of Mira, a saint and a poetess of the
eighteenth century, is given in detail. She originally
wrote in a Rajasthani dialect akin to the Gujarati language, and both language groups claim her as an early
poetess. Here are 112 of her devotional poems in the
original dialect (and English translations of some).

809.   Bazaz, Premnath. "Lalla: Harbinger of a New Age." Pp.
       123-138 in his *Daughters of Vitasta: A History of
       Kashmiri Women from Early Times to the Present Day*.
       New Delhi: Pamposh Publications, 1959.

       Lalla wrote philosophical poems. In these pages the
       writer has given her biographical sketch and printed
       her poems in Kashmiri dialects with the English transla-
       tions. She was influenced by both Brahminical and Is-
       lamic thought and suffered from the conflicts between
       the, two. Her poems express this conflict beautifully.

810.   Bhalla, P.N. "The Mother of the Company." *Journal of
       Indian History*, Vol. 22, No. 2/3 (1943), pp. 128-144.

       Munni Begam was the consort of Nawab Mir Jafar Khan
       and the mother and guardian of the future Nawabs. This
       article highlights the power she exerted in the house-
       hold affairs of the Nawabs and her relationship with
       the British Government. Based on original documents,
       the article does justice to her contributions.

811.   Bhatia, Krishan. *Indira. A Biography of Prime Minister
       Gandhi*. London: Augus and Robertson, 1970, 280 pp.
       (also New York: Praeger, 1974).

       The author evaluates Indira Gandhi's leadership during
       her apprenticeship to the Prime Ministership and dis-
       cusses her role during the war with Pakistan and the
       creation of Bangladesh in 1971. A journalistic biog-
       raphy. Many photographs.

812.   Bhattacharya, Panchanan. *Ideals of Indian Womanhood*.
       Calcutta: Goldquin and Company, 1921, 365 pp.

       Arundhati, Sita, Savitri, Gandhari, Gopa, Supriya,
       Samjukta, Pannabai, Padmini, Mirabai, and other women
       from Indian history are included in this collection;
       each represents a particular virtue--purity, self-abnega-
       tion, fidelity, righteousness, renunciation, philan-
       thropy, self-respect, duty, honor, and devotion.

813.   Bright, J.S. *Woman Behind Gandhi*. Lahore: Paramount
       Publications, 1944, vii + 160 pp.

       This is a biography of Kasturba, her early married
       life with Gandhiji, her support in South Africa and
       England, participation in the independence movement,
       and her last days in prison during 1942-44 in the
       Aghakhan Palace, where she passed away. In her memory,
       the Kasturba Memorial Trust was established. This book

contains information about this trust and remarks on
women by Gandhiji.

814. Brij Bhushan, Jamila. *Kamladevi Chattopadhyay: Por-
       trait of a Rebel*. New Delhi: Abhinav Publications,
       1976, 187 pp.

       Kamladevi was a freedom fighter. After India gained
       her independence, she retired from active politics and
       became a craftswoman, reviving old traditional handi-
       crafts and making handwoven cloth. In this biography
       based on interviews, newspaper clippings, photographs,
       etc., the author admires her withdrawal from party
       politics in order to uplift the rural craftsmen and
       craftswomen.

815. Brij Kishore. *Tarabai and Her Times*. Bombay: Asia
       Publishing House, 1963, 232 pp.

       As her family was politically and militarily oriented,
       she participated in these activities. The historical
       details in this book are gathered from the Marathi and
       Persian originals.

816. Brinda (Maharani of Kapurthala). *Maharani: The Story
       of an Indian Princess*. New York: Henry Holt and
       Company, 1954, 246 pp.

       A Rajput princess of Jubbal candidly describes her
       childhood, married life, and her travels around the
       world. She did not have a son, which made her anxious
       that the State might be left without an heir. Photo-
       graphs.

817. Brittain, Vera. *Envoy Extraordinary: A Study of Vijaya
       Lakshmi Pandit and Her Contribution to Modern India*.
       London: Allen and Unwin, 1965, 178 pp.

       Vijaya Lakshmi's biography is based on interviews with
       herself and her three daughters. It also contains
       press-cuttings of speeches and events, and letters and
       other such documents that describe her role as a freedom
       fighter and ambassador to various communist and non-
       communist countries. Her prison life as well as her
       achievements are discussed. Bibliography in the appendix.
       Her portrait is reproduced. Indexed.

818. Butler, Clementina. *Pandita Ramabai Sarasvati: Pioneer
       in the Movement for the Education of the Child-Widow
       of India*. New York: Fleming H. Revell Company, 1922,
       96 pp.

This book describes her life and the pioneering work
that she did in educating child widows of India.
"Sarda Sadan," an institution that she established,
encouraged people to educate child widows.

819. Carras, Mary. *Indira Gandhi in the Crucible of Leader-
      ship*. Bombay: Jaico Books, 1981, 289 pp.

      This is a psychobiography of Indira Gandhi by a
      political scientist who examines her traits, strengths,
      and weaknesses as well as her political philosophies
      against the backdrop of her childhood experiences.
      The author concludes that she overemphasized her role
      as mother during as well as after the emergency when
      she tried to promote her younger son Sanjay. By doing
      so she tarnished her image, and her political maneuvering
      became very apparent.

820. Caur, Ajeet, and Arpana Caur (eds.). *Dictionary of Indian
      Women Today*. New Delhi: India International Publica-
      tions, 1976, 659 articles, xlviii, iv pp. of index.

      Contains brief biographies and photographs of eminent
      women in almost all fields--art, education, social
      work, science, politics, and administration. Also in-
      cluded are some articles with such titles as "Women in
      India," "Women and the Arts," "Necessity for Legal
      Awareness," "Women in Administration," and a statewise
      list of women's organizations with addresses. This
      publication provides some idea of the achievements of
      Indian women--a sort of *Who's Who*.

821. Chapman, Mrs. E.F. *Sketches of Some Distinguished
      Indian Women*. London: W.H. Allen and Company, 1891,
      vi + 139 pp.

      Pandita Ramabai Saraswati, Dr. Anandibai Joshi,
      Sunitidevi, Maharani of Cooch Behar, Toru Dutt, and
      Cornelia Sorabji are the distinguished women; each one
      pioneered some movement or field during the last quarter
      of the nineteenth century. Their lives and works are
      described in such a wonderful manner that other women
      will be tempted to imitate them. The introduction
      gives a brief account of the factors affecting the wel-
      fare of Indian women and evaluates the contributions of
      these women.

822. Choksi, M. *India's Indira*. New Delhi: Orient Longman,
      1975, 180 pp.

The span covered is from her childhood to 1974. Many
photographs make this book attractive. The author portrays Indira Gandhi as a brave, dedicated master manipu-
lator and power-crazy leader.

823. Cousins, Margaret E. "Mrs. Rukmini Lakshmipathi, First
     Congress Woman M.C.C." *Modern Review*, Vol. 57, No. 6
     (1935), pp. 664-666.

     Mrs. Lakshmipathi was a freedom fighter; she was in-
     volved in salt making at Dandi as a part of the civil
     disobedience movement led by Gandhiji in 1930-31. She
     was imprisoned and after her release she became a mem-
     ber of the Madras Legislative Council in 1935 when the
     interim government was functioning under the Federal
     constitution.

824. D'cunha, S. *Mother of the Motherless: A Short Sketch
     of Life and Work of Mother Teresa.* Banglore: Society
     of St. Paul Dasarahalli, 1975, 80 pp.

     Based on Malcolm Muggeridge's book, this brief work
     sketches the life of Mother Teresa and her work with
     the Missionaries of Charity that she founded. Outlining
     the Christian philosophy of selfless service and dedica-
     tion, D'cunha praises this personality.

825. Dall, Caroline Healey. *The Life of Dr. Anandibai
     Joshee: A Kinswoman of the Pandita Ramabai.* Boston:
     Roberts Brothers, 1888, 187 pp.

     Dr. Anandibai Joshee was the first Hindu woman to be-
     come a doctor. Born in Poona, she married a widower
     from Kolhapur who sent her to study medicine at Women's
     Medical College in Pennsylvania. She returned to
     Kolhapur to practice medicine after getting her degree.
     This publication is based on her letters, which indicate
     that she met with lots of opposition but was able to
     withstand it. A very inspiring biography with a por-
     trait.

826. Das, Kamala. *My Story.* Jullundur: Sterling Publishers,
     1976, 195 pp.

     This is an autobiography of a poetess, expressing dis-
     satisfaction with her own married life and describing
     her extramarital affairs and sexual adventures. Her
     frankness in discussing such tabooed topics as in-
     fidelity, loyalty, and the sanctity of Hindu marriage
     in public created a stir when the book was published.

827. Desai, Bhadra. *Indira Gandhi: Call to Greatness.* Bombay: Popular Prakashan, 1966, 117 pp.

Bhadra Desai studies Indira Gandhi's girlhood, marriage, and separation from her husband in order to be an official hostess to her father. Jawaharlal groomed her for high office so that ultimately she was able to become the Prime Minister. Included here is a brief interview with Mrs. Gandhi.

827a. Doig, Desmond. *Mother Teresa: Her People and Her Work.* New York: Harper and Row, 1976, 175 pp. Illustrated.

Mother Teresa's work in Calcutta is highlighted. Excerpts from her speeches and written work are reproduced with a chronology of events and photographs. Makes interesting, convincing reading.

828. Dongerkery, Kamala S. *On the Wings of Time: An Autobiography.* Bombay: Bharatiya Vidya Bhavan, 1968, 246 pp.

Dongerkery's husband was the registrar of the University of Bombay, while she was active in women's education and freelance writing. She describes her childhood and siblings in Karnataka, marriage, her participation in women's organizations, and her travels abroad. Many photographs.

829. Drieberg, Trevor. *Indira Gandhi.* New York: Drake Publishers, 1972, 221 pp.

This is a political biography, focussing attention on her political career, beginning with participation in the freedom struggle, apprenticeship at Delhi at her father's palace, and her roles as president of party, cabinet minister, and then Prime Minister after the death of Lal Bahadur Shahstri in 1966. She then split away from party bosses, winning the general election in 1970 and establishing herself as an unchallenged leader. Excerpts from her speeches, a few political documents, and, of course, some photographs are reproduced here.

830. Dutt, G.S. *A Woman of India: Being the Life of Saroj Nalini.* London: The Hogarth Press, 1929, 143 pp.

Saroj Nalini's name is intimately associated with the women's movement. Her childhood, education, marriage, and her contribution to the freedom of women are described by her husband. It is very rare for an Indian

husband to write about his deceased wife. The foreword
is by C.F. Andrews and Rabindranath Tagore. Saroj
Nalini was influenced by the liberal thoughts and
ideals of the social reformers in Bengal, and in fact
she organized many associations in Bengal that are still
functioning for the betterment of women.

831. Dutt, Manmath Nath (ed.). *Heroines of India.* Cal-
      cutta: H.C. Dass, 1983, xl + 183 pp. (2nd ed. Cal-
      cutta: Society for the Resuscitation of Indian
      Literature, 1968).

      Sanjuneta, Padmini, Panna, Rani Durgabai, Rani of
      40 pages of introductory sketches briefly mention many
      more women from the ancient scriptures.

832. Dyer, Helen S. *Pandita Ramabai: The Story of Her Life.*
      New York: Fleming H. Revell, 1911, 197 pp.

      A biography in appreciation of the welfare work done
      by Pandita Ramabai, who established Sarda Sadan and
      worked selflessly for this organization.

833. Dyer, Helen S. *Pandita Ramabai: Her Vision, Mission and*
      Triumph of Faith. London: Pickering and Ingelis,
      1920, 174 pp.

      A biography of Pandita Ramabai, who worked for Indian
      women's welfare. Her devotion to educational activities
      and improving the lot of women of India is highlighted
      here.

834. Fisher, Welthy. *To Light a Candle.* New York: McGraw-
      Hill Book Company, 1962, 279 pp.

      Welthy Fisher was an American Methodist missionary
      who came to India and met Mahatma Gandhi. He advised
      her to come and work in a village. She settled down
      near Lucknow in Uttar Pradesh and founded a literacy
      village, where she started training teachers to go to
      villages and work for literacy. Even after her death
      the center is still functioning. This autobiography
      describes her earlier activities in China as a missionary
      and her work in India, illustrating her message "It is
      better to light a candle than to blame the darkness."

835. Ganapati, R. "M.S. and Her World of Music." *Bhavan's*
      Journal, Vol. 22, No. 7 (26 October 1975), pp.
      146-157.

The article is about M.S. Subbulaxmi, the famous
vocalist of India. The writer has interviewed her
about her family background, training in music, roles
in musical films, reflections on art and music, etc.,
and her achievement. This world-renowned personality
has performed at the United Nations and in many European
countries. Photographs and paintings.

836. Gandhi, Indira. *My Truth (presented by Emmanual*
Pouchpadass). Delhi: Vision Books, 1981, ix + 200 pp.

This book is a collection of Indira Gandhi's reminiscences written when out of power during March 1977 to
December 1979. She speaks of her childhood, girlhood
memories of the monkey brigade (little children's gang
during the struggle for freedom) and relates some anecdotes. The book can help the reader to understand her
enigmatic personality.

837. Gandhi, Indira. *Half the World: Thoughts of Indira*
Gandhi on Women. New Delhi: Directorate of Advertising and Visual Publicity, 1975, 38 pp.

A propagandistic publication by the governmental
agency, this leaflet describes her ideas about the
second-class citizenship enjoyed (!) by women.

838. Gandhi, Indira. *India: The Speeches and Reminiscences*
of Indira Gandhi, Prime Minister of India. Calcutta:
Rupa and Company, 1975, 221 pp.

She speaks about her insecure childhood, her memories
of her father and Gandhiji, and her family life. Twenty-
six political speeches and articles which she delivered
and published on different occasions from 1966 to 1972
are included.

839. Gandhi, M.K. "Kasturba." Pp. 5-13 in D.G. Tendulkar
et al. (eds.). *Gandhiji: His Life and Work*. Bombay:
Keshav Bhikaji Dhawale, 1944.

Gandhiji wrote this small piece in memory of his wife.
Photographs of important events from their last years
are included.

840. Ganguli, B.N. (ed.). *Social Development: Essays in*
Honour of Smt. Durgabai Deshmukh. New Delhi: Sterling
Publishers, 1977, viii + 303 pp.

Ms. Durgabai Deshmukh was a Gandhian sociopolitical
worker who did some pioneering work for the welfare of

women. In this commemorative volume, 14 papers are included, out of which only 4 do justice to her and review the work done by her in the field of rural and
social development by analyzing the solid data. The
others are only eulogies. This is hardly the way to
highlight the outstanding contribution of a notable
and dedicated social worker like Ms. Deshmukh.

841. Gayatri, Devi, and Santha Rama Rau. *Princess Remembers:*
      The Memories of the Maharani of Jaipur. Delhi: Vikas
      Publishing House, 1982, 328 pp.

      Every page of this book expresses the esteem in which
      the former Maharani of Jaipur was held. Born in a
      royal family, she was married to the Maharana of Jaipur.
      The biography covers her childhood and adolescence, her
      marriage, and widowhood. The authors describe the
      levelling process implemented by Mrs. Indira Gandhi
      when she deprived the Princes' privy purses. There is
      a brief mention of her career as an M.P. Illustrated
      and interesting references.

842. Guthrie, Anne. *Madame Ambassador: The Life of Vijaya*
      Lakshmi Pandit. New York: Harcourt, Brace and World,
      1962, 192 pp.

      This is a eulogizing biography of Vijaya Lakshmi
      Pandit and her family. Her involvement in the freedom
      movement, her subsequent role as ambassador, and her
      creditable performance in a diplomatic career are
      described in this biography with the help of many
      photographs.

843. Hutheesing, Krishna Nehru. *With No Regrets: An Auto-*
      biography. New York: Asia Press, John Day, 1945,
      160 pp. (also Toronto: Longmans, Green, and Bombay:
      Oxford University Press, 1952).

      This autobiography by Nehru's younger sister was
      written when the Quit India Movement was going on against
      British rule during 1942-43. Most of the national
      leaders were behind bars, and Jawaharlal Nehru was
      also imprisoned. The loneliness and insecurity suffered
      by the children in the Nehru family are brought out from
      personal experience.

844. Hutheesing, Krishna Nehru. *We Nehrus.* Bombay: Pearl
      Publications, 1967, 343 pp. (also New York: Holt,
      Rinehart and Winston).

The genealogy of the Nehru family and the privileged
position of Nehru thanks to close connections with
Gandhiji and the involvement in the freedom struggle
by all the members of the family are highlighted.
The book is well written and offers much inside information with photographs and index.

845. Hutheesing, Krishna Nehru. *Dear to Behold: An Intimate
      Portrait of Indira Gandhi*. London: Macmillan Com-
      pany, 1969, 221 pp.

The biographer is Indira's aunt. The biography had
been written when she won the elections of 1967. In
this biography, Indira Gandhi is described as a perfect
woman. The title "Dear to Behold" is the English
translation of Indira's first name "Priyadarshini."

846. Number omitted.

847. Jayanti, A.T. "Bhanu Athaiya, the Ultimate Crown of
      Glory." *Eve's Weekly*, Vol. 27, No. 20 (14-20 May
      1983), pp. 11-13.

The article is about Bhanu Athaiya, the first Indian
winner of the Oscar. Bhanu Athaiya is a costume
designer for Indian movies. She designed the costumes
for *Gandhi* and earned a name in the international
sphere. Bhanu Athaiya talks about her education, experience, hopes, and aspirations.

848. Jeffery, Mary Pauline. *Ida S. Scudder of Vellore: The
      Life Story of Ida Sophia Scudder*. Mysore: Wesley
      Press & Publishing House, Jubilee edition, 1951,
      xiv + 226 pp. Photos, ports.

This Jubilee edition of Jeffery's first biography of
Ida Scudder updates the earlier book and commemorates
the 50th anniversary of Dr. Scudder's work in Vellore,
India. Ida Scudder, born in a medical missionary
family that had served in India for two generations,
went to Vellore after graduation from Cornell Medical
College in 1899. Her numerous contributions to public
health and education included development of the Mary
Taber Schell Memorial Hospital (begun in 1902) and the
Christian Medical College (in 1918). A nursing school,
other hospitals, and health services also grew out of
her work. She has been compared with Albert Schweitzer
in her talent, zeal, energy, and dedication. Many
photos, well-documented biography. No bibliography or
index.

849. Jha, Manoranjan. *Katherine Mayo and India*. New Delhi:
      People's Publishing House, 1971, 128 pp.

      This is a biography of Katherine Mayo and her style
      of journalism. She was asked by British rulers to
      write a derogatory book on India, and she wrote one
      to satisfy their political motives. Her book, *Mother
      India*, became highly controversial. Mahatma Gandhi
      labelled the author a "Gutter inspector," as she ex-
      aggerated all negative aspects of Indian life. This
      book is a research report on her life and work.

850. Jog, N.G. (ed.). *Sumati Morarjee: Felicitation Volume:
      Service to Indian Shipping*. Bombay: I.M. Choksi for
      Sindhia Steamship, 1970, xvi + 250 pp. Front plates.

      Sumati Morarjee achieved heights in the shipping pro-
      fession, which is still an exclusively male-dominated
      field. A close disciple of Gandhiji (who used to be
      her house guest), she is a woman of extraordinary
      achievements. This is a collection of the tributes
      paid to her and her speeches and writings. Some articles
      on Indian shipping are also included. Several photo-
      graphs of Sumati Morarjee and Mahatma Gandhi, his per-
      sonal possessions, and his autograph in several Indian
      language scripts are reproduced.

851. Kalhan, Promilla. *Kamla Nehru: An Intimate Biography*.
      Delhi: Vikas Publishing House, 1973, 145 pp.

      This is an intimate biography of Kamla Nehru--Indira
      Gandhi's mother. Her marriage, exposure to nationalist
      ideas and participation in political activities, her
      relationship with her growing daughter, and her struggle
      with delicate health are dealt with in detail. In-
      teresting photographs and some personal letters, and
      passing references to Phiroze Gandhi, the late husband
      of Indira Gandhi, are provided.

852. Kalia, D.R., and M.K. Jain. *Eminent Indians: A Bib-
      liography of Bibliographies*. New Delhi: Marwah Pub-
      lications, 1977, 200 pp.

      In all 1544 entries are listed, around 400 relating
      to women. Some who's whos are listed to provide cross-
      references for the primary sources. This is the first
      such book to list as many biographies and autobiog-
      raphies as possible. Indexed.

853. Kamleshwar. "Rama Jain and the Jnanapith Award." *Illus-*

trated Weekly of India, Vol. 97, No. 9 (29 Feb. 1976),
pp. 10-12.

A tribute to Rama Jain, a patron of literary activity.
Influenced by Gandhian thinking, she instituted the
Jnanapith award, a very prestigious award given every
year to some literary figure.

854. Karanjia, R.K., and K.A. Abbas. *Face to Face with Indira Gandhi*. New Delhi: Chetana Publications, 1974,
127 pp.

Both authors of this coauthored biography are jour-
nalists. They interviewed the Prime Minister over a
span of 4 years, mainly on political questions. Unfortunately, the book lacks depth.

855. Karve, Anandibai. "Autobiography Translated from
Marathi." Pp. 58-79 in D.D. Karve (ed.). *The New
Brahmans: Five Maharashtrain Families*. Berkeley:
California University Press, 1963.

Anandibai writes about her childhood, marriage, and
widowhood at the age of eight years and her difficult
period at her in-laws' house. She entered Pandita
Ramabai's school for widows. Her second marriage to
Dr. D.K. Karve made her interested in widow welfare
work. She discusses all these events in a very frank
manner.

856. "Kasturba--Life and Reminiscences" and "Kasturba -- Work
Vision and View." Pp. 121-142, 143-190 in *Kasturba
Memorial*. Indore: Kasturba Gandhi National Memorial
Trust, 1962.

In both these articles, biographical details by
family and co-workers are given by way of homage. The
welfare work of Kasturba is also described.

857. Kaul, Jayalal. *Lal Ded*. New Delhi: Sahity Akademi,
1973, 147 pp.

The analysis of the life and work of Lal Ded, a great
saint of Kashmir, is mostly based on primary sources
with translations of 138 poems and a bibliography.

858. Kaur, Manmohan. *Great Women of India*. New Delhi: Sterling, 1970, 2 volumes, 36 and 45 pp., respectively.

Rani of Jhansi, Annie Besant, Kasturba Gandhi, Sarojini
Naidu, Rajkumari Amrit Kaur, Vijayalakshmi Pandit, and

Indira Gandhi are included in this collection as women
who had participated in the struggle for independence.

859. Khan, Abdul Majid. *Great Daughter of India: An Apprecia-
      tive Study of Mrs. Vijaya Lakshmi Pandit and Her Ideas
      in the Background of Nehru Family's Heroic Struggle
      for the Political Emancipation of India.* Lahore: In-
      dian Printing Works, 1946, 266 pp.

      Mainly about her political career, this book describes
      her role as a freedom fighter and how she came to be
      wedded to Gandhian ideals. Some specimens of her
      writings and public speeches are included. Photographs.

860. Khosla, G.D., T.S. Nagarajan, and P.D. Chandwadkar
      (picture eds.). *Indira Gandhi.* Delhi: Publication
      Division, Government of India, 1974, 152 pp.

      A brief biographical sketch, a chronology, and an
      album of photographs are the contents of this pictorial
      publication written for publicity purposes.

861. Kripalani, Sucheta. "An Unfinished Autobiography."
      Illustrated Weekly of India, 96, 1-2 and 9-10 (5-12
      Jan. and 2-9 March 1975), pp. 22-27, 22-26, 29-31, 35
      (also available by the same title, ed. by K.N. Vas-
      vani, Ahmedabad: Navjivan Publishing House, 1978,
      265 pp.).

      The author was a close associate of Gandhiji and was
      very active in the freedom struggle. She was the first
      woman to become Chief Minister of Uttar Pradesh--the
      largest and most populous state. She was married to
      Acharya Kriplani, who was also a freedom fighter. In
      this unfinished autobiography, she recalls the events
      of her political life. Unfortunately, she died before
      she could complete this account. The book includes a
      record of her public activities, her speeches, and
      tributes paid to her by national leaders on her death
      and some relevant photographs.

862. Kulkarni, V.B. "Chand Bibi." Pp. 53-59 in his *Heroes
      Who Made History.* Bombay: Bharatiya Vidya Bhavan,
      1965.

      Chand Bibi ruled over Ahmednagar. Her coming to
      power, military accomplishments, and her fall are
      described in this brief sketch.

863. Kulkarni, V.B. "Rani Durgavati." Pp. 60-67 in his

Heroes Who Made History. Bombay: Bharatiya Vidya Bhavan, 1965.

Queen Durgavati ruled Gondwana during the 16th century. Kulkarni in this brief sketch describes her rebellious attitude and courageous personality--she fought against Mughals in a spirited way.

864. *Lady Tata: A Book of Remembrance.* Bombay: printed at the Commercial Printing Press, 1932, 159 pp.

Lady Ratan Tata was a well-known social worker of Bombay, who was interested in improving the lot of women. Upon her death, the people paid rich tributes to her dedicated and selfless services. Reports of memorial meetings along with condolence resolutions are also included in this publication along with her letters, speeches, and photographs.

865. Madhavananda, Swami, and Ramesh Chandra Majumdar (eds.). *Great Women of India.* Mayavati: Almora, Advaita Ashrama, 1953, 551 pp.

This is a collection of biographical sketches of important women from all of Indian history--Hindus, Muslims, or Buddhists. Also included is an article about Shardadevi--this volume is published to commemorate the centenary of her birth. The contributors are all great scholars and specialists. Indexed. Contains photographs of religious places, paintings, sculptures, and portraits.

866. Mahadevan, T.M.P. "Andal." Pp. 70-75 in his *Ten Saints of India.* Bombay: Bharatiya Vidya Bhavan, 1971.

Anecdotes about this South Indian saint, a biographical sketch, and her devotional poems are brought together in this article.

867. Malhotra, L.K. "Begum Akhtar: Random Thoughts and Personal Reminiscences." *Sangeet Natak,* Vol. 37 (July 1975), pp. 16-20.

The writer knew this vocalist personally and recalls many incidents about Begam Akhtar's life, family, and her achievements in the field of music. Her style of singing and techniques are also described.

868. Masani, Shakuntala. *The Story of Indira.* Bombay: Vikas Publication, 1974, 164 pp.

This biography of Mrs. Indira Gandhi throws light on her childhood in Allahabad, where she imagined herself Joan of Arc and organized a "monkey brigade." It also deals with her education at Poona, Shantiniketan, and Oxford, a background that helped her to develop a powerful personality. It discusses the work of Mrs. Gandhi in political and social fields.

869.   Masani, Zaheer. *Indira Gandhi: A Biography*. New York: T.Y. Crowell, 1976, 341 pp.

This political biography is based on several interviews with Indira Gandhi prior to the emergency (June 1975). Just as the author was about to complete a eulogizing biography, emergency was declared. The last chapter reviews Gandhi's performance very critically and provides more details about her personal life and style of functioning. Photographs. Indexed.

870.   Mazumdar, Shudha (Geraldine H. Forbes, ed.). *A Pattern of Life: The Memories of an Indian Woman*. Columbia, Missouri: South Asian Books, 1977, 246 pp.

Shudha Mazumdar was a Bengali Hindu woman, reared and influenced by a Westernized father, and married to a civil servant. She met Saroj Nalini Dutt and started working in a women's organization. In this publication she recapitulates the major events of her 50 years and writes her memories in an autobiographical style. The editor has put her memories in proper historical perspective.

871.   Meherally, Yusuf (ed.). *Kamaladevi at the Crossroads*. Bombay: National Information and Publications Ltd., 1947, 226 pp.

This book on Kamaladevi includes her writing and speeches and a brief biography by the editor. She was very active in the women's movement and had her own particular perspective on the subject. Moreover, she was very close to Kasturba Gandhi and Sarojini Naidu; their biographical sketches are also included in this volume.

872.   Mehta, Usha. *I Travelled West*. Achalpur City: Sarawajanik Vachanalaya, 1966, 162 pp.

A social worker working in an ashram to rehabilitate lepers narrates her experiences.

873. Mehta, Vinod. *Meena Kumari*. Bombay: Jaico Publishing
      House, 1972, 187 pp.

      Meena Kumari was a very successful and renowned ac-
      tress on the Indian screen. Many spicy stories were in
      the air when she was popular. The author portrays the
      actress's birth, childhood, marriage, the roles she
      .performed, and the artist as a woman. She was rejected
      by her husband, became an alcoholic and ultimately
      died.

874. Mirabehn (Madaline Slade). *The Spirit's Pilgrimage*.
      New York: Coward McCann, 1960, 318 pp. (also London:
      Longman's).

      Miss Slade was the daughter of a British admiral.
      After reading a book about Gandhiji, she came to India
      in 1925 and actively participated in the freedom struggle
      and rural uplift work. Her urge to come to India and
      work with Gandhiji is recalled in a very convincing
      style.

875. Mohan, Anand. *Indira Gandhi: A Personal and Political
      Biography*. New York: Meredith Press, 1967, 303 pp.

      Mohan interviewed her teachers, relatives, and col-
      leagues as well as her domestic helpers after her elec-
      tion as Prime Minister and utilized these data in this
      flattering biography.

876. Moodgal, H.M., K.S. Majumdar, and R.K. Sharma (eds. and
      comps.). *Indira Gandhi: A Select Bibliography*. New
      Delhi: Gitanjali Prakashan, 1976, 275 pp.

      In all, 2,823 entries relating to her and by her are
      compiled by editors and organized according to subject.
      A chronology of the main events of her life from 1917-
      1976 and a bibliography of bibliographies are added.
      Indexed.

877. Morton, Eleanor (Elisabeth Gertrude Stern). *Women Be-
      hind Mahatma Gandhi*. London: Max Reinhardt, 1954,
      xii + 271 pp. (also Bombay: Jaico, 1961, 311 pp., and
      The Women in Gandhi's Life. New York: Dodd, Mead,
      1953, 304 pp.).

      Gandhiji's mother Putlibai, his wife Kasturba, Saro-
      jini Naidu, Vijayalaxmi Pandit, Mirabahen (Miss Slade),
      Annie Besant, Ansuya Sarabhai, Sushila Nayyar, Rajkumari
      Amrit Kaur, and others are considered. Based on per-
      sonal letters, conversations, informal interviews, and

clippings from the newspapers, this book throws some
light on the way that Gandhiji influenced their lives
and vice versa.

878.   Muggeridge, Malcolm. *Something Beautiful for God:*
       Mother Teresa of Calcutta. London: William Collins
       and Sons, 1971, 156 pp. Illustrated.

   Though a foreigner, Mother Teresa adopted India as
her country and started working for the teeming millions
of India. Through her founding order (Missionaries of
Charity), she has rendered humanitarian service. This
biography describes her life and work. Many photographs
illustrating her laudable work are given.

879.   Naidu, Gopalakrishna G.T. *The Holy Trinity, The Three*
       Saintly Ladies of Ecstatic Mysticism: Divine Mother
       Sri Sarada Devi, Sri Mirabai and Sri Andal. Coimba-
       tore: Mercury Book Company, 1974, 58 pp.

   The inspiring lives and teachings of these three
saints are described. In the author's words, "our purpose [of the booklet] will be amply served if our
readers get an insight into the beauty and truth inherent in the three Lady Saints whose innate glory is
delineated in the following pages."

880.   Naidu, Sarojini. *Speeches and Writings of Sarojini*
       Naidu. 3rd ed. Madras: G.A. Natesan, 1925, 444 pp.

   A brief biographical sketch and a collection of her
writings and speeches mainly focuses on the ills of
subjugation. She was a moving and powerful speaker,
her manner was both sarcastic and poetic.

881.   Nayyar, Sushila. *Kasturba: Wife of Gandhi.* Trans-
       lated from Hindi by the author. Wallingford: Penn-
       sylvania Pendle Hill, 1948, 71 pp. (also published
       as *Kasturba: A Personal Reminiscence.* Ahmedabad:
       Navjivan Publishing House, 1960, 102 pp.).

   The author was Gandhiji's personal doctor and very
close to both Gandhiji and his wife. After Kasturba's
death, at Gandhiji's request, she wrote this personal
biography. Gandhiji wrote a brief introduction describing his intimate relationship with his wife.
After Kasturba's death, the author looked after the
activities of Kasturba National Memorial Trust, which
is engaged in Women and Children's Welfare Work.

882. Nethercot, Arthur H. *The First Five Lives of Annie
      Besant*. Chicago: University of Chicago Press, 1960,
      419 pp.

      The evolution of Annie Besant from an English lady
      into a religious leader of the theosophy movement is
      highlighted in this publication. Her various roles as
      a wife, atheist mother, socialist labor leader, pro-
      moter of the home rule movement in India, and follower
      of Gandhiji are explained so as to do justice to her
      personality and her involvement in India.

883. Nethercot, Arthur H. *The Last Four Lives of Annie
      Besant*. Chicago: University of Chicago Press, 1963,
      483 pp. (also London: Rupert-Hart Davis, 1963).

      Annie Besant was an educator and a propagandist for
      India's freedom. She became interested in both mysti-
      cism and the Indian National Congress. Numerous photo-
      graphs.

884. Nijjar, Bakhshish Singh. *Maharani Jind Kaur: The Queen
      Mother of Maharaja Dalip Singh*. New Delhi: K.B. Pub-
      lications, 1975, 72 pp.

      Maharani Jind Kaur was the youngest wife of Ranjit
      Singh. Nijjar gives a historical account of her life
      and how the British rulers annexed Sikh Kingdom in
      Punjab during the 19th century. Mainly compiled from
      the British records, documents, and correspondence, a
      few items of which are appended.

885. Nikhilananda, Swami. *The Holy Mother: Being the Life
      of Sri Sarada Devi, Wife of Sri Ramakrishna and Help
      in His Mission*. Madras: Ramakrishna Math, 1962, 334 pp.
      (also New York: Ramakrishna Vivekananda Center, and
      London: George Allen and Unwin).

      A brief biographical sketch of Sarada Devi, dealing
      with her childhood, married life, and the true companion-
      ship that she enjoyed with her husband Sri Ramakrishna,
      especially as she was able to help him achieve his
      spiritual goal. After her husband's death, she managed
      mission activities. She headed the spiritual order,
      preached, and continued to work for the welfare of the
      Indian people.

886. Nilsson, Usha S. *Mira Bai*. New Delhi: Sahitya Akademi,
      1969, 70 pp. (Makers of India Literature Series.)

In this short pamphlet, Nilsson has included Mira's biography, conveyed her utmost devotion to Lord Krishna, and discussed her poetry by presenting a translation of 50 selected and representative poems.

887. Pandit, Chandra. *Nur Jahan and Her Family*. Allahabad: Dandewal Publishing House, 1978, 199 pp.

Based on primary source material, this biography explains how Jehangir yielded his power to Nur Jahan, who used it for the benefit of her natal family. Documents are quoted in an appendix which provide a primary source for further research in Moghul history.

888. Pandit, Vijaya Lakshmi. *So I Became a Minister*. Allahabad: Kitabistan, 1939, 154 pp.

Her speeches and writings and some autobiographical narrations are included. She became a minister in the interim government. Her sense of freedom and a desire to serve the country are well expressed.

889. Pandit, Vijaya Lakshmi. *The Scope of Happiness: A Personal Memoir*. New York: Crown Publishers, 1979, 333 pp.

Nearly one hundred photographs illustrate this personal memoir. Beginning from her childhood in the Nehru family and ranging to her participation in the freedom struggle, the experiences of her diplomatic career, and her role during the Emergency which Indira Gandhi (her own niece) imposed, she derives a sense of fulfillment from her life and achievements. A map of India and many photographs. Indexed.

890. Pandit, Vijaya Lakshmi. *Prison Days*. Calcutta: Signet Press, 1945, 130 pp.

The author wrote this diary in prison from August 1942 to June 1943 when the Quit India Movement was launched. It is an interesting personal account of her daily routine in jail and more often refers to her brother (Nehru) and Gandhi rather than her husband (Ranjit Pandit) and children.

891. *Pandita Ramabai Saraswati: The High Caste Hindu Woman*. 2nd ed. New York: F.H. Revell, 1901, 42 pp. (1st ed., 1887).

This brief monograph describes her childhood years, marriage, and widowhood. Her conversion to Christianity

and dedication to the betterment of Indian womanhood is
elucidated with the help of photographs.

892. Patel, Toni. *Chand Bibi*. Bombay: India Book House
      Education Trust, n.d., 32 pp. (Amar Chitra Katha,
      54).

      This well-illustrated children's book about Chand
      Bibi presents many episodes of her bravery, illustrating
      how she fought against the British and ruled Ahmednagar.

893. Poole, John J. *Famous Women of India*. 2nd abridged and
      revised ed. Calcutta: S. Gupta, 1954, 150 pp. (1st
      ed., *Women's Influence in the East: As Shown in the
      Noble Lives of Past Queens and Princesses of India*.
      London: Elliot Stock, 1892, 283 pp.).

      Biographical sketches of sixteen ideal women of royal
      families--Sita, Draupadi, Damayanti, Razia Sultana,
      etc. The publication assigns a fair share of historical
      importance to these women contrary to the popular be-
      lief.

894. Prabhu, E.K. (ed.). *Sati Kasturba: A Life Sketch, with
      Tributes in Memoriam*. Bombay: Hind Kitab, 1944, 87
      pp.

      Along with a brief biographical sketch of Kasturba,
      the editor has presented the tributes paid by various
      leaders after her death. This significant work relates
      how Kasturba acquired the status of Mother of the
      Nation as she worked shoulder to shoulder with her
      husband Mahatma Gandhi in the freedom struggle.

895. Qudri, Sayyid Ahmad-Ullah. *Memoirs of Chand Bibi: The
      Princess of Ahmednagar*. Translated from Urdu by
      Mohammed Hayat Quraishi. Hyderabad: Tarikh Office,
      1939, 128 pp.

      This political biography based on Persian sources
      gives the genealogical details of relevant dynasties.
      With tables and plates of the paintings inscribed on
      her grave.

896. Raina, Vimala. *Ambapali*. Bombay: Asia Publishing
      House, 1962, 439 pp.

      Ambapali was a prosperous court dancer at the time
      of Bimbisar. This biographical novel explains how she
      was forbidden to marry and forced to use her talents
      for the King and his courtiers. Later she joined a

Buddhist monastery to become a Bhikhuni (nun) after
she grew to hate the life she was compelled to live.

897. Rajwade, Madhav. "Rani Ahilyabai Holkar." *Illustrated
     Weekly of India*, Vol. 94, No. 32 (12 Aug. 1973), pp.
     22-23, 25, 27.

     A short sketch of her life--how she followed non-
     violence and promoted a just rule.

898. Ramaswami, Aiyar C.P. "Srimati Sarojini Naidu." Pp.
     107-111 in his *Biographical Vistas: Sketches of Some
     Eminent Indians*. Bombay: Asia Publishing House,
     1968.

     The writer knew Sarojini Naidu quite well, first as
     a poetess and later as a crusader for the women's libera-
     tion movement and a freedom fighter. In these few
     pages he records his impressions of her life and work.

899. Ranade, Meena. *Ahilyabai Holkar*. Bombay: India Book
     House Education Trust, n.d., 31 pp. (Amar Chitra
     Katha).

     Ahilyabai's life history is set forth in this
     children's book.

900. Ranade, Ramabai. *Himself: The Autobiography of a Hindu
     Lady*. Translated from Marathi. New York: Longmans,
     Green and Company, 1938, 253 pp.

     Ramabai Ranade was the wife of Justice Mahadeo Govind
     Ranade. Her husband encouraged, educated, and trained
     her for social service so that she was able to estab-
     lish Seva Sadan in Bombay and Poona, an institution for
     children and women's education and welfare.

901. *Rani Durgavati*. Bombay: India Book House Education
     Trust, n.d., 31 pp. (Amar Chitra Katha, 104).

     Rani Durgavati's life is illustrated in this book
     for children.

902. Rau, Dhanvanti Rama. *An Inheritance: The Memoirs of
     Dhanvanti Rama Rau*. New Delhi: Allied Publishers,
     1977, 305 pp.

     Lady Rama Rau was born in an affluent Kashmiri Pandit
     family and married to a high official in 1919. Her
     intercaste-interstate marriage created a sensation.
     Her husband was Indian Ambassador to the United States

for some time and then became Governor of the Reserve
Bank of India. Lady Rama Rau herself was a pioneer in
women's organizations and family planning. In this
autobiography she recalls her past and highlights the
major socio-cultural changes in India.

903. Rau, M. Chalpathi, et al. *Indira Priyadarshini*. New
       Delhi: Popular Book Services, 1966, 116 pp.

As soon as Indira Gandhi became Prime Minister, this
biography by an admirer was published. Her childhood
years, participation in the Vaner Sena (monkey brigade),
the chronology of her life, some political cartoons
by the cartoonist Ranga, and many photographs have
found a place in this book.

904. Ray, Renuka. *My Reminiscences: Social Development
       During Gandhian Era and After*. New Delhi: Allied
       Publishers, 1982, ix + 294 pp.

This autobiography of a freedom fighter and participant in the political processes is written in order to
explain to a younger generation how events were shaped
by the previous generation. The social reform movements, fight for equality and justice, and the sort of
awakening which prevailed 40 years ago no longer exist
in India. The present political leaders' apathy toward
social inequality and injustice is lamented. As a
freedom fighter in her youth, she had such ideals and
aspirations for Independent India that the corrosion
of ethical values pains her. As an active member of
the Constituent Assembly of India and Provisional Parliament during 1942-52 and a Minister for Relief and
Rehabilitation in the West Bengal Government, she has
contributed a lot. The book contains a bibliography,
letters written by Gandhiji to the author, an index,
and some photographs.

905. Reddy, Muthulakshmi S. *Autobiography of Dr. S. Muthu-
       lakshmi Reddy*. Madras: M.K.J. Press, 1964, xii +
       177 pp.

The author's childhood, education, and her children's
and women's welfare work are described in detail. Her
role as a social reformer has been described at particular length. Original documents are reproduced, and
photographs make this autobiography a well-documented
personal account.

906. Reddy, Muthulakshmi S. *My Experiences as a Legislator*.
      Madras: Current Thought Press, 1930, 246 pp.

      While narrating her own experiences as a legislator,
      the author shows how a woman can convert her own family
      concerns into national ones, for example, the welfare
      of children and women, and the abolition of the devdasi
      and child marriages. She also presents her memories
      of childhood.

907. Roy, Chowdhury Bulu. *Madame Cama: A Short Life Sketch*.
      New Delhi: People's Publishing House, 1977, 34 pp.

      Bhikhaji Rustom Cama became a revolutionary in Europe
      during 1902-1935. She devised the first national flag
      out of her sari. This leaflet briefly describes her
      activities with the help of documents and photographs
      in appendices.

908. "Dr. Rukmabai. A Pioneer Medical Woman of India."
      World Medical Journal, Vol. 11, No. 1 (1964), pp.
      35-36

      This brief article presents a portrait of Dr. Rukmabai,
      who went to study at the London School of Medicine in
      1894. She was also a rebel and fought a court case against
      her husband as he was too possessive. The article
      describes her medical career. Portrait attached.

909. Saha, Panchanan. *Madame Cama (Bhikaji Rustom K.R.)*
      "Mother of Indian Revolution." Calcutta: Manisha,
      1975, 47 pp.

      A brief biography of Madame Cama is given in this
      booklet, which describes the freedom struggle which
      she led in Europe. She lived abroad but her heart was
      in India. How she devised the first Indian national
      flag in Germany is also described.

910. Sahgal, Nayantara. *Prison and Chocolate Cake: Auto-
      biography of the Daughter of Vijaya Lakshmi Pandit
      and Ranjit Pandit*. New York: Alfred A. Knopf, 1954,
      234 pp. (also London: Victor Gollancz).

      The author reviews the spirit behind the Indian strug-
      gle for freedom, the pervasive idealism, and how national
      leaders acted in the most dignified way to achieve
      the goal. This book documents the history of the in-
      dependence movement from 1927 to 1947 which Gandhiji had
      led. Sahgal and her sisters were adolescent freedom

fighters. Her memories of travels abroad and in India
are recounted.

911.   Sahgal, Nayantara. *From Fear Set Free*. New York: W.W.
       Norton, 1963, 240 pp. (also London: Victor Gollancz,
       1962).

       This sequel to *Prison and Chocolate Cake* evaluates
       India's independence and the role of the writer's
       maternal uncle as a Prime Minister and reveals the
       facts about her marriage and motherhood.

912.   Sahgal, Nayantara. "The Making of Mrs. Gandhi." *South
       Asian Review*, Vol. 8 (April 1975), pp. 189-210.

       The author offers a clinically objective analysis of
       the pre-emergency situation of India. Sahgal theorizes
       that Mrs. Gandhi's upbringing was responsible for her
       style of political functioning—self-willed and bent
       upon fulfilling her thirst for power.

913.   Sahgal, Nayantara, Chandralekha Mehta, and Rita Dar
       (eds.). *Sunlight Surrounded You*. New Delhi: Nayan-
       tara Sahgal, 1970, 176 pp.

       To celebrate Vijaya Lakshmi's 70th birthday, all three
       daughters joined hands and published selected tributes
       to their extraordinary mother as a birthday bouquet.
       A very interesting and personal publication.

914.   Sahota, S.S. *Indira Gandhi: A Political Biography*.
       Jullundur: New Academic Publishing Company, 1972,
       193 pp.

       This biography covers the period of Gandhi's becoming
       head of state, the 1967 elections, the Congress Party
       split in 1969, the midterm elections, the creation of
       Bangladesh, the general elections of 1972, and the
       Simla Agreement. A personality profile is added.

915.   Sanger, Margaret. "Who Can Take a Dream for Truth and
       Depth but not Tumult?" In her *Margaret Sanger: An
       Autobiography*. New York: W.W. Norton and Company,
       1938, pp. 461-492.

       In the late thirties, Margaret Sanger travelled all
       over India to promote the birth control movement. She
       met important persons (Mahatma Gandhi and Rabindranath
       Tagore) who did not agree with her because Gandhi be-
       lieved in self-control and abstinence rather than birth

control devices. However, she got positive responses
from women's meetings.

916. Sarangpani, M.P. "Mrs. Sarojini Naidu." *Modern Review*, Vol. 39, No. 1 (1926), pp. 98-107.

A very informative article about Sarojini Naidu, well
illustrated with many family photographs.

917. Sarin, L.N. *Indira Gandhi: A Political Biography*. New
Delhi: S. Chand and Company, 1924, 127 pp.

After she took over as Prime Minister, she managed to
break away from the Congress Party and its syndicate.
The biography relates her announcement of policies of
democratic socialism and her establishment as an unchallenged leader.

918. *Sarojini Naidu*. New Delhi: Publications Division,
Government of India, 1975, vii + 175 pp.

"A highly perceptive biography which brings out the
warmth and richness of an extraordinary personality,"
Seeta Badrinath reviewed this publication in *Indian
and Foreign Review*. Sarojini Naidu's love and respect
for Gandhiji and her participation in the freedom
struggle are described.

919. Satavadhani, D. Rajasekhara. *Heroines of Hindustan*.
Proddutur: Janaki Printing Works, 1938, vi + 151 pp.

The heroines include Samyukta, Koorma Devi, Krishna
Kumari, Joshi Bai, Veeramati, Dewul Devi, Tarah Bai,
Karnavati, Padmini Bai, Padma, Jodha Bai, and all great
women of India famous for idealism and specific actions.
Most of the heroines in this book were from Rajasthan.

920. Saxena, T.P. *Women in Indian History--A Biographical
Dictionary*. New Delhi: Kalyani Publishers, 1979,
114 pp.

In this biographical dictionary, an attempt has been
made to present a brief biographical sketch of all
women whose names appear in the pages of history. The
dates of birth, death, and important historical events
in the life of each woman are given. Very few contemporary famous women are listed. Alphabetically arranged
by last name.

921. Scharlieb, Mary. *Reminiscences*. London: Williams and
Norgate, 1924, xi + 239 pp.

Based on her diaries, this book is about her decision
to become a doctor so that Indian women could be treated.
She struggled hard to obtain a degree in medicine in
Madras in the 1870's as England would not permit women
to receive medical education. She then established a
hospital in Madras--Royal Victoria Hospital--and taught
at Medical College in Madras. She mainly concentrated
on prenatal care, venereal disease, and women's diseases.
Prejudice against women and social backwardness posed
problems even for an Englishwoman.

922. Scudder, Dorothy Jeasons. *A Thousand Years in Thy
 Sight: The Story of the Scudders of India.* Shelter
 Island, New York: Author, 1970, vii + 418 pp.

Four generations of the Scudder family devoted their
services to medical missionary work. This illustrated
biography focuses on Ida Scudder, who was born in 1870,
attended Women's Medical College in Pennsylvania, and
graduated from Cornell University in 1898. After her
return to India she devotedly worked for mothers' and
children's health at Vellore. Her niece Ida Belle Scudder
came to work at the Vellore Medical Complex in the 1930's.
This book contains a glossary, a bibliography, and a
genealogical chart.

923. Sen, Ila. *Indira Gandhi: A Biography.* London: Peter
 Owen, 1973, 198 pp. (also published Calcutta: Rupa
 and Co.).

Indira Gandhi's evolution into omnipotent leader is
described by a family acquaintance. Her early life,
her married life with her husband Feroze Gandhi, the
beginning of her political career as a party boss, and
the toppling of some state governments, the war with
Pakistan, the creation of Bangladesh, and her foreign
policy are also described. Photographs.

924. Sen, Ila. "Sarojini Naidu." Pp. 109-121 in her *Testa-
 ment on India.* London: George Allen and Unwin Ltd.,
 1939.

The author considers Sarojini one of the greatest
modern women. In this article, she gives her biographical sketch, describes her disposition, personality, and
character and summarizes her work as a soldier in the
independence movement.

925. Sen, Ila. *Wives of Famous Men.* Bombay: Thacker and
 Company, 1942, xiii, 122 pp.

Biographical sketches of the wives of world states-
men are the subjects of this publication--Madame Chiang
Kai-shek, Mrs. Stalin, Mrs. Roosevelt, Mrs. Churchill,
etc. Indian wives are included, e.g., Kasturba Gandhi
and Kamla Nehru. The national spirit, fearlessness,
and companionship that both these Indian women prized
are stressed.

926. Sen, S.P. (ed.). *Dictionary of National Biography*.
     Calcutta: Institute of Historical Studies, 1972, 4
     Volumes, 480, 418, 562, 465 pp., respectively.

     Prominent men and women from all walks of life are
     covered in this national biography. General format
     followed is: (a) personal and family details, (b) early
     life, (c) career history, (d) personality, and (e) gen-
     eral estimate. The contributors are all eminent scholars
     and specialists. Many distinguished women are covered.
     Some references for further reading are also given.

927. Sen, Sushama. *Memoirs of an Octogenarian*. New Delhi:
     Hilly Chatterjee and Jal Pradeep Sen, 1971, 706 pp.

     Born in a famous Brahmosamajist family (P.K. Sen),
     this octogenarian recalls her childhood and her partici-
     pation in political activities and social welfare work,
     etc. Illustrated with letters and photographs, it is
     a remarkable publication.

928. Sengupta, Padmini. *Pandita Ramabai Saraswati: Her
     Life and Work*. Bombay: Asia, 1970, 364 pp.

     The Pandita Ramabai Centenary Memorial Committee re-
     quested this detailed biography covering her life and work.
     Sengupta discusses her childhood, marriage, widowhood,
     and social reforms, especially her work with child
     widows.

929. Sengupta, Padmini. *Pioneer Women of India*. Bombay:
     Thacker, 1944, 195 pp.

     25 eminent and accomplished women of the 19th and
     20th centuries are covered in brief sketches with
     photographs.

930. Sengupta, Padmini. *Portrait of an Indian Woman*. Cal-
     cutta: Y.M.C.A. Publishing House, 1956, 200 pp.

     Kamla Ratnam Sathiavadhan was a renowned social worker,
     educator, and an editor of *Indian Ladies' Magazine*.

The author is her daughter, who describes in this intimate biography her mother's activities, intellectual
capacity, and creativity.

931. Sengupta, Padmini. *Sarojini Naidu: A Biography*. Bom-
      bay: Asia Publishing House, 1966, 359 pp.

      This is a full-length biography of Sarojini Naidu.
      Her formative years and youth, her poems, and later
      her active participation in the non-cooperative, civil
      disobedience movement which Gandhiji led against the
      British rule are all covered. Her poems are quoted,
      and her letters are used to elucidate her personality.
      Contains photographs.

932. Sengupta, Padmini. *Toru Dutt*. New Delhi: Sahitya
      Akademi, 1968, 94 pp. (Makers of Indian Literature.)

      This is a literary biography of Toru Dutt, a poetess,
      discussing the international influence that helped her
      to crystallize her thoughts about writing. Also
      describes her loneliness, her friendship with Clarissa
      Bader, and her early death. A critical evaluation of
      the poems and novels is also given.

933. Sharma, Hira Lal. *Ahilyabai*. New Delhi: National
      Book Trust, 1969, 123 pp. (National Biography.)

      Based on Marathi and Hindi primary and documentary
      sources, this eulogizing biography describes in detail
      her life and her training that enabled her to assume
      the leadership of a state.

934. Sharma, P.L. *World's Greatest Woman*. Delhi: Indian
      School Supply Depot, Publication Division, 1972,
      407 pp.

      Sharma considers Indira to be India; she is the only
      leader who can rule India as she alone is capable of
      inspiring the masses.

935. Singh, Gurcharan S. "A Sikh Heroine of the Ghadar
      Party: Gulab Kaur." *Journal of Sikh Studies*, Vol. 4,
      No. 2 (1977), pp. 93-98.

      Gulab Kaur was nicknamed the "lioness." She partici-
      pated in the Gadar Movement during 1920-1935, went
      abroad, returned to India, and fought against the
      British. This article is primarily based on the oral
      accounts of her associates.

936. Singh, Khushwant. *Indira Gandhi Returns*. New Delhi:
      Vision Books, 1979, 184 pp.

      This political biography highlights the events which
      brought Smt. Indira Gandhi back to power in 1979 after
      she was voted out in 1977. According to the author,
      she possesses charisma, the ability to get things done,
      energy, stamina, and a mastery of political strategy
      and tactics. Drawing on his knowledge of Mrs. Gandhi
      and using the material he gathered through a series of
      interviews, the author evaluates her as a person and
      as a leader.

937. Soltav, B. Eleanor. "Edith Louisa Young, M.D." *Medical
      Women's Federation Newsletter* (March 1930), pp. 62-63.

      Dr. Young qualified in 1901 at the London School of
      Medicine. She spent 24 years in India as a medical
      missionary and built the Rohmatpur Hospital in Palwal.
      This brief article praises her selfless service to
      Indian people.

938. Sorabji, Cornelia. *"Therefore": An Impression of
      Sorabji Kharsedji and His Wife Franscina*. London:
      Oxford University Press, 1924, 87 pp.

      Cornelia Sorabji, the first woman lawyer of India,
      here presents her memories of her parents. Both her
      parents were Parsi but converted to Christianity and
      became involved in the social reform movement. Both
      of them were interested in matters pertaining to women
      and, therefore, encouraged their daughter to pioneer
      legal education. Illustrated.

939. Sorabji, Cornelia. *India Calling: The Memories of Cor-
      nelia Sorabji*. London: Nisbet and Company, 1934,
      308 pp.

      Cornelia recalls her childhood and youth, her educa-
      tional experiences in England as well as in India. She
      describes the social reform work that she started at
      the League of Social Reform Work and the League of
      Social Service (which she herself established). She
      encouraged women to participate in political spheres.
      Illustrated.

940. Swain, Clara A. *A Glimpse of India: Being a Collection
      of Extracts from the Letters of Dr. Clara A. Swain,
      First Medical Missionary to India of the Women's
      Foreign Missionary Society of the Methodist Episcopal*

Church in America. New York: James Pett and Company, 1909, ix + 366 pp.

These letters written by Dr. Swain to her sister mostly describe her life in India. She was the first medical missionary to establish a hospital in Bareilly in 1870. Then she worked in Khetri as a private physician to the Queen. These letters narrate her involvement in medical work for the welfare of women. Photographs and portraits.

941. Thoburn, J.M. *Life of Isabella Thoburn*. Cincinnati: Jennings, 1903, 373 pp.

Isabella was a Methodist missionary mainly interested in education of women. She spent more than three decades in India and contributed toward women's welfare through education.

942. Tilak, L.B. *A Follow After: An Autobiography*. Bombay: Oxford University Press, 1950, iv + 353 pp. (translated from Marathi by E. Josephine Inkster).

Laxmibai, the wife of Narayan Vaman Tilak, writes about her life, her marriage at the age of eleven, and the quarrels between husband and wife. Mr. Tilak converted to Christianity and that created some unforeseen problems for Laxmibai. One common interest of the couple was social service and, amidst many contradictions and differences of opinion, this kept them together. Interesting rendering of unusual problems, and, of course, her frankness must be appreciated.

943. Vasudev, Uma. *Indira Gandhi: Revolution in Restraint*. Delhi: Vikas Publishing House, 1974, 582 pp.

The ingredients of Indira Gandhi's life (power, leadership, and image building) are described in an appreciative manner. Based on interviews and published and unpublished correspondence, the book stresses the salient characteristics of her personality. Many photographs decorate the book.

944. Vasudev, Uma. *Two Faces of Indira Gandhi*. New Delhi: Vikas Publishing House, 1977, 208 pp.

The book depicts the personal and political transformation of Indira Gandhi. The dual personality which became apparent during 1975-1976 when the internal emergency was imposed has been described in a penetrating

analysis. Her indulgence of her son Sanjay is criticized.

945.   Vaswani, K.N. (ed.). *Sucheta: An Unfinished Autobiog-*
          raphy. Ahmedabad: Navjivan Publishing House, 1978,
          265 pp.

       Sucheta Kriplani was a freedom fighter and first
       woman chief minister of a state. She married a Gandhian
       freedom fighter, Acharya J.B. Kriplani. Her autobiog-
       raphy was being serialized in *Illustrated Weekly of In-*
       dia, but unfortunately before she could complete it, she
       died. This publication covers her political role, her
       public activities, her writings and speeches. Tributes
       to her are included.

946.   Verma, H.N., and Amrit Verma. *Eminent Indian Women*.
          New Delhi: Great Indian Publishers, n.d., 180 pp.

       Seventy-five great women of prehistoric, Vedic,
       Upanishadic, Epic, Jain, Rajput, Islamic, Moghul, and
       modern periods are listed in chronological order. In-
       formation in brief is provided for each woman. Further
       references are listed in almost all cases. A very
       useful encyclopedic type of work.

947.   Verma, Hari Narain, and Amrit Verma. *Indian Women*
          Through the Ages. New Delhi: Great Indian Publishers,
          1976, 203 pp.

       The authors maintain that *Indian Women Through the*
       Ages is a dictionary and not a social study. The book
       identifies important women in the variegated history
       of this country. Brief biographical sketches of 3,000
       women have been arranged alphabetically. The book was
       published in the International Women's Year in 1976.
       A short bibliography is attached.

948.   Verma, Shrikant. *Seven Hundred Days: An Appraisal*.
          New Delhi: Published by Author, 24, Akbar Road, 1982,
          95 pp.

       A member of Parliament, coordinator of publicity for
       Congress I (Indira Gandhi's political party) has pub-
       lished this booklet for private circulation. Topics
       covered are the sixth plan, commerce, industry, energy,
       housing, communication, tourism, education, and parlia-
       mentary affairs in a way so that a positive picture
       can be presented for publicity purposes. This is not
       an objective appraisal, but Indira Gandhi's leadership
       is evaluated.

949.   Willcoxen, Harriet. *First Lady of India: The Story of Indira Gandhi*. New York: Doubleday, 1969, 143 pp.

This biography runs from childhood to prime minister-ship. Her marriage, attachment to her father, separation from her husband, becoming a party president and then minister, from which she was elevated to Prime Minister, are dealt with here.

950.   Wilson, Dorothy Clarke. *Dr. Ida: The Story of Dr. Ida Scudder of Vellore*. New York: McGraw-Hill Book Co., Inc., 1959, 358 pp.

Ida Scudder was a third-generation medical missionary to India, following in the footsteps of her father and grandfather. She decided to enter medicine to serve the women of India, and in 1895 she enrolled in the women's medical college of Pennsylvania. In 1899 she completed her studies at Cornell Medical College (which was opened to women the previous year) and was com-missioned to raise funds for a woman's hospital in Vellore, near Madras. This illustrated biography re-counts the work and personal life of Dr. Scudder in India until 1959. In that year on her 88th birthday, she was given an award by Cornell for her contributions to medical education, public health, and international understanding.

951.   Wilson, Dorothy Clarke. *Palace of Healing: The Story of Dr. Clara Swain, First Woman Missionary Doctor and the Hospital She Founded*. New York: McGraw-Hill Book Company, 1968, x + 245 pp.

Clara Swain came to India as the first woman missionary doctor in 1869 when strict caste taboos and the seclu-sion of women prevented their treatment by male doctors. There was, thus, a desperate need for women doctors and for training in medicine for Indian women. Dr. Swain opened the first women's hospital in India. For nearly 30 years she combined education, evangelism, and medical care for Christian, Hindu, and Mohammedan women. The hospital at Bareilly is now called the Clara Swain Hos-pital. This biography describes the slow pace of social change in India.

952.   Wilson, Dorothy Clarke. *Take My Hands: The Remarkable Story of Dr. Mary Verghese*. New York: McGraw-Hill Book Co., Inc., 1963, 216 pp.

Mary Verghese graduated from the Christian Medical College at Vellore, India, where she was influenced by

its founder Dr. Ida Scudder to become a surgeon. Short-
ly after graduation, an accident made Dr. Verghese a
paraplegic. This biography tells how she managed to
overcome her physical handicap and was able to perform
delicate operations while seated in her wheelchair.
She became a rehabilitation specialist for leprosy
patients. The book emphasizes the role of her Christian faith in reconstructing her life. "Without the
accident," Dr. Verghese is quoted as saying, "I might
have been only an ordinary doctor."

953.   Wiser, Charlotte Viall. "'Madam President' in the
         Chair in India: A Woman's Hands and Her Fiery Words
         Guiding the Indian National Congress." *Asia*, Vol.
         26, No. 7 (1926), pp. 634-682.

Sarojini Naidu was president of the Indian National
Congress in 1926. Her presidential address was both
poetic and fiery. Excerpts from her speech on the role
of women in the struggle for independence and photographs of the Congress are included.

954.   Wodeyar, Sadashiva. *Rani Chennamma*. New Delhi: National
         Book Trust, 1977, 153 pp.

This book provides a short historical background
about Rani Chennamma, the first head of a princely
state in India to rise against the mighty British Em-
pire. She was a woman of indomitable courage and
patriotism. Contents based mostly on archival sources.

955.   *Women in India Who's Who*. Bombay: National Council
         of Women, India, 1935, 91 pp.

During 1932, the British Government appointed a
Who's Who committee. Mr. Mishri of Patna compiled the
names of and other relevant information about eminent
women. Members of the ruling states, pioneers, and
a general section are the three main sections under
which information is collected. Indexed. This was the
first *Who's Who* for the women of India.

956.   *Women Saints of East and West. Shri Sarada Devi (The
         Holy Mother) Birth Centenary Memorial*. London:
         Ramkrishna Velanta Centre, 1955, xviii + 274 pp.

Spiritual traditions of India are described, and in-
formation about women saints of Hinduism (Avvaiyar,
Kareikkal Ammaiyar, Andal, Akka Mahadevi, Bahinabai,
Mirabai, Sarada Devi, Gauribai), of Buddhism, and

Jainism is given by various famous authors. Parts I
and II provide biographies of the saints of Eastern
countries, and Parts III and IV provide information
about women saints of Christianity, Judaism, and
Sufism. The foreword is written by Vijaya Laxmi Pandit
and the Introduction by Kenneth Walker. Swami Ghanananda
and Sir John Stewart Wallace have acted as advisors
for this memorial volume. Indexed. Portrait of Sarada
Devi.

957. Zakaria, Rafiq. *Razia: Queen of India*. Bombay: Popular Prakashan, 1966, 159 pp.

Razia, the only woman to hold the throne at Delhi,
reigned for four years in the 13th century. The author
highlights the progressive policies she adopted as a
ruler. The introduction lists the sources on which
this novel-cum-biography is based.

XI

WOMEN IN DIFFERENT COMMUNITIES

Though Hindus are in the majority in India, there are large Jain, Buddhist, Muslim, Zoroastrian, Sikh and Christian communities. Studies of women belonging to these categories are gathered in this section. These communities are religious minorities in a secular state such as India. These minorities have their own cultures. Since India does not have a uniform civil code, women in these communities are guided by religious laws of their own: Muslim women are guided by the *Quran* and the tenets prescribed in the scripture. Many of them still live in seclusion, wear a veil, and are victims of segregation of sexes. Zoroastrian women enjoy more rights than Muslim women. Unfortunately, no in-depth study has been made of these women so far.

958. Bhatty, Zarina. "Status of Muslim Women and Social Change." Pp. 99-112 in B.R. Nanda (ed.). *Indian Women from Purdah to Modernity*. New Delhi: Vikas Publishing House, 1976.

   The writer compares the status of Muslim women and Hindu women. She feels that Muslim women have not yet achieved equality and they are far from the reach of social justice. Still governed by the laws or religious tenets as prescribed in the *Quran*, they are treated as if they were inferior to men.

959. Bhatty, Zarina. "Muslim Women in Uttar Pradesh: Social Mobility and Directions of Change." *Social Action*, Vol. 25 (Oct.-Dec. 1975), pp. 365-374.

   The position of Muslims in North India is influenced by the system of social stratification of Ashrafs (land-owners) and non-Ashrafs (converts to Islam). This paper analyzes their life styles, patterns of marriage, education and work and brings out the fact that Muslims are also a heterogeneous community in India. With the help of diagrams, Bhatty explains social mobility and directions of change.

960. Brij Bhushan, Jamila. *Muslim Women: In Purdhah and out of It*. Delhi: Vikas Publishing House, 1981, 133 pp.

Jamila Brij Bhushan's sensitive approach to the problems of Muslim women makes informative reading. Most of the problems that beset Muslim women are discussed at length. Women from all economic strata are studied through interviews. Purdah, polygamy, easy divorce, and destitution are the problems of Muslim society. Brij Bhushan recommends some changes in Muslim laws, e.g., abolition of unilateral divorce and polygamy to improve the status of Muslim women.

961. Cooper, Elizabeth. *The Harem and the Purdah: Studies of Oriental Women*. London: T. Fisher and Unwin, 1915, 312 pp., 31 plates.

Will the oriental woman ever be able to escape from those traditional and inherent influences which have been wrought into the very warp and woof of Eastern humanity? This book offers some insight into the traditional beliefs, pitiable conditions in harems, rituals, superstitions, and laws pertaining to marriage and divorce in the East.

962. Dastoor, Aloo J. "Women in Zoroastrianism." *Journal of Gujarat Research Society*, Vol. 37, No. 3 (1975), pp. 2-16.

Before Zoroastrians migrated to Western India, the high status enjoyed by Parsi women in Persia had declined. How it improved in recent times in India is beautifully described in this research article with historical evidence from the primary sources.

963. Debnath, Dhirendra. "Sikh Women in Religion and Customs." *Folklore (Indian)*, Vol. 10, No. 2 (1969), pp. 55-62.

Sikh women's position from the 15th century when the religion was founded by Guru Nanak to the present is traced in this survey.

964. Ehrenfels, U.R. (Von). "Aboriginal Womanhood and Culture Contact." *Eastern Anthropologist*, Vol. 3, No. 1 (1949), pp. 48-54.

The article examines the tribal women's status in two southern states--Tamil Nadu and Kerala--where these women are exposed to the matrilineal system.

Tribal women's status seems very low. Exposure to
other cultures does not always seem to change this
situation. Some programs for welfare work among tribal
women are suggested.

965. Elwin, Verrier. "Tribal Women." Pp. 203-213 in Devki
     Jain (ed.). *Indian Women*. New Delhi: Publications
     Division, Ministry of Information and Broadcasting,
     Government of India, 1975.

     Elwin Verrier was a Christian missionary and noted
     anthropologist who worked with aboriginal people in
     India. He describes tribal women's life styles, charac-
     teristics, traditional beliefs and religious ceremonies,
     etc. Tribal women are free, self-reliant, respected by
     their men. Some photographs illustrate the life and
     manners of tribal women.

966. Garg, B.M. "Status of Women in Tribal Communities in
     India." *Indian Journal of Social Work*, Vol. 21, No. 2
     (1960), pp. 191-197.

     This inconclusive article describes women of various
     tribes and their life in general. The economic, re-
     ligious, social, and domestic spheres are studied.

967. Ghananand, Swami. "Improved Status of Women in Jainism
     and Buddhism: Introduction." Pp. 139-143 in Rama-
     krishna Vedant Centre. *Women Saints of East and West:
     Shri Sardadevi Birth Centenary Memorial*. London:
     Ramakrishna Vedanta Centre, 1955.

     The founders of Jainism and Buddhism, Mahavira and
     Gautam Buddha, believed in social equality. Both these
     religions came into existence as a reaction against
     orthodox Hinduism; so they provided opportunities to
     women for spiritual advancement.

968. Gill, Pritam Singh. "Social Status of Women." Pp. 91-
     97 in his *Heritage of Sikh Culture, Society, Morality
     and Art*. Jullundur: New Academic Publishing Company,
     1975.

     The status of Sikh women vis-à-vis that of Hindu,
     Buddhist, and Christian women is compared. The Sikh
     religion does not consider women to be evil, so the
     perception of women is favorable in Sikh culture.

969. Handoo, Chandrakumari, and Swami Ghananand. "Women
     Saints of Buddhism and Jainism." Pp. 144-158 in

Ramakrishna Vedanta Centre. *Women Saints of East
and West: Sri Sarada Devi Memorial*. London: Ramakrishna Vedanta Centre, 1955.

Gopa, Gautami, Kisa Gotami, Supriya, Ambrapali,
Sanghmitra were Buddhist nuns and famous women who
embraced Buddhism and devoted themselves to spiritualism. Brief biographies of them are provided here.
Similarly, Mallinath and Marudevi were Jain saints
Information about many less famous women is given in
this chapter.

970. Horner, I.B. *Women Under Primitive Buddhism: Lay Women
and Alms Women*. London: George Routledge & Sons,
1930, 392 pp. (reprinted in 1975 by Oriental Publishers, Delhi).

The social status of the laywoman in Pre-Buddhist
and Buddhist periods as mothers, daughters, wives, and
widows is described. The book also throws light on the
historical position of almswomen. Based on the *Jataka*
and *Tripitaka*, the book shows careful scholarship.
Indexed.

971. Husain, Sheikh Akhtar. *Marriage Customs Among Muslims
in India: A Sociological Study of Shia Marriage Customs*. New Delhi: Sterling Publishers, 1976, 226 pp.

This is a revised version of a Ph.D. thesis accepted
by the University of Lucknow, but the book avoids any
sociological analysis. Among the Shia sect, the custom
of Murah (temporary marriage) exists. After several
Murah, some people enter permanent marriage (Nikah).
One comes to know and understand the social structure
by studying marriage customs. Divorce laws among Muslims are guided by the religious scriptures, according
to which men have the advantage over women.

972. Hyder, Qurratulain. "Muslim Women of India." Pp. 187-
202 in Devki Jain (ed.). *Indian Women*. New Delhi:
Publications Division, Ministry of Information and
Broadcasting, Government of India, 1975.

The position of Muslim women in the 19th century is
reviewed in this chapter, which covers such major
issues as education, literature, and legal as well as
political issues bearing on Muslim women. The religious
influence still continues.

973. Jacobson, Dorothy Ann. "Hidden Faces: Hindu and Muslim

Purdah in a Central Indian Village." Ph.D. Dissertation, Department of Anthropology, Columbia University, 1970, 554 pp. (University Microfilms 73-16,209).

The reasons for the observance of purdah are examined.
Photographs.

974.   Number omitted.

975.   Jones, Violet Stanford, and L. Bevan Jones. *Woman in*
       Islam: A Manual with Special Reference to Conditions
       in India. Lucknow: Lucknow Publishing House, 1941,
       455 pp.

       The authors discuss the position of women in Islam
       with special reference to conditions in British India.
       The manual was prepared for Christian missionaries
       working in India. The book quotes from Islamic re-
       ligious texts to explain the conditions. Bibliography.

976.   Karkaria, Bachi J. "Parsi Women: Are They Really More
       Liberated?" *Illustrated Weekly of India*, Vol. 96,
       No. 36 (7 Sept. 1975), pp. 30-33.

       The status of Parsi women, their education, and their
       marriage laws are discussed at length to prove that
       Parsi women enjoy equality in all spheres. Photographs
       illustrating customs, etc., are given.

977.   Khan, Mazhar Ul Haq. *Social Pathology of the Muslim*
       Society. Delhi: Amar Prakashan, 1978, 196 pp.

       Khan analyzes the decline of the Muslim people be-
       cause of purdah and polygamy. Women and children suffer
       from backwardness. Women's personalities do not de-
       velop; they remain insecure under constant fear of re-
       jection. They are ignorant and not allowed to develop
       a sense of worth or achievement. Religious tenets
       debar women from making any progress.

978.   King, Ursula. "Women and Religion: Image and Status of
       Women in Some Major Religious Traditions." *Social*
       Action, Vol. 25 (July-Sept. 1975), pp. 277-291.

       The article describes the social, economic, and poli-
       tical emancipation of women and how social pressures
       affect the religious traditions. King deals with the
       religious ideals, women and Indian religions, and women
       in Jainism, Buddhism, and Christianity.

979. Mahapatra, Piyushkanti. "Jain Women and Their Folklife
      Through the Ages." *Folklore (Indian)*, Vol. 10, No. 1
      (1969), pp. 26-33.

      The position and the status of Jain women are dis-
      cussed in this essay. Based on early Jain literature,
      scriptures, epigraphs, and traditional oral communi-
      cations, this article emphasizes that Jainism gave
      complete freedom to women to enter the ascetic order.
      They contributed toward the political and administrative
      activities. Their socioreligious life is also described
      in this informative article. Many references are cited.

980. Meer, Hassan Ali. *Observations on the Mussulmauns of
      India: Descriptive of Their Manners, Customs, Habits
      and Religious Opinions Made During a Twelve Years
      Residence in Their Immediate Society*. Delhi: Oxford
      University Press, 1974, 442 pp.

      An Englishwoman married to a Muslim writes about her
      observations and impressions during a 12-year period.
      She describes the tenets of Islam, festivals, cere-
      monies, purdah and seclusion of women, polygamy and
      childrearing practices that she observed during the
      early 19th century in North India.

981. Omvedt, Gail. "The Downtrodden Among the Downtrodden:
      An Interview with a Dalit Agricultural Labourer."
      Signs: Journal of Women in Culture and Society,
      Vol. 4, No. 4 (1979), pp. 763-774.

      The author talks to Kaminibai, an untouchable agricul-
      tural worker, in order to find out the work patterns of
      men and women. The interview reveals Kaminibai's
      feelings of oppression and frustration. She feels
      doubly oppressed as a woman and as a Dalit.

982. Papanek, Hanna. "Purdah: Separate Worlds and Symbolic
      Shelter." *Comparative Studies in Society and His-
      tory*, Vol. 15, No. 3 (1973), pp. 289-325.

      Sex segregation through various types of the purdah
      system is the subject under study. Purdah segregates
      women from men in Muslim society, curtails social
      freedom, and restricts exposure. The writer also states
      that under the guise of honor and status, purdah re-
      stricts and suppresses women's freedom.

983. Paul, Diana Y. *Women in Buddhism: Images of the Femi-
      nine in Mahayan Tradition*. Berkeley, California:
      Asian Humanities Press, 1979, xxii + 333 pp.

   This book examines the ambivalent way in which women
   are regarded in the Buddhist tradition. Women have
   been seen as potential dangers to and distractors of
   men's spiritual uplift as well as guides of great insight and power who are sometimes equal to men. The
   author explores the various roles of women, e.g.,
   temptress, mother, nun, daughter, with the help of
   ancient Buddhist texts. Some of the material has been
   translated into English from Sanskrit and Chinese for
   the first time. Originally, the book was a doctoral
   dissertation. The foreword is by I.B. Horner, author
   of *Women Under Primitive Buddhism* (970). The book contains a glossary, a bibliography, and an index.

984. Paul, S.K. "Muslim Ladies in India." Pp. 399-400 in
      History Congress 21, 1958, Trivandrum, Proceedings.
      Bombay: The Congress, 1958.

   A summary of this paper lists the names of some Muslim
   women such as Gulbadan Begum, Nurjahan, Mumtaz, etc.,
   who were influential in Indian politics from the 14th
   through the 19th centuries. Based on the data of
   visiting experts (Ibn, Batula, etc.), the paper highlights the contributions of these Muslim women.

985. Rallia Ram, Mayavanthi. "Muslim Women in India:
      Dilemma of Change." *Mainstream*, Vol. 11, No. 27
      (1973), pp. 19-22.

   In this brief article, the writer concentrates on
   the reform movement in the Muslim community. The demand
   for relaxation in the religious laws and the reper-
   cussions of these changes are discussed.

986. Rallia Ram, Mayavanthi. "Modernization and Muslim
      Women." *Mainstream*, Vol. 14, No. 48 (1976), pp. 22-23.

   In this article, the author summarizes a survey of
   Muslim women in Uttar Pradesh and Kashmir regarding
   their attitudes toward education, social equality, and
   freedom. Housewives were conservative, and professional women seemed to be leaning toward liberalism.

987. Rathuamal, Sita. *Beyond the Jungle: A Tale of South
      India*. London: William Blackwood, 1968, 253 pp.

      This is the autobiography of a tribal woman from
      Nilgiri Hills in South India, who went to an English
      school and became a nurse. She compares her tribal
      life with her present life. Some illustrations.

988. Roy, Shibani. *Status of Muslim Women in North India*.
      Delhi: B.R. Publishing Corporation, 1979, 250 pp.

      An empirical study based on field work in such cities
      as Delhi and Lucknow where Muslims live in large num-
      bers. The study assessed the extent and quality of
      changes that have taken place within three generations
      and their effect on the status of women. Education,
      employment, marriage, and the observation of purdah,
      etc., are studied. The author concludes that religious
      tenets act as constraints to the acceptance and assimi-
      lation of progressive and egalitarian ideas.

989. Sachidananda. "Social Structure, Status and Mobility
      Patterns: The Case of Tribal Women." *Man in India*,
      Vol. 58, No. 1 (1978), pp. 1-12.

      Tribal societies from Gujarat to West Bengal, the
      northeastern and the southern parts are studied as to
      the type of social structure. The status of tribal
      women is better in matrilineal tribal societies than
      in nontribal culture. Though some changes are taking
      place, female status does not much depend on economics;
      social structure determines the status.

990. Sangave, V.A. *Jaina Community: A Social Survey*. Bom-
      bay: Popular Book Depot, 1959, xviii + 480 pp.

      Jain social institutions, customs, habits, and manners
      are studied in this survey. Information about Jain
      women saints, teachers and preachers, education for
      women, and women's contribution to literature is pro-
      vided. The forms of marriage in the Jain community
      and property rights among women are discussed in one
      chapter.

991. Sarkar, R.M. "Women in Tribal India Through Customs
      and Traditions." *Folklore* (Calcutta), Vol. 9, No. 12
      (1968), pp. 458-467.

      Anthropological parameters (matriliny, patriliny,
      polyandry and polygamy) are used to study the status
      and position of tribal women. Sarkar observes that

their position is somewhat better in matrilineal and polyandrous societies as compared to patrilineal and polygamous ones.

992. Shah, Umakant Premchand. "Great Women in Jainism." Pp. 275-284 in Swami Madhavananda and Rameshchandra Majumdar (eds.). *Great Women in India*. Mayavati, Almora: Advaita Ashram, 1953.

The writer has included in this chapter biographies of many Jain women who managed their homes and families and yet devoted some time to religious activities. Some information about nuns and their activities is also given.

993. Sharma, Arvind. "How and Why Did the Women in Ancient India Become Buddhist Nuns?" *Sociological Analysis*, Vol. 38, No. 3 (1977), pp. 239-251.

With the help of autobiographical material, Sharma explains that women became Buddhist nuns, not because of any dissatisfaction or frustration in their personal lives, but because they were spiritually drawn to Buddhism. The author has examined 42 cases out of 68 cases in *Therigatha* and reached this conclusion.

994. Shashi, S.S. *The Tribal Women of India*. Delhi: Sundeep Prakashan, 1978, vi + 163 pp.

Shashi says in the preface that "A tribal woman occupies an important place in the socio-economic structure of her society. She dominates in the tribes of Eastern India like Garos and Khasis but faces hardships among various tribes of Western Himalayas, particularly the Kinners and Gaddies." The young women of the Muria, Oraon or Adi Naga tribes enjoy the colorful life of their youth dormitory, but the Bhil women observe Purdah. The author describes the role and the status of a tribal woman in her society. Data are drawn from many anthropologists' works. 5 appendices, 18 photographs, a bibliography, and an index.

995. Smith, Wilfred Cantwell. *Modern Islam in India: A Social Analysis*. 2nd ed. London: Victor Gollancz Ltd., 1946, 344 pp.

This publication came out during the days of the British Raj and gives information on the status of Islam in India. At many points throughout references to women in Islam and the problems related to women are made.

996. Sultan, Jahan Begum. *Al-Hijab: Or Why Purdah Is Neces-sary?* Calcutta: Thacker, Spink and Company, 1922, 212 pp.

The queen of Bhopal, a princely state in subjugated India, explains why seclusion of women is necessary and purdah is essential. She argues that purdah gives women privacy and security.

997. Talim, Meena. *Women in Early Buddhist Literature.* Bombay: University of Bombay, 1972, 242 pp.

The book offers insights into the way of life during the Buddhist period and the monastic life of women. The general atmosphere in which Buddhist women were brought up is described. The last chapter discusses the life of women during the Brahminical, epic, and Jain periods.

998. *Tribal Women in India.* Calcutta: Indian Anthropological Society, 1978, iv + 199 pp.

The Indian Anthropological Society published a volume on various aspects of tribal women in India to celebrate the International Women's Year. Chapters by scholars in the field concern the female population, the status of tribal women in all parts of India, a case study of the nomadic Gadulia Lohar women, the role of women in the tribal economy, tribal women and beauty culture, etc. Photographs, tables, graphs, and references at the end of every chapter.

999. Vreede-De Stuers, Cora. *Purda, A Study of Muslim Women's Life in Northern India.* Assen, Netherlands: Royal Van, Giorcum, 1968, xii + 128 pp.

On the basis of field work in North India, this book discusses two main aspects (kinship and purdah) of the observance of Muslims in Delhi and in Aligarh. Based on interviews and participant observations, these brief case histories have many interesting anecdotes. Orig-inally written in French as articles, the book contains some authentic photographs, notes, a glossary, and a bibliography.

1000. Wazir, Hasan, and Fatima Sakinatul. "Indian Muslim Women: A Perspective." Pp. 22-25 in Shyam Kumari Nehru (ed.). *Our Cause: A Symposium by Indian Women.* Allahabad: Kitabistan, 1938.

The backward condition of Muslim women at the end of
the 19th century, Sir Syed Ahmad Khan's movement to
educate only Muslim men on western lines, the first
school for Muslim girls in 1896, and the general
awakening against the orthodox forces are described
in this brief chapter.

1001. Zaidi, H.M. *The Muslim Womanhood in Revolution:
        Being an Exhaustive Survey of Modern Movements Among
        the Muslim Women All Over the World with Special
        Reference to Their Social, Educational and Political
        Awakening.* Calcutta: King's Palace, 1937, 140 pp.

        Pages 104 to 124 describe Indian Muslim women.
        The princesses of Hyderabad and Bhopal (princely
        states) were progressive enough to fight for Muslim
        women, to secure economic freedom for them, and to
        ameliorate the social status through legal reforms.
        This comprehensive survey offers a comparative view-
        point.

1002. Zaidi, S.M.N. *Position of Women Under Islam.* Cal-
        cutta: The Book Tower, 1935, 154 pp.

        The author surveys the position of women under
        Islam as described in the *Quran* and in Muslim tradi-
        tions. It also mentions the Muslim women's movement
        in different countries, including India. Some of the
        princely rulers were progressive enough to promote
        women's education and raise their status.

XII

FILMS

Unless otherwise indicated, films in this section are
produced by the Film Division, Ministry of Information and
Broadcasting, 24 G. Deshmukh Marg, Bombay 400 026. This
list is prepared from the catalogues, and, as such, it is
not exhaustive but selective. Films available in Canada and
the United States are indicated so that interested parties
can buy or borrow the print. Films are alphabetically arranged as it was not possible to view each film so as to
classify them according to subject. However, an effort
has been made to explain, in a line or two, the films' contents.

Films Produced by Film Division

1003. *Amrita Sher Gil*. Produced and directed by B.D. Garga,
       1969, 19 min., color, 16 and 35 mm.

       She was a painter, her mother was an Indian, and
       her father was a Hungarian.

1004. *Banssthali*. Produced by Mohan N. Wadhwan, directed
       by Dilip Jamdar, 1966, 10 min., black and white,
       16 and 35 mm.

       Banssthali is an institution imparting liberal arts
       education to women.

1005. *Begum Akhtar*. Produced through Issar Films, Bombay,
       1971, 17 min., black and white, 16 and 35 mm.

       She was a famous singer, known as Gazal Queen and
       Thumri Queen.

1006. *Bharat Natyam*. 1956, 13 min., color, 16 and 35 mm.

       Dancer Kamala demonstrates the Bharat Natyam dance
       and explains the beauty of it.

1007.   *A Daughter Is as Good as a Son*. Produced and directed
        by K.T. John, 1971, 13 min., black and white, 16 and
        35 mm.

        The film depicts the changing status of women.

1008.   *Deserted Women*. Produced through Fact Films, Bombay,
        1956, 18 min., black and white, 16 and 35 mm.

        Rescue homes and rehabilitation of deserted women
        are shown.

1009.   *Dry Leaves*. Produced through Cine Cooperatives
        Limited, Bombay, 1961, 19 min., black and white,
        16 and 35 mm.

        The film is about the dowry system.

1010.   *Eroticism in Hindu Sculpture*. 1968, 20 min., color,
        16 and 35 mm.

        Scenes from Puri, Konark, Belur, Khajuraho.

1011.   *The Farmer's Wife*. 1972, 30 min., color, 16 and 35 mm.

        A farmer's wife's role in agriculture and homemaking
        is depicted.

1012.   *Feminine Fashions*. 1953, 11 min., black and white,
        16 and 35 mm.

        Clothes, particularly saris, from various parts of
        India are shown.

1013.   *For the Family*. Produced and directed by Ama Private
        Ltd., 1959, 22 min., black and white, 16 and 35 mm.

        A woman becomes a teacher to supplement the family
        income despite her husband's objection.

1014.   *Girl Guides of India*. Produced through Rustom P. Mas-
        ter, Bombay, 1964, 11 min., black and white, 16 and
        35 mm.

        Activities of Girl Guides in India are depicted.

1015.   *The Goddess Comes Home*. 30 min., black and white,
        16 and 35 mm.

        A married woman returns to her father's home for
        Durga Puja festival.

1016. *Indian Women*. 1969, 20 min., black and white, 16 and 35 mm.

> Indian women are interviewed as to Gandhi's and Kasturba's influence on their lives.

1017. *Invitation to an Indian Wedding*. Produced by Ezra Mir, directed by Ramesh Gupta, 1961, 19 min., color, 16 and 35 mm.

> A wedding in Northwestern India.

1018. *Life Begins Anew*. 1969, 18 min., black and white, 16 and 35 mm.

> A film about destitute women.

1019. *Maa*. Produced through Art Films of Asia Private Ltd., Bombay, 1956, 23 min., black and white, 16 and 35 mm.

> Problems of unwed mothers' children are depicted.

1020. *Madhubani Paintings*. Produced by Miniature Films, directed by Debabrata Roy, 1971, 15 min., color, 16 and 35 mm.

> A film of a village in Bihar, where women painters united and established a cooperative for marketing their folk art products.

1021. *Our Indira*. Produced by Pramod Pati, directed by S.N.S. Sastry, 1973, 15 min., black and white, 35 mm.

> Indira Gandhi's activities.

1022. *Rangoli*. Produced by Mushir Ahmed, directed by Dilip Jamdar, 1968, 16 min., color, 16 and 35 mm.

> A documentary of floor and ground designs created by women for auspicious occasions.

1023. *Shringar*. 1960, 29 min., color, 16 and 35 mm.

> Hairstyles of Indian women.

1024. *The Story of Dr. Karve*. Produced by Ezra Mir, directed by Neil Gokhale and Ram Gokhale, 1958, 21 min., black and white, 16 and 35 mm.

> The life of Maharashi Karve and the establishment of an educational institution for women's uplift. A widow's miserable life is portrayed.

1025.   *Sunrise and Mud Walls*.   1960, 26 min., black and white, 16 and 35 mm.

Activities of social welfare institutions are shown.

1026.   *The Village and I*.   Produced through H.D. Sethna, Bombay, 1958, 20 min., black and white, 16 and 35 mm.

Training of a young widow for social welfare work is depicted.

1027.   *Village and Women*.   1955, 24 min., black and white, 16 and 35 mm.

Women participating in community development projects are depicted.

1028.   *We Want to Live*.   Produced by Pramod Pati, directed by B.N. Mehra, 1970, 18 min., black and white, 16 and 35 mm.

A film about prostitutes and how to rehabilitate them.

1029.   *Who Seeks the Light*.   Produced through G.R. Sethi, Bombay, 1964, 19 min., black and white, 16 and 35 mm.

Social welfare activities for women in rural India.

1030.   *Wives and Wives*.   Produced by Ezra Mir, directed by Pramod Pati, animation by G.K. Gokhale, 1962, 4 min., color, 16 and 35 mm.

The role of housewives in national development is portrayed.

1031.   *Women and Education*.   1957, 14 min., black and white, 16 and 35 mm.

A young college girl's life and educational opportunities are portrayed.

1032.   *Women in Industry*.   1962, 9 min., black and white, 16 and 35 mm.

Special provisions for women working in industry are shown--creches, accommodation for shift workers, etc.

1033.   *Women in White*.   1951, 11 min., black and white, 16 and 35 mm.

Life of a nurse is portrayed. The amount of dedication this profession requires is made clear.

1034. *Women of India*. Produced by Mohan Wadwani, directed
by Ramesh Gupta, 1964, 17 min., black and white,
16 and 35 mm.

General interest film depicting the position of
women from ancient India to present times.

1035. *Women Workers*. 1960, 24 min., black and white, 16
and 35 mm.

Rural women in economic activities are portrayed.

1036. *A Women's University*. 1976, 12 min., black and white,
16 mm.

It is a film about Shrimati Nathibai Damodar Thackersey Women's University on the occasion of its 60th
anniversary, depicting various facilities for women's
higher education.

Films Produced and Distributed by
Film Finance Corporation,
White House, Walkeshwar Road,
Bombay 400 006

1037. *Kanku*. Directed by Kantila Rathod, 1970, 100 min.,
black and white.

The life of a widow, relates how she was sexually
exploited by the village money lender.

1038. *Maya Darpan*. Directed by Kumar Shahani (Hindi dialogue, French titles), 1972, 100 min., color.

A single girl's struggle to break away from the
traditional ideas of marriage.

1039. *Sara Akash*. Directed by Basu Chatterji, Dialogue in
Hindi, titles in English, 1970, 100 min., black
and white.

Young married couple's life--the misunderstanding
between them is the theme of the film.

1040. *Uski Roti*. Directed by Mani Kaul (Hindi dialogue
with French titles), 1970, 130 min., black and
white.

Life of a truck driver's wife who is rejected by
her husband and yet waits on the highway to give him
his lunch packet.

Films Distributed and Available
in Canada and the United States

1041. *The Arithmetic of People*. 30 min., black and white,
      16 and 35 mm., Distributed by University of Michigan
      Television Center, 310 Maynard Street, Ann Arbor,
      Michigan 48108.

      Birth control programs for women are considered.

1042. *Balasaraswathi*. Directed by John Frazier, 1963,
      20 min., color, 16 mm., Distributed by Center for
      the Arts, Wesleyan University, Middletown, Connecti-
      cut 06457.

      Film about the famous dancer and her performances
      during the 1960's.

1043. *Bharata Natyam*. 1951, 11 min., black and white,
      16 mm., Distributed by University of California,
      Extension Media Center, Berkeley, California 94720.

      A demonstration and interpretation of the Bharat
      Natyam dance.

1044. *Charulata*. Directed by Satyajit Ray (Bengali dia-
      logue, English and French titles), 1965, 115 min.,
      black and white, 16 and 35 mm., Distributed by
      Contemporary Films, McGraw-Hill, 330 West 42nd
      Street, New York, New York 10020.

      An educated wife feels neglected by her busy hus-
      band. The wife becomes attracted to her husband's
      cousin. From a story by Tagore.

1045. Number omitted.

1046. *Couples in India*. Directed by David Ruskin, 1972,
      30 min., color, 16 mm., Distributed by Martha Stuart
      Communications, 66 Bank Street, New York, New York
      10014.

      Birth control and parenthood are discussed.

1047. *Courtship*. Produced by Guy Glover, 1961, 2 parts,

30 min., black and white, 16 mm., Distributed by National Film Board of Canada, 1251 Avenue of the Americas, New York, New York 10020.

Comparison of Eastern and Western marriages. International marriages are discussed.

1048. *Devi*. Produced and directed by Satyajit Ray (Bengali dialogue and English titles) 1960, 96 min., black and white, 16 and 35 mm., Distributed by Audio Film Center, 34 Macquesten Parkway South, Mount Vernon, New York 10550.

A daughter-in-law's plight. She ends her life because her father-in-law dreams that she is an incarnation of the Goddess Kali.

1049. Number omitted.

1050. *Four Families*. Produced by National Film Board of Canada, directed by Ian McNeill, 1965, 2 pts., 30 min. each, black and white, 16 mm. Distributed by New York University Film Library, 43 Press Annex, Washington Square, New York, New York 10003.

In the first part, Margaret Mead describes the Indian family--its child-rearing practices and its relation to the national character. Other families studied are French, Canadian, and Japanese.

1051. *Helen: Queen of the Nautch Girls*. Produced by Ismail Merchant, directed by Anthony Kramer, 1972, 30 min., color, 35 mm. Distributed by New Yorker Films, 43 W. 61st Street, New York, New York 10023.

Helen is an Anglo-Burmese dancer, working in the film industry in Bombay. The film tells us about her career.

1052. *The Householder*. A feature film directed by James Ivory, story and script by Ruth Prawer Jhabvala, 1963, 100 min., black and white, 16 mm., Distributed in the United States by Film Images, 17 W. 60th Street, New York, New York 10023.

Life of a newly married school teacher and his wife.

1053. *An Indian Pilgrimage: Ramdevra*. Produced by South Asian Area Center, University of Wisconsin, directed by Joseph W. Elder, Mira Reym Binford, and Michael

Camerini, Filmmakers, 1975, 25 min., color, 16 mm.
Distributed by South Asia Area Center, University
of Wisconsin, 1242 Van Hise Hall, Madison, Wisconsin 53706.

1054. *Indira Gandhi: A Heritage of Power*. Produced and
       directed by Paul Saltzman, 1976, 21 min., color,
       16 mm. Distributed by Eccentric Circle Cinema
       Workshop, Greenwich, Connecticut.

       Indira Gandhi discusses her childhood, her father
       Pandit Jawaharlal Nehru (former Prime Minister) and
       Mahatma Gandhi's impact on her government.

1055. *Indira Gandhi of India*. 1967, 52 min., color, 16 mm.
       Distributed by Time-Life Multimedia Distribution
       Center, 100 Eisenhower Drive, Paramus, New Jersey
       07652 and University of Washington, Audio-visual
       Services, B-54 Administration Building AC-30,
       Seattle, Washington 98195.

       An Indira Gandhi interview.

1056. *Kanchenjungha*. Directed by Satyajit Ray, 1962, 102
       min., color, 16 and 35 mm. Available from Audio
       Film Center, 34 Macquesten Parkway South, Mount
       Vernon, New York 10550.

       A story of two daughters in a well-to-do Bengali
       family, who rebel against traditional expectations.

1057. *Mahanagar*. Directed by Satyajit Ray (Bengali dialogue,
       English titles) 1963, 122 min., black and white,
       16 and 35 mm., Distributed by Audio Film Center,
       35 Macquesten Parkway South, Mount Vernon, New
       York 10550.

       A wife starts working because of her husband's poor
       earnings; his suspicious nature creates tensions in
       the family.

1058. *Marriage: Indian Styles*. 30 min., black and white,
       16 and 35 mm. Available from University of Michigan
       Television Center, 310 Maynard Street, Ann Arbor,
       Michigan 48108.

       Wedding ceremonies of Muslim, Sikh, South and North
       Indians are shown.

1059. *One Man's Family*. 1975, 27 min., color, 16 mm. Dis-
       tributed by Asterisk Productions, Toronto, Canada.

Population problems of India are examined. Giving birth to sons enhances status; barren women are afraid.

1060. *Radha's Day: Hindu Family Life.* Directed and written by H. Daniel Smith, 1969, 17 min., color, 16 mm. Distributed by Film Rental Center, Syracuse University, 1455 E. Colvin Street, Syracuse, New York 13210.

A teenage daughter's day in a South Indian family is portrayed.

1061. *Rana.* 1977, 19 min., 16 mm. Distributed by Wombat Productions Inc., Little Lake, Glendale Road, Ossining, New York 10562.

Film portrays family life of a 21-year-old Muslim university student.

1062. *Saris and Careers.* 30 min., black and white, 16 and 35 mm., Available from University of Michigan Television Center, 310 Hayward Street, Ann Arbor, Michigan 48108.

Three professional women scientists are interviewed regarding employment and marriage.

1063. *The Serpent Deities: Art and Ritual in South India.* Directed by Clifford Jones, 1976, 18 min., color, 16 mm. Distributed by Bullfrog Films, Inc., Box 114, Milford Square, Pennsylvania 18935.

Serpent worshipping in Kerala by women worshippers is depicted.

1064. *Welthy Fisher.* 1967, 30 min., black and white, 16 mm. Distributed by Indiana University, Audio-visual Center, Bloomington, Indiana 47401.

Welthy Fisher was an American woman who promoted literacy in Lucknow, North India.

XIII

BIBLIOGRAPHICAL PUBLICATIONS

1065.   Arora, Ved Prakash. *Women: A Selected Bibliography.*
        Regina, Saskatchewan: Provincial Library, 1972,
        52 pp.

1066.   *Bibliography of Cost Benefit Studies on Family Plan-*
        ning in India and I.U.C.D. Studies in India. Bom-
        bay: Demographic Training and Research Centre,
        1970, 21 pp.

1067.   Bombay (Presidency) Women's Council. *Handbook of*
        Women's Work, 1928-1929. 2nd ed. Bombay: Women's
        Council, Government of Bombay, 1929. 87 pp.
        1st ed. was published in 1920.

1068.   Bullough, Vern, et al. (eds.). "Area Studies: India."
        In their *A Bibliography of Prostitution.* New York:
        Garland Publishing, 1977, x + 419 pp.

1069.   Chandra, Jagdish (compiler). "Indian Costumes." Pp.
        260-261 in his *Bibliography of Indian Art and*
        Archaeology. Vol. 1, Indian Art. Delhi: Printers
        Prakashan, 1978.

1070.   Chitalia, K.S. (ed.). *Directory of Women's Institu-*
        tion, Bombay Presidency. Bombay: Servants of India
        Society, 1936, 71 pp.

1071.   Caur, Ajeet, and Arpana Caur (eds.). *Directory of*
        Indian Women Today. New Delhi: India International
        Publications, 1976, 10, xlviii + 659 + iliv pp.

1072.   Dadachanji, Fareddun K. (comp.). *List of Hindu Chari-*
        ties in Bombay. Bombay: Social Service League,
        1919, 91 pp.

1073.   Dasgupta, Kalpana (ed.). *Women on the Indian Scene.*
        New Delhi: Abhinav Publications, 1976, xii + 391 pp.

1074. Gidwani, N.M., and K. Navalani (comp. and eds.). *A Guide to Reference Materials on India*. Jaipur: Saraswati Publications, 1974, 2 vols., 3000 pp.

1075. India (Republic) Office of the Registrar General. *Bibliography of Census Publication in India*. Delhi: Manager of Publications, Government of India, 1972, 520 pp.

1076. "Indian Costumes: A Select Bibliography." *Cultural News from India*. Vol. 3, No. 2 (1962), pp. 27-30.

1077. Jacobs, Sue-Ellen. *Women in Perspective. A Guide for Cross-Cultural Studies*. Urbana, Illinois: University of Illinois Press, 1974, pp. 39-48. Devoted to the women of Ceylon, India and Nepal.

1078. Kapil, Krishan K., and Devendra N. Saxena. "A Bibliography of Family Planning Knowledge, Attitude, and Practice Studies in India, 1951-68." *Demographic Training and Research Centre Newsletter*, No. 26 (1968), pp. 19-38.

1079. Karkal, Malini. *Annotated Bibliography of Studies on Age at Marriage in India*. Bombay: International Institute for Population Studies, 1971, 25 pp.

1080. Khandwala, Vidyut K. (ed.). *Education of Women in India 1850-1967: A Bibliography*. Bombay: S.N.D.T. Women's University, 1968, 115 pp.

1081. Krishnamurthy, K.G. *Research in Family Planning in India*. Delhi: Sterling Publishers, 1968, 180 pp.

1082. Lakhanpal, Saru Krishna. *Indian Women: A Bibliography*. Saskatoon: University of Saskatchewan, 1967. 14 pp.

1083. Lytle, Elizabeth. *Women in India: A Comprehensive Bibliography*. Public Administration Series No. 10, Monticello, Illinois: Vance Bibliographics, 1978, 29 pp.

1084. Malhotra, K.C. "Bibliography of Iravati Karve's Works." *Bulletin of Deccan College Research Institute*, Vol. 31-32 (1970-71), Pt. II (1971-72), i-viii pp.

1085. Patankar, Tara. *A Bibliography on Fertility Studies in India*. Bombay: Demographic Training and Research Centre, 1969, 38 pp.

1086. Patterson, Maureen L.P. *South Asian Civilizations: A Synthesis of Selected Resources*. Chicago: University of Chicago Press, 1981, xxxvii + 853 pp.

1087. Pattison, Mattie, and Shakti Chhaya (comps.). *Annotated Bibliography of Research Related to Home Science in India*. Baroda: Faculty of Home Science, Maharaja Sayajirao University of Baroda, 1967, 262 pp.

1088. Pearson, J.D. (ed.). *South Asian Bibliography: A Handbook and Guide*. Hassocks, Sussex: Harvester Press, 1979, 381 pp. Also published by Atlantic Highlands, New Jersey.

1088a. Pontes, Hilda, and Nayantara Sahgal. *Bibliography of Indian Writing in English* (Series 2). New Delhi: Concept Publishing Company, 1985, x + 95 pp.

1089. Rihani, May. *Development as If Women Mattered: An Annotated Bibliography with a Third World Focus*. Washington, D.C.: New Transcentury Foundation (Overseas Development Council), 1978, 137 pp.

1090. *A Select Bibliography on Women of India*. Research Unit on Women's Studies, S.N.D.T. Women's University, Bombay. New Delhi: Allied Publishers, n.d., x + 131 pp.

1091. Sen, S.P. (ed.). *Dictionary of National Biography*. Calcutta: Institute of Historical Studies, 1972-74. 3 Vols., lviii + 418, 562, 465 pp.

1092. Sharma, Prakash C. *Female Working Role and Economic Development: A Selected Bibliography*. Monticello, Illinois: Council of Planning Librarians, 1974, 16 pp.

1092a. Vashishta, B.K. (ed.). *Encyclopaedia of Women in India*. New Delhi: Praveen Encyclopaedia Publications, 1978, 4 parts, 518 pp.

1093. Ward, Barbara E. *Women in the New Asia: The Changing Social Roles of Men and Women in South and South East Asia*. Paris: UNESCO, 1963, 529 pp.

1094. *Who's Who of Indian Women, International*. Madras: National Biographical Centre, 1977, 109 pp.

1095. *Women in India: Who's Who?* Bombay: National Council of Women, India, 1935, 91 pp.

1096. Yaquin, Anwarul, and Anwar, Badri. *Protection of Women
       Under the Law: An Annotated Bibliography*. New
       Delhi: Deep & Deep Publications, 1982, 200 pp.

1097. Young, Katherine K., and Arvind Sharma. *Images of the
       Feminine, Mystic, Philosophic and Human in the
       Buddhist, Hindu and Islamic Traditions: A Bibliog-
       raphy of Women in India*. Chico, California: New
       Horizons Press, 1974, 36 pp.

XIV

ENGLISH LANGUAGE PERIODICALS
CONTAINING ARTICLES ABOUT WOMEN'S STATUS,
POSITION, INTERESTS, PROBLEMS, AND ISSUES

1098. *Association of Medical Women in India.* Monthly
       (1909).* Bombay.

1099. *Beautiful Working Woman* (for working mothers and
       career women). Monthly (1973). Bombay.

1100. *Centre Calling.* Monthly (1966). New Delhi: Depart-
       ment of Social Welfare, Government of India.

1101. *Eve's Weekly.* Weekly (1947). Bombay.

1102. *Family Planning News.* Monthly (1960). New Delhi:
       National Institute of Family Planning.

1103. *Femina.* Fortnightly (1959). Bombay.

1104. *Home Life.* Monthly (1975). Bombay.

1105. *Indian Ladies' Magazine* (1901-1918, 1927-1938). Cal-
       cutta.

1106. *Indian Social Reformer.* Weekly (1894-1952). Madras/
       Bombay.

1107. *Journal of the Indian Housewife.* Monthly (1977).
       Madras.

1108. *Kumari.* Monthly (1967). Beawer.

1109. *Manushi.* Bi-monthly (1979). New Delhi.

1110. *Modern Review.* Monthly (1907). Calcutta.

*The year that publication began is given in parentheses.

1111. *Our World*. Monthly (1967). New Delhi: Delhi Poly-
        technic for Women.

1112. *Shreemati Nathibai Damodar Thackersey Women's Univer-
        sity Report*. Annual (1916). Bombay.

1113. *Shreemati Nathibai Damodar Thackersey Women's Univer-
        sity Research Unit on Women's Studies Newsletter*.
        Monthly (1977). Bombay.

1114. *Social Welfare*. Monthly (1954). New Delhi: Publica-
        tions Division, Central Social Welfare Board.

1115. *Today*. Quarterly (1962). New Delhi: Young Women's
        Christian Association of India.

1116. *Women on the March*. Monthly (1957). New Delhi:
        Published by All India Congress Committee, Indian
        National Congress.

1117. *Women's Era*. Fortnightly (1973). New Delhi.

1118. *Women's Own Weekly*. Weekly (1960). Bombay.

1119. *Women's Voice*. Fortnightly (1969). New Delhi.

AUTHOR INDEX

References are to *entry* numbers.

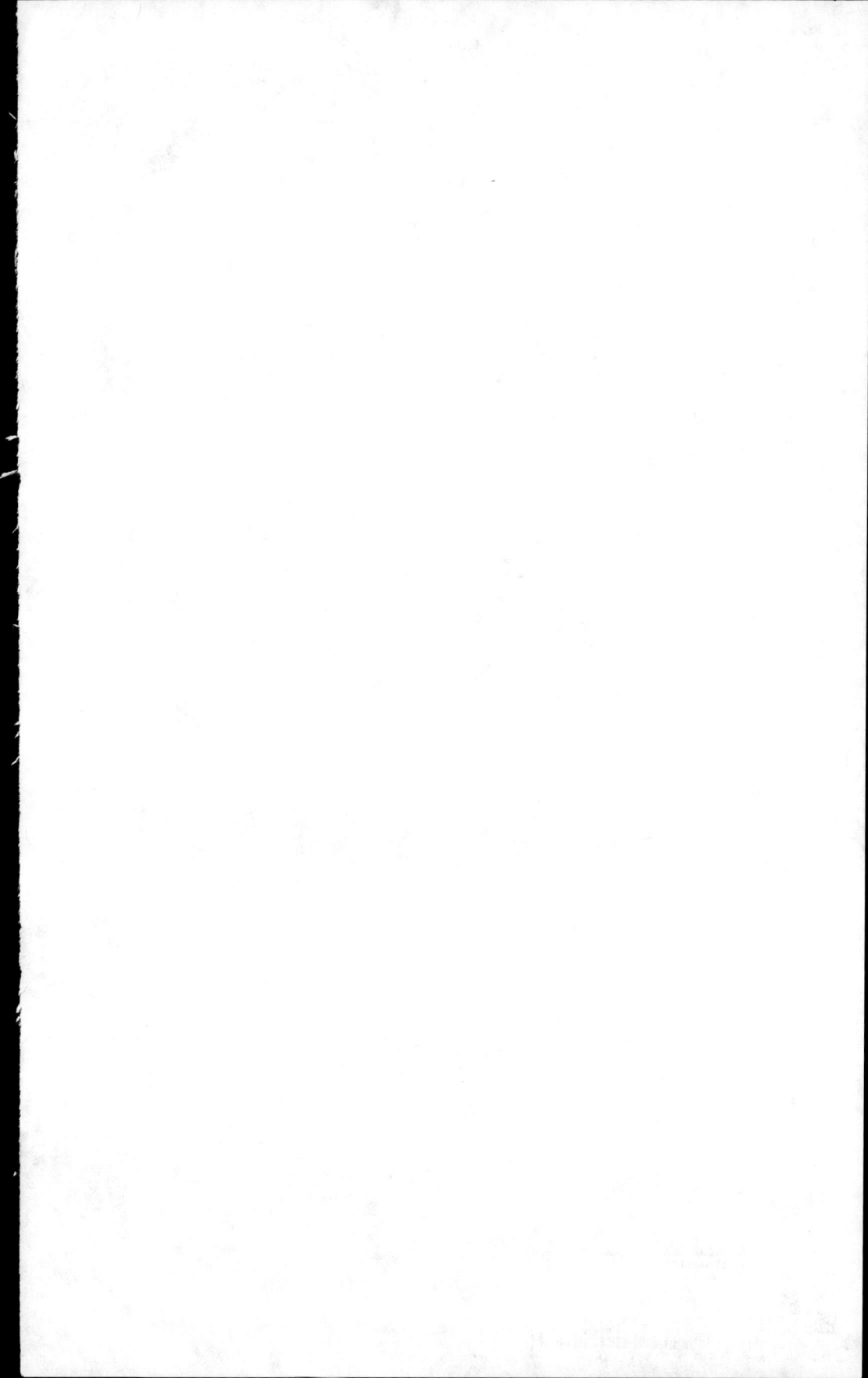

For Product Safety Concerns and Information please contact our EU
representative GPSR@taylorandfrancis.com
Taylor & Francis Verlag GmbH, Kaufingerstraße 24, 80331 München, Germany